I0792950

LOST GHOST TOWNS OF TELLER COUNTY

LOST GHOST TOWNS OF TELLER COUNTY

JAN MACKELL COLLINS

THE History PRESS

Published by The History Press
Charleston, SC
www.historypress.net

First published 2016

Manufactured in the United States

ISBN 978.1.46713.512.2

Library of Congress Control Number: 2016930762

Notice: The information in this book is true and complete to the best of our knowledge. It is offered without guarantee on the part of the author or The History Press. The author and The History Press disclaim all liability in connection with the use of this book.

CONTENTS

Contents

PREFACE

I cannot remember the first time I ever saw a ghost town. My parents, who had rambled around the back country of the Southwest for much of their own childhoods, continued the habit as adults. On a weekend, vacation or sometimes even the evenings after my dad got off work, our family could be found exploring just about anywhere. From the hot and dusty deserts of Southern California to the lush mountains of Colorado and places in between, we scouted out faded trails to see where they led.

The family hobby suited us. My mom would read to us on the road about where we were going and what we might see. She always had a history book of some sort on hand. Our explorations led us to some stunning places during the 1960s and '70s. It was the perfect time to visit long-abandoned towns, ranches and whistle-stops before they sank back into the earth and ceased to exist at all. In Colorado, the names of these places now run together like a list of old friends. I never have outgrown the temptation to climb to the tops of old decrepit mills, step into abandoned houses, dig around in ancient dumps and photograph lone tombstones standing in a field.

Teller County in particular has always been one of my favorite places. I hold very fond memories of getting caught in a wicked rainstorm at Elkton, taking refuge in a house where furniture, including an old piano, remained as a testament to the newly wedded couple who once lived there. Wrapping paper from their gifts lay about, as well as a note explaining how the groom was in a terrible car accident days after the ceremony. I don't know if he lived.

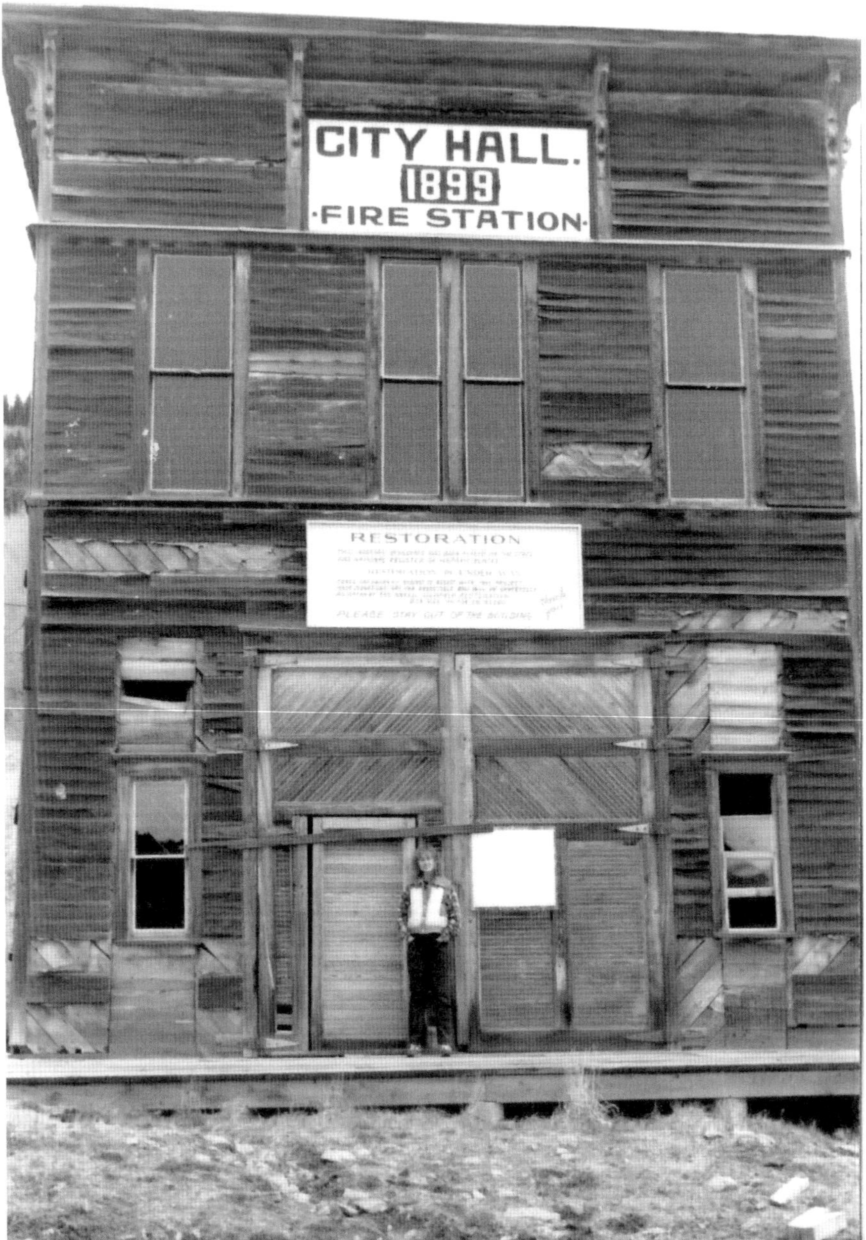

The author in front of Goldfield City Hall, Cripple Creek District, 1985. The structure still stands and is well preserved. *Jan MacKell Collins.*

Preface

The day I finally found Manchester, my worries about locating the actual town dissolved when I spotted the sunken ground where two of the only buildings once stood. I was elated the day I was given directions to the old cemetery at Gillett. Most recently, my insatiable yearning to find Alnwick was satisfied, even though nothing is left of the village but an empty pasture. Finding nothing where there once was something is common when "ghost-towning," but the satisfaction of at least finding the place remains the same.

The title of this book is no mistake. Populated places, such as Woodland Park, Divide, Florissant, Cripple Creek and Victor, do not appear in this book because they are still inhabited. Likewise, towns like Crystola and Goldfield that no longer have their own municipalities are excluded because they still have residents and remain known by their original names. Rather, included here are the settled places that are truly lost, some forever, as the landscape on which they perched has been literally changed by one circumstance or another.

Teller County's history is truly amazing. So much was going on at various times that the population was truly of a transient nature, with inhabitants lasting anywhere from a few weeks to decades before dying or moving on. Our pioneers exhibited great courage in their struggles to survive in some pretty remote places. Some of the most interesting history in America transpired here, often carried out in rustic and primitive buildings that no longer stand.

I am thankful that I was able to visit certain towns and other places that are now gone and even happier that I get to share their stories now. In writing this book, I was pleasantly surprised to uncover—or, at least, solve the mystery of—camps and towns I have never written about before. One thing is for sure: The ghostly western world of yesteryear is slowly fading to dust. Today's rides down history trails often yield piles of only what was, not what might have been. Sometimes, there is only a bare patch of ground left. Other times, a cemetery or a few buildings might mark the spot. If we're lucky, the place has been carefully preserved, watched over and even fenced to prevent access. But the numbers of those few survivors are small compared to what has been lost to time, weather, progress and vandalism.

Because Teller County's ghost towns are such a precious and endangered resource, readers will note the absence of clear directions to most of these places. Visiting a ghost town, even when there is little or nothing left, is a privilege future generations may not have. Please show the ultimate respect when seeking these wonderful landmarks of history.

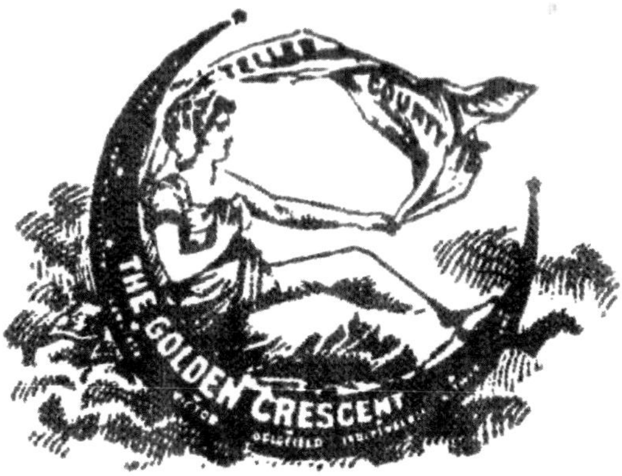
TELLER COUNTY
THE GOLDEN CRESCENT

ACKNOWLEDGEMENTS

Because I have been writing about the people, places and events around Teller County for a number of years, my list of thank-yous seems simply enormous. Some of the people who have encouraged, helped, supported and advised me are no longer living. Many others remain as excellent colleagues, fellow history buffs and friends who, like me, continue to love this special place with all their hearts. One of them is my friend and mentor Richard Wayne Johnson, founder of the Cripple Creek District Museum in 1953 and still president of the board of directors when he died at the age of eighty-three. "Cripple Creek is like a disease," he once said of the famed gold district that is the heart of Teller County. "Once it gets into your system, you will never get it out again."

While Dick Johnson remains at the top of the list of people to whom I owe my gratitude, there are many, many others. They include but are not limited to Missie Trenary and Dick Tremayne, current stewards of the Cripple Creek District Museum; Linda Bretag and the staff at the Teller County Courthouse in Cripple Creek; Yvette at the El Paso County Clerk and Recorder; Shaun Boyd of the Douglas County History Research Center in Castle Rock; and everyone else who has answered my inquiries. Special thanks go to my editors, Artie Crisp and Julia Turner, who are having to learn to put up with me.

I am also so thankful for the many historians who gladly conducted early research on the towns of Teller County and shared invaluable information about them. My hat is off to Robert L. Brown, Perry

Eberhart, Marshall Sprague, Leland Feitz, Mel McFarland, Dr. Thomas J. Noel and so many others who have written about the ghost towns of Teller County.

Lastly, I have to thank my best friend, traveling buddy and husband, Corey, who has allowed me to drag him down many dusty trails and over barbed-wire fences to see what is on the other side.

INTRODUCTION

The great gold rushes that helped settle the West are ingrained in American history as some of the most exciting times our country would ever see. The gold rushes of Colorado were especially amazing, spanning from the Pikes Peak Gold Rush of 1859 to all new gold discoveries at Cripple Creek in 1891. Colorado's first gold rush was so named because prospectors heading to the region used Pikes Peak, elevation 14,114 feet, as a landmark. The peak, which towers above Colorado Springs on one side and Teller County on the other, was named for explorer Zebulon Pike. As the Pikes Peak Gold Rush unfolded throughout the 1860s, prospectors traversed an ancient trail used by local Ute Indians that wound up through a pass at the base of the peak. Eventually dubbed Ute Pass, this trail became known as one of the quickest ways for easterners wishing to access the western slope of Colorado. A few rest stops popped up over time, mostly ranches but one or two mail stops and supply towns, too. By the time El Paso County was formed as one of Colorado's original counties in 1861, Ute Pass had become known as the gateway from Colorado City (a supply stop west of today's Colorado Springs) to the western gold fields.

Pioneers and early surveyors making their way up Ute Pass found some ranches already settled by squatters. Legal homesteaders were allowed to settle on 160-acre tracts of land starting in 1873. The gold discoveries at Cripple Creek altered these places dramatically. The Cripple Creek District is formed from an extinct volcano that was so large it actually imploded in on itself rather than erupting. A unique field of rich minerals was created as the molten mass melted, flowed into the cracks and crevices caused by the explosion and hardened over time. Ranchers within this "caldera" included the Womacks, whose son, Bob, was sure there was gold in the area. When young Womack was finally able to convince everyone of the rich gold deposits, prospectors by the thousands flocked to the area as more towns were established both within and outside the Cripple Creek District. The Cripple Creek District directory of 1894 perhaps described it best:

> *Over the quiet hills and vales there came a change. Where once no sound was heard save the halloo of the herdsman, clatter of hoofs and horns and jingle of spur bells, there came the crushing, rending roar of dynamite, tearing the rocks asunder, the crunching and grinding and rattling of wheels, the shouting of mule drivers and freighters, with sounds of saw and axe and hammer. A town grew up like magic, prospectors thronged the hills—and there was solitude no more.*[1]

Within a short time, a series of other mining districts, camps, towns and cities sprang up throughout the western portion of El Paso County. Some of these places never evolved further than small camps where transient miners lived and worked. Others were founded as whistle-stops with the coming of the railroads. Still more bloomed into thriving metropolises that, in time, rivaled bigger cities in Colorado and beyond. A few were settled with high hopes of becoming large cities, only to fold within a few years or even months. Some towns never even made it off the ground.

City directories for the Cripple Creek District began publishing in 1893, but due to the ever-moving population, it was a limited effort at best. "The first edition of the Cripple Creek Directory is now placed in circulation," announced the editors, but added, "In the compilation of this book the publishers have been careful to exclude the names of non-residents. The general makeup of a new town is such as to make the work very difficult; however, we will say that neither labor nor expenses has been spared to make this directory complete and accurate, and we believe it will prove reliable."[2] Indeed, the population of the area swelled and shrank accordingly as those who couldn't gain good work or prosperity moved on. For every person who left the district, however, another one arrived.

In 1899, city officials in Cripple Creek successfully formed Teller County. The new county was carefully carved from parts of El Paso, Park and Fremont Counties. Teller County measures a mere 559 square miles, but much activity occurred within its boundaries during the 1890s and early 1900s. The Teller

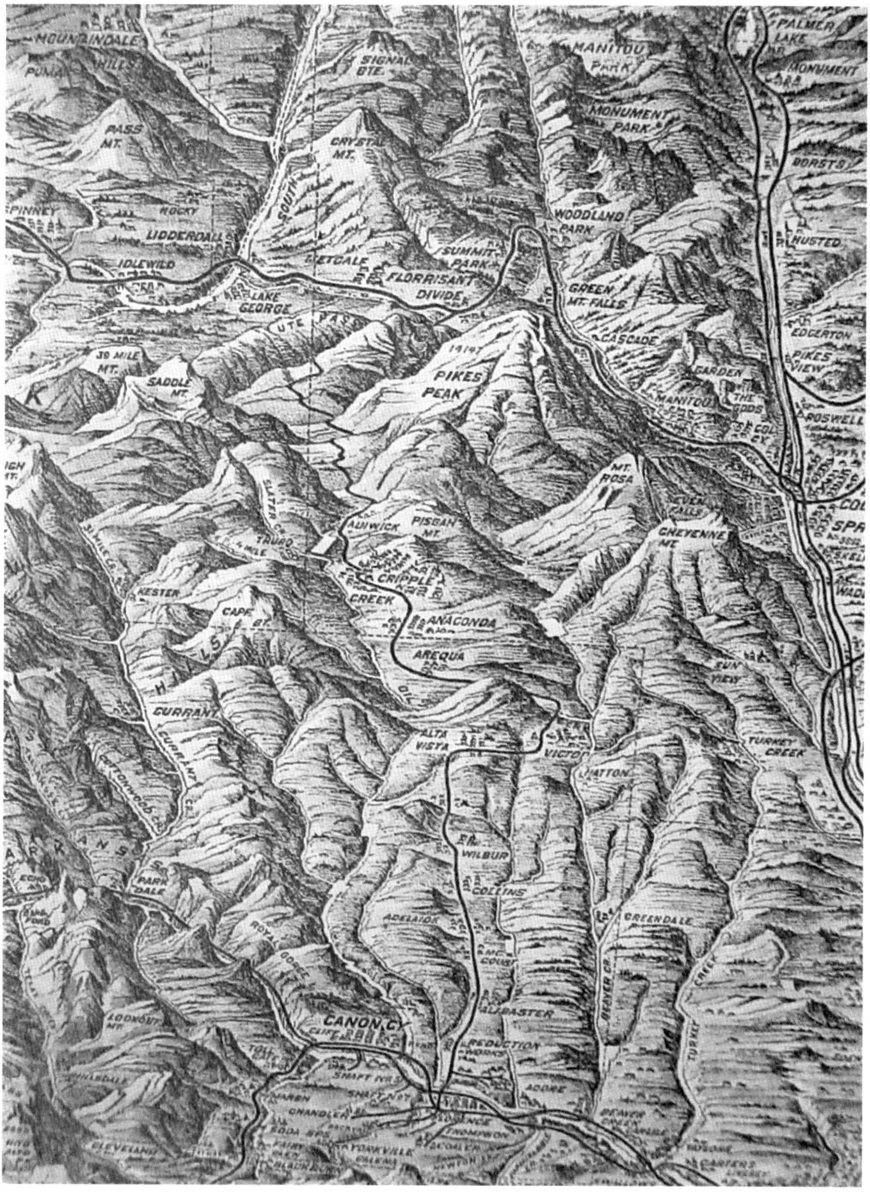

A map of El Paso County, circa 1892, shows Teller County before it was formed in 1899. *Jan MacKell Collins.*

County of the turn of the twenty-first century was rife with historic events, including two labor wars. Get-rich-quick schemes, insurance frauds, historic fires, murders and more have made for a most interesting history. More than a few honorable figures, including Colorado governor Ralph Carr and a slew of celebrities, also called Teller County home. For a time, the Cripple Creek District made Teller County known to folks worldwide.

Because of the hardened minerals left by the giant caldera in the Cripple Creek District, hard-rock mining was primarily employed in Teller County. Placer mining, wherein a fellow with a pan scooped up river sand and shook out the gold, was far less common. Thus, in time, digging, blasting and processing ore in the Cripple Creek District became harder and more expensive. Gold miners fell under the impression that there was little more gold to be had that was worth digging for, and people began moving away from the Cripple Creek District. Subsequently, the rest of Teller County downsized as well.

In an attempt to lessen the perils created by the Great Depression, President Franklin Delano Roosevelt signed the Gold Reserve Act in 1934. Doing so raised—and capped—the price of gold at thirty-five dollars per ounce. Although there were still some working mines in the county, most of them dwindled away in time. Times were changing; railroads were shutting down, wagon roads were falling out of use, historic ranches were changing hands and many of the towns established on behalf of the gold boom were being abandoned.

By the 1950s, many of Teller County's towns and camps had faded into obscurity. Surviving places, such as Woodland Park, Cripple Creek and Victor, turned to tourism as a new industry. Museums were established as residents of Teller County looked for ways to draw visitors to the area. The cap on the price of gold was finally repealed in 1971 by President Richard Nixon, just as new techniques to extract hard-rock gold were being employed. A renewed interest in mining, combined with increased tourism, kept Teller County alive.

Of particular interest to many tourists were the county's numerous ghost towns. While the Cripple Creek District remained a key destination to see such places, others slowly faded away. A few were incorporated as part of local ranches or were subsequently purchased by private interests. Especially in the last twenty-five years or so, many ghost towns have fallen in the wake of modern mining operations and in the name of progress. Even so, history buffs, local residents and others who hold Teller County near and dear to their hearts have worked tirelessly to support the history of these places. While many of the towns may be gone, each place still has lots of stories to tell. Here are some of them.

PART I

RANCHING AND RESORT TOWNS

1

BISON PARK

The City of Victor's Private Playground

Local legend records Bison as a logging camp dating to the 1860s and that it was located between Cow Mountain and Pikes Peak near today's Cripple Creek District. The east fork of West Beaver Creek feeds today's Bison Reservoir, which, in turn, drains into Bison Creek running south. In 1874, Quincy King, who had just recently discovered the eventual resort of Seven Lakes, partnered with two other men to form the "Smith, King and Unrue" mining claim in Bison Valley on the east fork of Beaver Creek.[3]

The few mine diggings aside, the area remained a pristine and most scenic park. Here, a quiet wooded valley opened into wide green meadows surrounded by towering rock formations. Cabin ruins in the woods today attest to times when people worked or lived in the area. The remaining treasures include a small Victorian home built in 1893. A spacious floor plan allowed for two bedrooms, a parlor, a dining area and a kitchen.

Two years after the home was built, on July 2, 1895, a plat map for the "Bison Park Town Site" was surveyed by R.W. Bradshaw and filed in El Paso County. The map reads more like an advertisement, with the following description:

> *Bison Park is a romantic and picturesque place. It is in the main mineral belt south of the Peak and is already surrounded with good mines. It is also on the established route of the* [Colorado Springs & Cripple Creek District] *Railroad. Hence it is destined to become a town of considerable importance. Moral: Buy lots while they are cheap.*

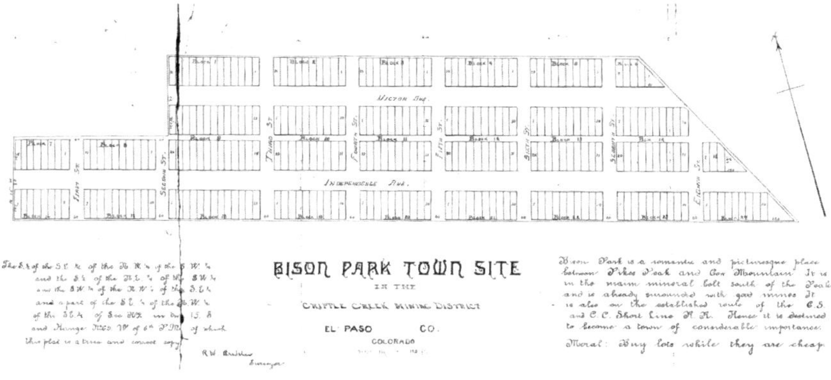

The Bison Park town site map encouraged folks to buy lots "while they are cheap." *Teller County Assessor, Cripple Creek, Colorado.*

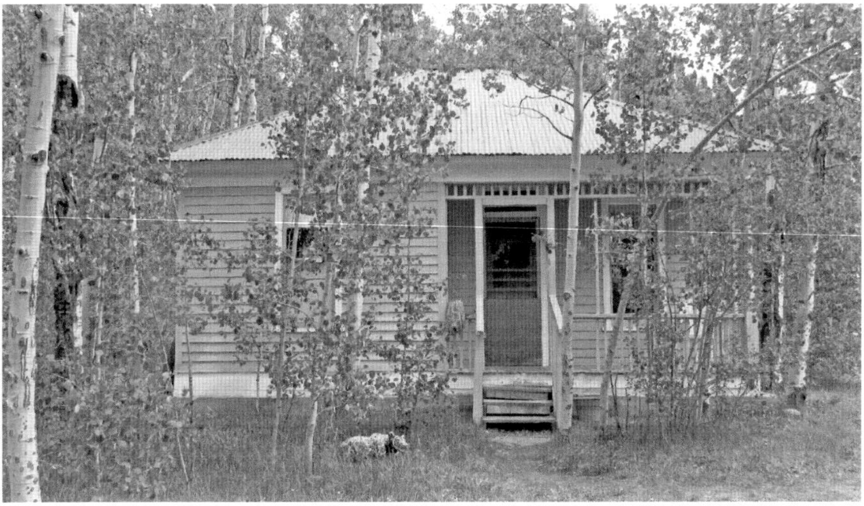

The caretaker's house at Bison Reservoir is maintained and still used today by the members of the Gold Camp Fishing Club. *Jan MacKell Collins.*

Alas, the railroad declined to pass by Bison Park's remote location, and Bison Park's plat map shows that the town was vacated in September 1895. In July 1901, the City of Victor proposed purchasing 213 acres of the park from the owner, a woman named Mary Miller, for $10,000. The city wanted to build a reservoir as a water supply for residents.[4] The Altman Water Company, which already sold water to Victor, raised a slight ruckus at the idea. In the end, however, the city successfully completed the purchase.

Bison Reservoir was constructed in about 1901. Several claims—namely, the Park Placer, Park Placer No. 2, Old No. 9 and a small portion of the Maggie A—were covered with water.[5]

In more modern times, Bison continues to serve as Victor's water supply but is also home to the Gold Camp Fishing Club. Membership to the club is extended to only Victor property owners, who take much pride in maintaining the area's natural setting and historic sites. Much of the park is surrounded by Bureau of Land Management (BLM) land. Numerous members actively volunteer their time, money and labor to Bison Reservoir. The grounds are frequently the scene of weddings, memorials, fishing tournaments and a host of other activities. In essence, visitors to Bison respect the land and its surroundings so that future generations can enjoy this natural playground for many years to come.

2

CLYDE

A Happy Ranching Community

Prior to the gold boom in the Cripple Creek District, folks wishing to access today's Teller County used a series of wagon and stage roads to reach various ranches and other places of note. The oldest of these was the Cheyenne & Beaver Toll Road Company, which began in Cheyenne Canyon near Colorado Springs and joined what is today known as Gold Camp Road. The route was originally established in 1875.[6] Two years later, the name of the road was changed to the Cheyenne & Beaver Park Toll Road. At the confluence of Bison Creek and Middle Beaver Creek, a new wagon road veered off toward Seven Lakes, a budding resort just below the summit of Pikes Peak. A stage stop was established at this junction that would later be known as Clyde.[7]

Though only a stop on the toll road, Clyde had amenities that included a place to stay for the night, food and libations. Clyde prospered as the last stop before the ascent to Seven Lakes. The road from Colorado Springs also flourished, its name changing again in 1879 to the Cheyenne, Lake Park and Pikes Peak Toll Road Company. With the gold boom in the Cripple Creek District beginning in 1891, the road through Clyde gained even more popularity as the shortest route to the district from Colorado Springs. Promoters, including the Colorado Springs Chamber of Commerce, spent upward of $18,000 to improve the toll road.[8]

As the few merchants of Clyde prospered from miners and other travelers, a post office opened under the name of Seward in August 1896. The name was changed to Clyde in October 1899, after the son of resident George

McCarthy. The post office application explained that the office would serve thirty-five people and was expecting to serve one hundred or more in time.[9] Families at Clyde were of the hardworking variety with lots of children. Being far away from good medical facilities especially took its toll on babies in this remote spot. Unable to afford tombstones or reach nearby graveyards in winter, many ranch families simply buried their stillborn or deceased infants on the family property. Most of these graves were never marked and have been forgotten over time.[10]

The Colorado Springs & Cripple Creek District Railroad, later dubbed "the Short Line," was built through Clyde in 1899. The railroad was developed by mine owners sick of paying expensive freight fees to the Florence & Cripple Creek and the Midland Terminal Railroads, both of which also served the Cripple Creek District. Irving Howbert, president of Colorado Springs's First National Bank at the time, convinced the mine owners to finance their own railroad. The Short Line was a limited success; even with the renowned Seven Lakes Resort above town abandoned, passengers still favored accessing trails to Pikes Peak from Clyde.[11]

The Cripple Creek District directory for 1900 notes that George McCarthy was serving as postmaster at "Clyde City" while working on the side as a miner. There were other miners, too, and a sawmill operator named W.S. Garber who rented a home from P. McNeny. The house was located next to the post office building, owned by a Mr. Swink. In May 1900, Garber, hoping to cash in on insurance money for his household goods, burned both buildings.[12] Counting Garber, the entire population, according to the 1900 census, numbered only twenty-nine people. The post office closed in September.[13]

Clyde, as well as a number of satellite camps, remained home to prospectors and ranchers for many more years. One outlying community was Saderlind, identified on a 1901 Short Line timetable as a stop roughly 2.2 miles from Rosemont and 6.0 miles from Clyde.[14] That same year, the Short Line engaged in a fare war with the Colorado Midland and Midland Terminal railroads, which ran from Colorado Springs and Divide to the Cripple Creek District. The railroads had been charging two dollars for a round-trip ticket, but the Short Line won by charging just twenty-five cents. The resurgence of interest in Clyde was so good that Frank Cady, postmaster at the nearby community of Love, submitted a new application to reopen the post office there. Cady cited 140 people as living in Clyde proper, with the total number of people using the post office as 300. The post office successfully reopened in September 1901.[15]

With the post office back in place, a new railway station and water tank were constructed in November. There was also a school. Among the best natural features was Cathedral Park, just around the bend from Clyde along the railroad. The "sublime scenery, fantastic rocks and cathedral spires" of this amazing formation beckoned passengers from the Short Line, which offered daily excursions to the park. Awaiting patrons were a dance pavilion complete with a corrugated iron roof, a five-room "dwelling" and two refreshment stands installed by the railroad. It was perhaps around that time that an artificial lake was constructed at Clyde for recreational purposes.[16]

There was little crime around Clyde, but in 1904, assassins Harry Orchard, Johnnie Neville and Neville's son Charlie camped near Clyde. The group was working on behalf of the striking miners during a most violent and tumultuous labor war in the Cripple Creek District. Orchard was orchestrating a plan to blow up the depot at the Cripple Creek District town of Independence, which the group did successfully on June 5. Thirteen men were killed and several others injured.[17]

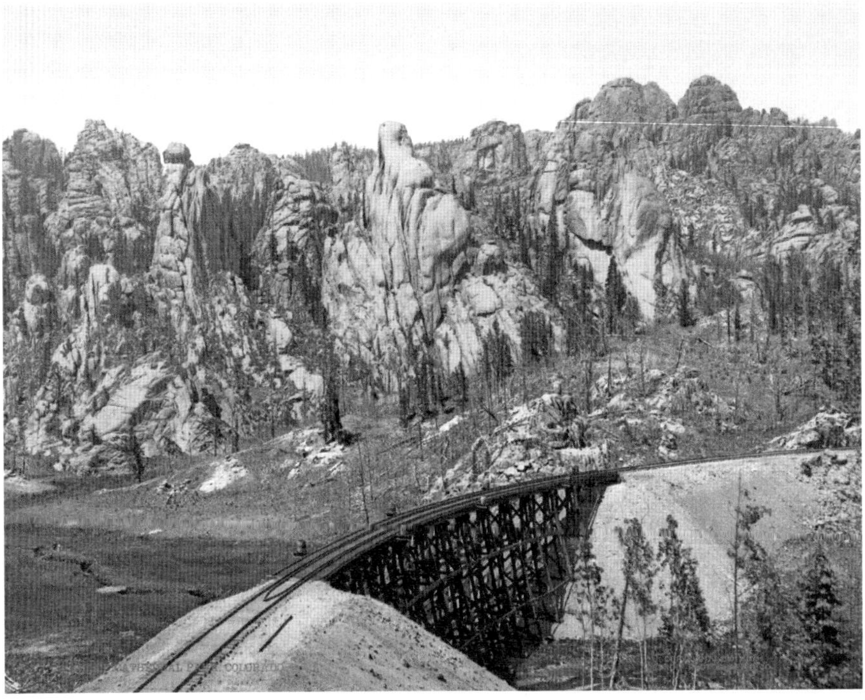

Cathedral Park, shown here in 1901, was a favored picnic ground along the Colorado Springs & Cripple Creek District Railroad. *Jan MacKell Collins.*

Throughout the early 1900s, Clyde's population remained at a mere handful of residents. In 1905, when the number was around fifteen citizens, the figure included Joseph and Elmira Schneider. Joseph worked as a section boss on the Short Line, but the family homestead eventually grew into a large ranch totaling two thousand acres. Those who knew Schneider remembered when he bought his first car. In learning how to work the newfangled machine, Schneider would yell, "Whoa!" and, cussing at the vehicle, jump to safety when it went out of control.[18]

People at Clyde in 1908 included schoolteacher Miss J.E. Kenton, as well as station agent and postmaster Chas. F. Redman. But the tiny village could hardly justify its post office, which closed a final time in September 1909. When the population shot up to eighty-three residents in the 1910 census, the figure included numerous temporary railroad workers. Eighteen section hands shared quarters in the railroad's section house, ten of them being Greek immigrants. Eight others were Japanese. Also living in Clyde were schoolteacher Harry G. Goves, employees of the Clyde Timber Company and the McCarthy family, including young Clyde, who was now eighteen years of age. Young McCarthy and his brothers were employed as farmers on the family homestead.[19]

The 1910 census at Clyde also is notable because at the time, several satellite camps surrounded the community. They included Bald Mountain, Bunker Hill District, Rosemont, Saderlind, Summit and Seven Lakes. The five residents at Bald Mountain included prospectors Frosty Clemens, Frank Nelson and James Snodgrass, all widowers in their forties and fifties. Clemens, in particular, was a character of sorts whose name has become legend in his part of the country. Born in 1865 in Missouri, Clemens was allegedly a cousin of Samuel Clemens, better known as the prolific writer Mark Twain. By the time he arrived in the area, Clemens was a widower who apparently had been prospecting for some time. Local folklore cites that he dug several mines but never found much. Ultimately, according to legend, he died in 1916, when "he pulled a permanent lid of gravel down over himself in one of his mines." It is also believed that he built what is now known as Frosty Clemens Trail in Frosty Park.[20]

The Bunker Hill District was located on Bunker Hill between Bald Mountain and Rosemont. Residents of the district were all farmers, most of whom had departed the area by the time of the 1920 census. Part of the reason for their exodus might have been because the Pike National Forest was formed and took over much of the land. A ranger station was built at Clyde between 1912 and 1917. The new forest designation mattered little since, by that time, the Cripple Creek District mines were dwindling and fewer people were using the Short Line. When the dance pavilion roof at Cathedral Park collapsed during a heavy snow, nobody bothered to rebuild it.[21]

Longtime homesteaders in the twentieth century included Isadore and Minnie Meyers, who moved to Clyde from the Cripple Creek District town of Goldfield in 1914. The Meyerses' daughter Glenora remembered that the schoolhouse was just one room with a dozen or so students. She also gave a complete description of the family home. The house was a one-and-a-half-story cabin made from square logs. The bottom floor contained the front room, kitchen and the Meyerses' bedroom. Their many children slept on the second floor in a large room, with a curtain dividing the girls from the boys. There was a cellar and an outhouse, and water was carried from Middle Beaver Creek across the road.

Glenora remembered that "there never was any shortage of snow in winter. Sometimes, the snow drifts were so high that we could walk over the tops of the fences. Of course, to go anywhere, the road had to be shoveled out by hand or plowed out with what was called a go-devil. This was a triangular shaped contraption that was weighted down with rocks or sometimes with us kids and pulled by our faithful team of horses." In winter, the family would take trips to Victor with hot rocks wrapped in newspapers to keep everyone's feet warm. Beginning in about 1917, the Meyerses alternated their time between Clyde and a nearby place they called simply "Camp" near Gould Creek. The family felled and sold timber at Camp. They were also farming by 1920. After Minnie died in Colorado Springs in 1926, Isadore continued alternating his time between there and Camp. He died in 1961 and was buried in Manitou Springs.[22]

In about 1918, the telegraph office at Clyde was replaced by a telephone system so engineers on the Short Line could talk with the dispatcher. In 1920, however, the Short Line ceased operations altogether, and residents of Clyde were counted in the population of Victor during the census that year. Longtime residents remembered that in about 1921, a particularly heavy rainstorm threatened to break the dams at Seven Lakes above town. The local children were sheltered in the second story of the sturdy ranger station until the danger passed. Everyone survived, and in 1922, the old railroad bed gained new life when W.D. Corley purchased it at auction for $370,000. Corley, a coal operator turned capitalist, beat out three other bids, including one representing mining and freighting millionaire A.E. Carlton. Corley tore up the tracks, filled in the trestles and turned the rail bed into

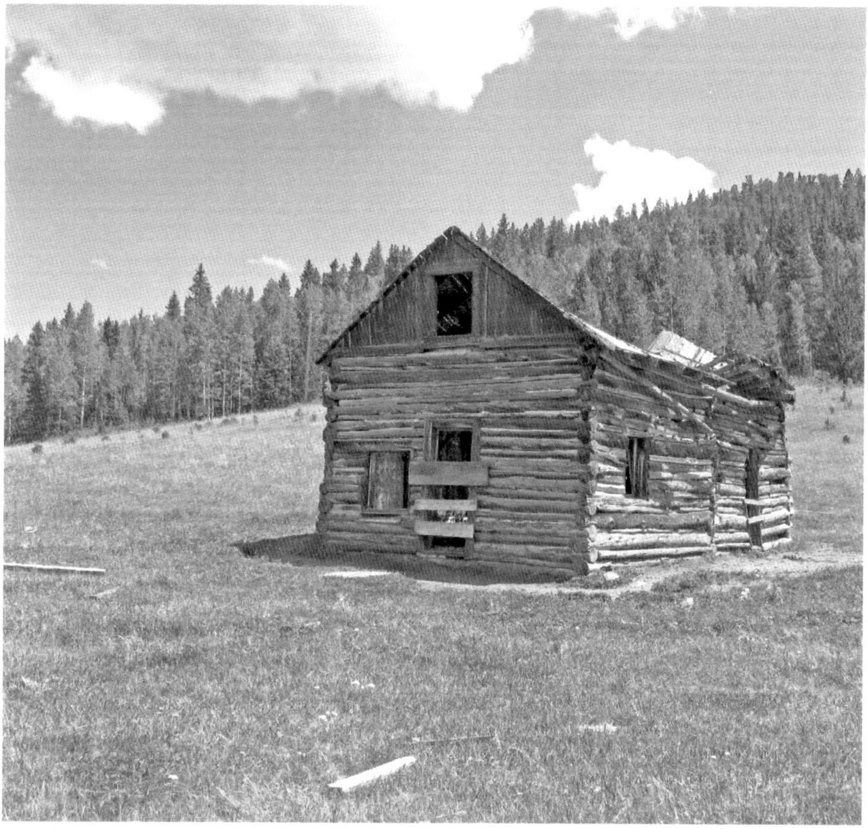

The Meyers homestead is one of a handful of structures surviving at Clyde. All of them are now on private property. *Jan MacKell Collins.*

the Corley Mountain Highway toll road. The toll was $1 and, on a good day, reaped $400 in fees.[23]

The toll road enabled others at Clyde to prosper as the area remained a popular picnic ground. In 1924, Jim and Helen Schneider moved into the former Clyde Pavilion and converted two of its rooms to living quarters. In 1927, a new post office application was submitted by the Clyde Eating House but was denied. During the 1930s, Pike National Forest took over the Corley Mountain Highway, renaming it Gold Camp Road and opening it for free to all. The Schneiders and their children continued living off the land. They grew hay, harvested block ice from some nearby caves and traded hand-churned butter to Seven Lakes caretaker Clyde Reynolds in exchange for trout. The Clyde School closed in 1936.

Into the 1940s, Clyde next served as a stopover for mule trains training soldiers from Camp Carson (today's Fort Carson) in Colorado Springs. The soldiers gave the Schneider children candy bars and bought moonshine from the family.[24] By 1947, one of the Schneider children, Hank, was living with his wife, Ida, in the old school. There also was a hotel at Clyde called the Clyde Inn. The inn didn't last long, for Clyde resident Frances Kramer remembered the hotel being closed up and shuttered during the 1950s. The building was later purchased by some investors from Colorado Springs, but it burned to the ground on September 9, 1954. Clyde's last school survived, however, and was purchased by Robert and Laverne Rayburn that same year for only $1,500. The Rayburns installed a door between the attached teacherage and the schoolroom, expanded the kitchen and added a second bathroom, fireplace, back door and picture window.[25]

The Bradley family, who had purchased property during the 1940s, continued buying other area ranches, including that of the Schneiders, throughout the 1960s. In 1974, Chuck Bradley subdivided lots at Cathedral Park and tried to sell them, but the effort was in vain. Picnic tables that had been present at Clyde were dismantled by the Forest Service during the 1980s even as Gold Camp Road remained a popular tourist destination. When Teller County commissioners attempted to close the old railroad tunnel outside town in 1988, residents of Clyde and others complained until the tunnel was reopened.[26] These days, the school and former ranger station are all that really survive of old Clyde. The rest of the historic area remains as private ranching property.

3

HIGH PARK CITY

A Ranching and Farming Paradise

If nothing else, the road on which High Park City was located served as the first route for prospectors and other travelers wanting to reach the Arkansas Valley from the Cripple Creek District. The High Park City & Cripple Creek Toll Road was first incorporated by John K. Witcher, R.K. Potter and S.P. Maderia of Cripple Creek in 1896. An alternate route skirted around the base of Mount Pisgah outside Cripple Creek and through Box Cañon, with an intersecting road leading to what would soon be High Park City.[27]

The High Park area seemed lucrative enough, as area farmers could grow crops and sell their goods in the Cripple Creek District, as well as Cañon City. There were prospectors, too. J.M. Kellogg was locating claims around High Park for the firm of Barbee, Bastian and Kellogg in January 1896, and gold ore from the Red Oak Lode was assaying at twenty-three dollars per ton.[28] The *Cripple Creek Morning Times* of February 6, 1896, reported that three other miners by the names of Grant, Wagner and Griffith were busy prospecting in the area.

Prospectors, ranchers and farmers would all benefit from the newly proposed High Park City, although mining was a primary focus. "Robert Boath was in yesterday from High Park and reports a flourishing condition of things, both as to mining prospects and as to High Park City," said Chicago's *Mining and Industry Review* magazine on February 13. "A number of buildings are now underway and a livery barn, hotels, restaurants and other enterprises will soon be open for accommodation to the public."

Everyone was hopeful that the Cripple Creek District's gold veins extended to High Park. "A good deal of prospecting is being done in the neighborhood of High Park," reported the *Colorado Transcript* newspaper in faraway Golden. "The district is constantly spreading out." Even before it was platted, T.P. Rigney of Cripple Creek was selling lots in the new town. The plat map was filed in El Paso County on March 5, 1896, by the Greatest Gold Belt Mining Company. Most of the streets bore the names of local minerals. Progress was quick, as reported in Leadville's *Herald Democrat* a few weeks later. "High Park City, one of the new mining camps in El Paso County, now has a dozen buildings completed and as many more in process of construction."[29]

High Park City's post office opened in June 1896. The population was guessed to be around one hundred people. In time, however, it was clear that mining prospects were not as good as expected, and the post office closed in June 1899. The 1900 Cripple Creek District directory described High Park as a "small settlement between Cripple Creek and the Bare Hills." In fact, the Bare Hills post office, in Fremont County, was servicing High Park City. It is no wonder, since business had slowed down considerably. According to the directory, only eleven men lived there, some with wives and children.[30]

The 1900 census is a bit more telling. High Park City consisted mostly of ranchers and farmers. In town, there were two boardinghouses run by Mary Mitchell and Minnie Allen, respectively. The presence of a cook indicates there might have been a restaurant. The population also included

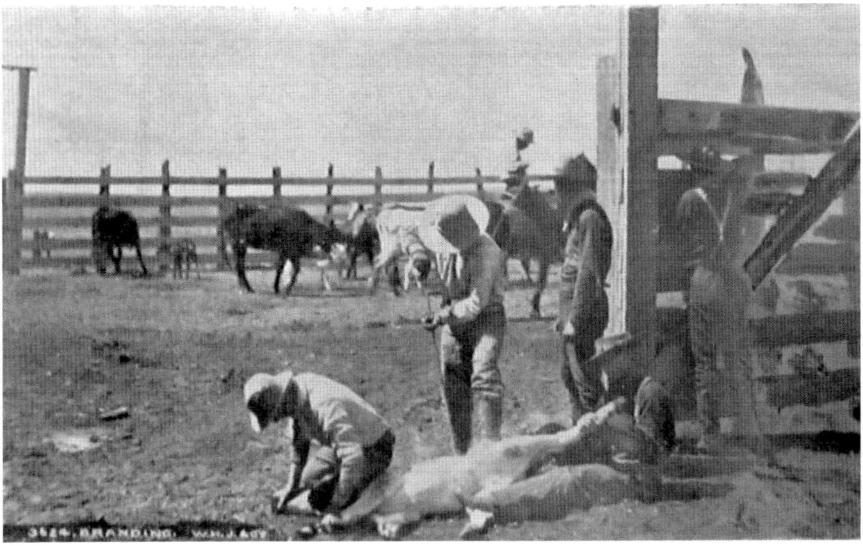

An early photograph, circa 1896, depicts cowboys at branding time in Teller County. *From Hall,* Official Cripple Creek Up to Date.

a sawmill owned by Robert K. Potter and Nelson Hackett, a veterinarian, a bookkeeper, a schoolteacher and two wood choppers but only six miners. Almost all the residents were married and had children.

For a time, High Park City did experience a brief resurgence, and the post office reopened in 1902. When postal authorities closed it again in 1913, local residents rallied a protest and the office reopened once more in 1914. Finally, in 1917, as the Cripple Creek District mining operations continued closing and people left the area, the post office closed one last time.[31] That was the end of High Park City, which today is no more than a wide spot in the road.

4

LOVE

A Community of Many Uses

The engaging community of Love began as a local ranch. With the coming of a toll road and later a railroad, however, Love blossomed into a well-known community and rest stop on the way to the Cripple Creek District. The story of Love begins in 1875, when the Cheyenne & Beaver Toll Road was established. The road ran through the ranch of John Love, who had homesteaded roughly five and a half miles west of the settlement of Clyde a few years prior. In the 1880 census, John and Charles Love were found on their ranch raising cattle. Love's father, Joel, was appointed Colorado Springs postmaster in 1888.[32]

Although ranching was the main staple at Love, mines began appearing as the gold boom in the Cripple Creek District began in 1891. Early newspapers mentioned that Winfield Scott Stratton, destined to become the district's first millionaire, stayed or stopped at the Love Ranch on his way to the area before making his millions. Love's ranch often served as a stopover for those traveling to and from Cripple Creek, and particular mention has often been made that some guests stayed because they were too intoxicated to make it all the way to their final destinations.[33]

About half a mile from the ranch, a small community was being settled by 1892. This place was first known as Beaver Park since it was situated along Beaver Creek. There was already a town called Beaver Park being platted closer to the Cripple Creek District, however, and the two were sometimes confused. When a graveyard was established soon afterward, it was called Beaver Creek Cemetery. Unfortunately, the cemetery's exact location has

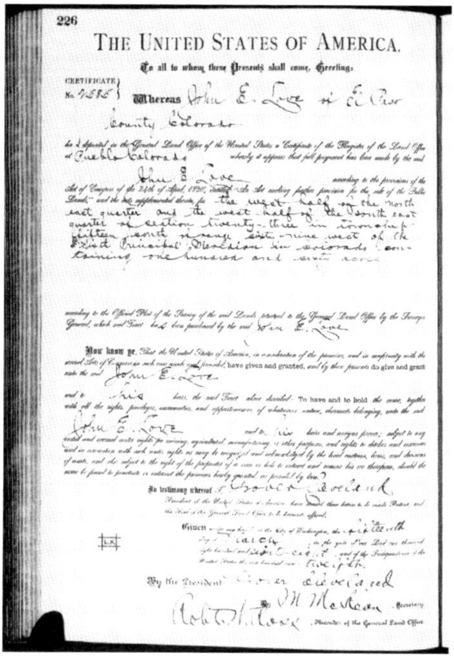
226

THE UNITED STATES OF AMERICA.

To all to whom these Presents shall come, Greeting:

CERTIFICATE No. 4585

Whereas John E. Love of El Paso County Colorado

has deposited in the General Land Office of the United States a Certificate of the Register of the Land Office at Pueblo Colorado whereby it appears that full payment has been made by the said John E. Love according to the provisions of the Act of Congress of the 24th of April, 1820, entitled "An Act making further provision for the sale of the Public Lands," and the acts supplemental thereto, for the west half of the north east quarter and the west half of the south east quarter of section twenty-three in township fifteen south of range sixty-nine west of the Sixth Principal Meridian in Colorado containing one hundred and sixty acres

according to the Official Plat of the Survey of the said Lands, returned to the General Land Office by the Surveyor General, which said Tract has been purchased by the said John E. Love

Now know ye, That the United States of America, in consideration of the premises, and in conformity with the several Acts of Congress in such case made and provided, have given and granted, and by these presents do give and grant unto the said John E. Love and to his heirs, the said Tract above described: To have and to hold the same, together with all the rights, privileges, immunities, and appurtenances of whatsoever nature, thereunto belonging, unto the said John E. Love

By the President: Grover Cleveland

Recorder of the General Land Office

John Love first patented his land in 1888. The document was signed by President Grover Cleveland. *BLM/GLO website.*

proven to be quite elusive. Various graveyard directories for Teller County have pinpointed the place as being just northwest of Pringtime Reservoir on the old Love ranch, but other sources have suggested different locations. Most of those buried there are children, including one or two children of Henry Charles and Margaret Rathke, as well as Roy Harold McCallister, an eight-year-old who died after an accidental shooting. The burials took place in 1896 and 1897, respectively. Other children buried in the cemetery include two babies from the Waters family and members of the Love family.[34]

As the Cripple Creek District continued developing, an increase in traffic and population merited opening a post office in December 1894. To avoid conflicts with the other Beaver Park, the new post office was christened Love. An ore-processing plant, the Colorado Springs Mill, also opened to service smaller mines in the area.[35] What John Love had to say about these developments remains unknown, for by 1896, the rancher and his family had moved to Delta on Colorado's western slope.[36]

The move might have been a wise choice, for soon Love was subject to the lawlessness often suffered by rural towns. Early in 1898, Constable Michael Hayes of the city of Victor went to Love to serve a warrant on Charles Nichols for some unknown crime. Nichols shot the officer, who died from his wounds. The killer was sentenced to life at the state penitentiary in Cañon City. Six months into his sentence he tried to escape but was apprehended. In June 1899, Nichols tried to escape once again. This time, he was successful, and because his wife still lived at Love, authorities banked on the outlaw trying to come home. A posse soon descended on the village. "It is said that when Nichols is met by the posse, some one will shoot," predicted the *Cripple Creek Morning Times*, "and it is rumored around [Cripple Creek] Nichols will

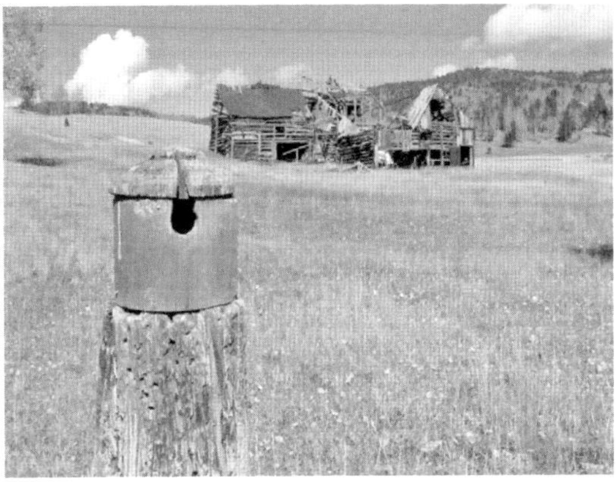

The barn in the background is all that remains of Love today. *Jan MacKell Collins.*

never be taken alive, unless he is taken by surprise." The next day, the paper reported that Nichols had indeed been apprehended but at the town of Rockvale in Fremont County. He surrendered without incident, but Cañon City deputy sheriff Thomas Tobin was accidentally shot by another officer. He was expected to live.[37]

One other bizarre incident marred the otherwise placid life at Love. The same day on which Nichols was apprehended, a group of fishermen found the body of Adolph Huffman lodged against a large rock in West Beaver Creek a mile and a half below Love. A scissor and tool sharpener by trade, Huffman had recently been seen "lying behind an embankment apparently asleep, with his grinding machine standing nearby in front of a house at or near Love." Coroner Dunn of Victor and two assistants were called. Unfortunately, Huffman's body was too decomposed for transport back to Victor for burial preparation, so the men loaded the body into a coffin and buried it near the spot where it was found.[38]

By 1900, Love still had its post office, as well as a store and a school taught by Miss Nora Smith. The population was seventy-five, although citizens were listed in the Cripple Creek District directory under the jurisdiction of the nearest town, Altman. Residents consisted of miners and timber men, postmaster and grocer F.W. Cady and Samuel Cashmaker of the Love Saloon.[39]

Love was on the decline by 1902, when the post office closed. The *Cripple Creek District Directory* shows most of the residents employed as miners, cowboys and ranchers. There was also a dairy serving up butter and cream. The community's continued decline coincided with that of the Cripple Creek District. When the Colorado Springs & Cripple Creek District Railroad ceased service past Love in 1920, most residents moved away.[40] Today, the town site lies within the privately owned Beaver Park Ranch.

5

MANITOU PARK

THE DREAM OF DR. WILLIAM BELL

In 1869, a township commonly known as Bergen's Park was surveyed at the top of Ute Pass just beyond today's Woodland Park along Highway 67. The park was named for an early prospector who, in 1861, was known to be living near Missouri Gulch.[41] Few others lived in the area, and Bergen's Park remained fairly quiet until the arrival of Dr. William Abraham Bell.

Bell was a British physician who came to America in the 1860s. After working briefly as a photographer, he found himself in Colorado, where he met General William Jackson Palmer. The general was founding a new town, Colorado Springs, and the two men became business partners. Palmer went on to found his town in 1871, while Bell founded his own town, Manitou, just up the road in 1872. The men also explored the region thoroughly. Upon visiting Bergen's Park, Bell saw the perfect spot for establishing a resort and began buying out several local homesteaders to the tune of eleven thousand acres.[42]

In 1873, Bell built a three-story hotel and some cabins made from tents with wood floors. Soon, wealthy families from the East and even Europe began visiting the park. Within a year, a wagon road was planned from Bergen's Park that would lead east to the town of Monument in El Paso County and west to the city of Fairplay in Park County. Even as plans for the road were delayed, Bell next developed a trout hatchery. In 1874, he imported 100,000 eastern brook trout eggs from New York. As the eggs hatched, fish were sold to shops in Colorado Springs and Leadville. The hatchery ran successfully as late as 1890.

When Bell discovered there was already another place in Colorado called Bergen Park in 1875, he changed the name of his resort to Manitou Park. The name now tied in with Bell's city of Manitou and brought more visitors from Colorado Springs. Within a short time, Manitou Park became a true vacation destination. The park was beautiful; there were ample trout, and one could experience "the beneficial effects of Pine timber upon delicate lungs."[43]

Bell made money other ways, too. Because sawmills and logging were a big industry in the area at the time, he built his own sawmill at Manitou Park in 1880. H.D. Fisher of Chicago was hired to run the operation, which was quite a project. A Denver & Rio Grande narrow-gauge locomotive was even hauled to the site, and a tiny, unnamed railroad was built, spanning seven to nine miles from Cantrell's Gulch to Drury Gulch. Subsequently, Fisher became a chief promoter for the Colorado Midland Railroad when it began chugging up the Ute Pass.[44]

In 1886, as the Colorado Midland Railroad tracks reached the top of Ute Pass, rancher Daniel Steffa established his own whistle-stop some miles down the road and decided to call it Manitou Park. Bell immediately objected on the grounds that train passengers would confuse the new place with his resort. He successfully petitioned for Steffa to change the name of his Manitou Park to Belmont and also made sure stagecoach service was available between the two places.[45]

Bell continued purchasing land throughout 1888, and Manitou Park expanded to twenty-six thousand acres. Unfortunately, the hotel also burned that year. Cottages around the hotel survived, however, and a new hotel, built in 1889, contained fifty to sixty rooms and a fancy ballroom. There were also a bowling alley, a billiards parlor, an outdoor pavilion, stables, carriage houses, a blacksmith shop, a golf course and even tennis courts. General Palmer and his wife, the cultured Queen Mellen Palmer, were frequent visitors.[46]

In 1890, the name of Belmont was permanently changed to Woodland Park, and a few months later, Manitou Park opened its own post office. Bell's next project, Manitou Lake, was constructed and drew even more guests. One of them, Francis Chomondeley Thornton, built a lavish summer home at the shore. For a time, the area around the home was known as Thornton Village. Other subresorts of Manitou Park included Garden of Eden, which was platted by Matthew Davis in April 1891, and Pine Grove, which was platted by Hannah Johnson in June.[47]

Manitou Park's post office was short-lived, closing in February 1892. Then Bell carved a new town out of Manitou Park and called it Torrington.

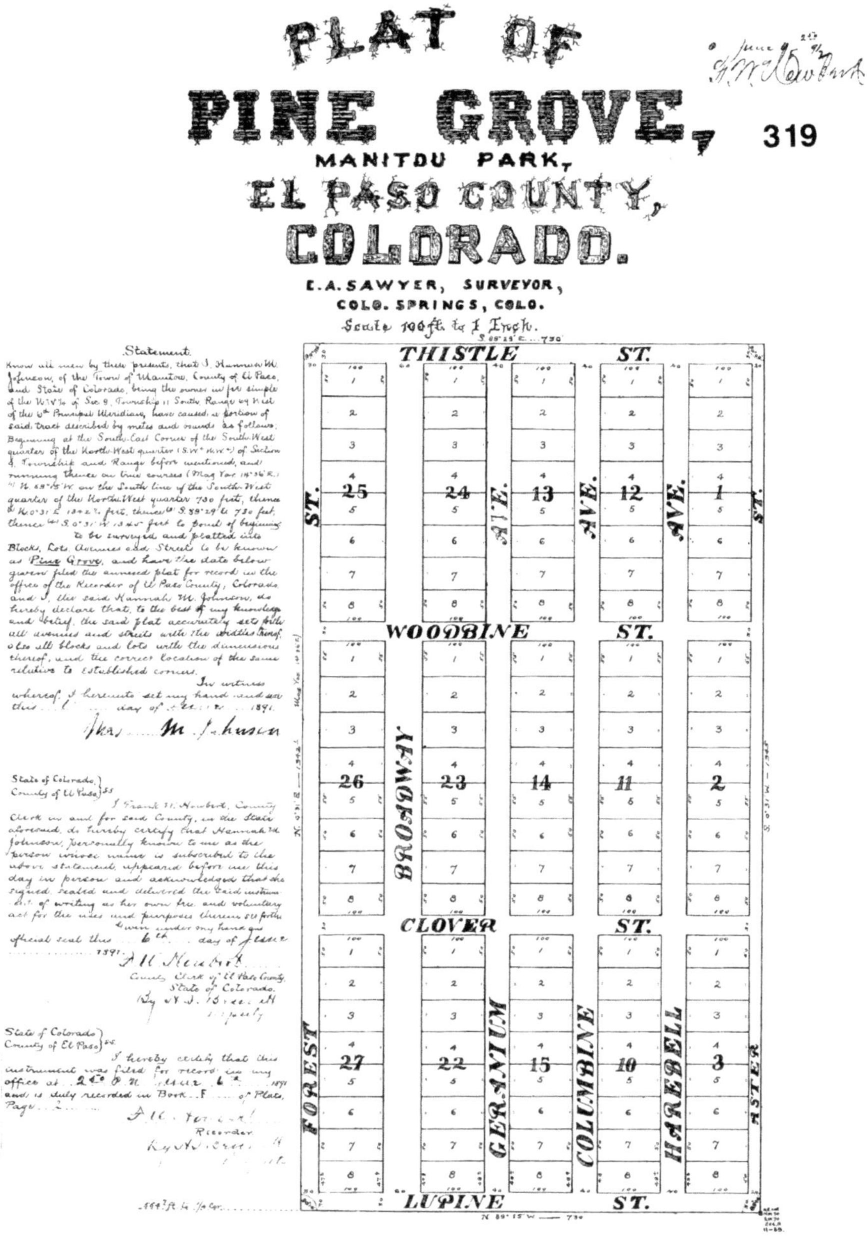

Pine Grove was one of the resort communities established at Manitou Park. *El Paso County Clerk and Recorder.*

This newest endeavor was located on the east side of Manitou Lake. There was a saloon, general store, carpentry shop and livery, and a new post office opened there in September 1896. Back at the main resort in 1899, another fire burned the second Manitou Park hotel, along with the casino with its own amusement hall. Once again, however, the cabins were saved and could still accommodate upward of one hundred guests at a time. By 1900, Henry Law of Lanter City was operating a sawmill at Torrington, but not much else became of the town. Part of it was vacated in 1903, just months before the post office closed.[48]

In 1909, the year of General Palmer's death, Bell deeded the remainder of Manitou Park to Colorado College in Colorado Springs. The decision was fitting since Palmer was the one who founded the college. Thus, the end of Manitou Park was the beginning of a new life for the area. Palmer had long voiced his concern for conservation of the forests in the park. Accordingly, Colorado College established the Colorado School of Forestry. In 1937, the Works Progress Administration built a lovely six-building complex at Manitou Park. The structures were built with native sandstone from Missouri Gulch.[49] Today, the Forest Service continues to use the buildings, and outdoor enthusiasts and campers continue to enjoy the scenic views and campgrounds around Manitou Lake.

6

ROSEMONT

RESORT TO RESERVOIR

When the Cheyenne & Beaver Park Toll Road Company was formed along today's Gold Camp Road, Rosemont served as a "halfway" station where travelers could rest. In 1877, Charlie Hancock ran the station, a large log cabin with a tin roof that offered food, lodging and libations. Rosemont's name was fashioned after Mount Rosa nearby.[50]

Services at Rosemont coincided with the improvement of another road at Clyde that ran toward the resort of Seven Lakes in 1878. The man making the improvements was Dr. Mayo G. Smith, who was planning to buy Seven Lakes. Smith also owned one of two ranches at Rosemont at the time. Another prominent rancher was Henry C. Rathke, who, in 1888, homesteaded 160 acres on what is now the site of Rosemont Reservoir. Rathke took up residence in an old cabin that had been abandoned. Two years later, his homestead was recognized, and he paid $200 for the land. Rathke built a sizeable ranch and began raising oats.[51]

Rosemont gained popularity with the discovery of gold in the Cripple Creek District. Soon, prospectors from the district were trying their luck in the area. By 1901, as the Colorado Springs & Cripple Creek District Railroad laid tracks near the town, Rosemont had evolved into a whistle-stop. In time, the community was home to 350 people and even a school.[52] There was not, however, a fire department, as evidenced by the burning of C.F. Pinson and Henry Seigfried's lumberyard in September 1901. "There are no facilities for extinguishing the blaze," explained the *Aspen Democrat* newspaper. "The fire will have to burn itself out."

Although it was first believed the fire was caused by a locomotive from the CS&CCD Railroad, it was soon learned that Seigfried and Pinson had recently been notified that the government planned to seize most of their lumber operation. The lumber that was said to rightfully belong to Pinson and Seigfried, as well as their equipment, had conveniently been moved just before the blaze began. The fire was finally put out on October 2 after burning eighty acres. There was no further news as to whether Seigfried and Pinson were charged.[53]

At long last, a post office opened at Rosemont in March 1903. The following year, plans were in the works for a summer resort there that would include "the building of a large artificial lake and a $10,000 hotel." Three hundred acres had been purchased for the site, but alas, the resort never materialized. At the very least, Rosemont was the site of a tree nursery in 1905 for the Pikes Peak Forest Reserve Project to reseed trees in the area.[54]

Rosemont's population numbered fifty in 1908 and included both prospectors and timber men. Mrs. May Day's Summit Lunch Room, where railroad passengers could stop for a bite, also opened. There was also a telephone operated by H.M. Loveland, whose wife was a music teacher. Helen Ritchel was superintendent of the school, and James Wilder offered services as justice of the peace. Henry and S.P. Yates rounded out things with a general merchandise and hotel, respectively.[55]

Rosemont clearly aspired to be more than just another railroad stop. The community's elite status was given an even bigger boost in 1918, when Spencer Penrose, plagued by water shortages after expanding his marvelous Broadmoor Hotel in Colorado Springs, began buying water from Rosemont. The water was drawn from Cheyenne Creek and piped to a reservoir near the hotel. Within a year, Rosemont's population had grown by one hundred people. C.C. Lane ran a general store as well as a real estate company. Lane's wife ran the Rosemont Lodge.[56]

In spite of its quiet and scenic vistas, Rosemont never did become a resort. The post office closed in 1926, and in 1935, the City of Colorado Springs Water Department built an expansive reservoir to supplement the water supply exclusively for the Broadmoor. The reservoir was expanded in 1962, and by the 1980s, Rosemont was home to just a caretaker's house and one cabin. One of the structures was formerly a lodge where Penrose once entertained guests.[57] Today, Rosemont-Penrose Reservoir is open for fishing seasonally and is accessible only by foot.

7

SEVEN LAKES

A Remote Retreat

Back in 1872, Quincy King, a simple carpenter, chanced to discover a beautiful valley with a chain of seven glacial lakes. The area was located just below the summit of Pikes Peak on the west side of Almagre, aka Baldy, Mountain. The lakes ranged in size from "ten or twelve acres" to "seventy or eighty acres." All were within easy walking distance of one another, feeding into Middle Beaver Creek.[58] Seven Lakes, as the place would be known, provided magnificent views, gorgeous meadows, ample water and an easy jaunt to the top of Pikes Peak. A resort was born.

By 1874, King had partnered with two other men, M.W. Smith and William Unruh, on a mining claim in nearby Bison Valley. Unruh left in 1876, but a new partner, David L. Welch, joined the team. Just a year later, the Cheyenne & Beaver Park Toll Road Company was formed expressly to create a better road to reach Seven Lakes.[59] By 1878, the high-altitude resort was a favorite among tourists, even though its elevation was between ten and eleven thousand feet. In June, a group of visitors consisted of sixteen campers, ranging in age from a nine-month-old boy to a seventy-three-year-old woman. The group pitched tents near the lakes and were visited the next day by proprietors King and Welch.

More visitors in July included a party who stopped at Seven Lakes on their way to the Pikes Peak summit via Marsh and Brent's "burro train." Among the nine people was Miss Kate Mailler, correspondent for the *St. Joseph (Missouri) Herald* newspaper. "The party camped Monday night in the two commodious tents that were provided," reported the *Colorado Springs*

Gazette on July 20. "Mr. King very hospitably entertained the party during a part of the time."[60]

Visitors to Seven Lakes remembered seeing a large hotel under construction. Hand-hewn boards were cut from native logs using only a whipsaw. Each of the two stories had a porch, and the structure was topped by a tin roof and central chimney. There were twenty rooms in all. Even before it was completed, the Seven Lakes Hotel was receiving rave reviews. "When there is a hotel on the shores of these lakes, and we can take refuge there for a week at a time, we can defy the Colorado sun and leave it to do its worst on the plains," wrote one reporter. "It cannot scorch us at the lakes."[61]

With the hotel completed, Seven Lakes saw a marked increase in traffic. In September, a Dr. Edwards and family stayed at Seven Lakes for ten days. During his time there, Edwards managed to shoot an amazing amount of wildlife but missed a cinnamon bear guessed to weigh one thousand pounds. Seven Lakes even made a suitable winter camp, what with improvements to the road and the abundance of deer, grouse rabbit, fox and bison.[62]

Although King and Welch seemed satisfied with their resort, they were not beyond selling the place. Noted author Helen Hunt Jackson, who had visited Seven Lakes, seemed less than impressed with the endeavors of the two men, writing:

> *They had wild dreams that merely by sheltering and feeding people who came up there, they could lure them into staying a long time. They had still wilder dreams of stocking the lakes with fish, cutting bridle paths to the tops of all the high peaks, keeping donkeys, guides, and all sorts of hunting equipments, and so making a "summer resort" of the place. Of course, they failed miserably. To build even a log house where every pound of nails must be brought twenty miles by horse or mule, a twenty miles' steady climb, is dear work. The poor fellows had to give up, with a good deal less than their "labor for their pains," and their log house fell into the hands of a strange man.*[63]

The "strange man" was Dr. Mayo G. Smith, a prominent physician from Colorado Springs. For about two years, Smith worked on improving the road from his ranch at Rosemont to the resort.[64] In May 1880, he purchased the King and Welch claim for $1,500. In the meantime, Welch and his wife, Emma, sold their interest in the hotel to King. The sale included

> *nine bedsteads with beds & bedding for the same; one heating stove No. 36 & one cooking stove with furniture & appurtenances for hotel purposes; two dozen common chairs and two rockers; lot of table furniture consisting of two castors, plates, cups and saucers and side dishes sufficient for the accommodation of about sixteen persons, also 4 bracket lamps, 4 hand lamps, 4 mirrors, 2 dining tables, 2 kitchen tables and a number of tools.*

In November, King deeded over his entire share to Smith for $1,000.[65]

Smith aspired to take up where King and Welch left off. A grand reopening of the hotel was staged in July 1881. Advertisements for the resort in Colorado Springs proclaimed, "The Seven Lakes house is now open for the reception of guests. Conveyances leave for this resort every Thursday morning." By September, Seven Lakes was noted as being "a very popular resort since the trail has opened to it. The house is but four miles from the summit of Pikes Peak."

Other improvements through 1882 included a bowling alley and billiard room. The hotel closed during the winter months, reopening in June with the grand announcement that "this is one of the best located mountain resorts in Colorado, and is destined to be very popular with all tourists." Shortly afterward, however, Seven Lakes came under fire when the state of Colorado announced that Smith's ownership was invalid until surveys had been conducted and land patents had been obtained. Smith duly filed a claim for his 160 acres in October. Witnesses that he owned the land included G. Odle, who lived in the hotel. Testimony revealed the presence of several more buildings—including an icehouse, a corral, a shed and a stable—on the property.[66]

His battle won, Smith kept up improvements on the road to Seven Lakes. There was even talk of building a railroad to the summit of Pikes Peak that would pass by the hotel. The railroad never came to fruition, and by October 1884, Smith had hired Mr. and Mrs. L.B. Farrar to run the hotel. "Our tent is pitched on the banks of Heart Lake, one of the seven at the foot of Bald Mountain," reported some visitors from Kansas. "At night we accepted an invitation to join the guests at the hotel in an entertainment. The hosts Captain and Mrs. Farrar made our stay very enjoyable…We have slept in one of the beds at the Lake hotel and eaten at the table, and of all places east or west in Colorado we like it the best."[67]

In 1885, Smith next leased the resort to E.B. Curtis and L.T. Gray, but in the end, running the resort was simply too expensive. When the lease expired, Smith sold Seven Lakes Resort to George W. Thorne of New York. The selling price was only $4,000. In November, the new owner was working on fencing in the property and adding a wing to the hotel, but there was also another deal on the table. On March 9, 1886, Thorne partnered with Colorado Springs businessman Irving Howbert to create the Colorado Springs Land and Water Company. The idea was to use the lakes as a water supply to the city. Thorne happily sold the water rights to the company to the tune of $5,000. The Beaver Water Supply Company was formed on March 10, and on April 2, Thorne sold the entire Seven Lakes property to the company for $9,000—not a bad deal for a $4,000 investment.[68]

The new company retained former lessee Everett Curtis and partner H.H. Stevens. More improvements were made to the Seven Lakes Hotel, including the addition of a third story. Platforms were installed for those using tents. Advertisements in June read, "Elevation 11,000 feet. Hotel now open. Access by the romantic Cheyenne Road, or by Bear Creek trail. Loveliest views in Colorado. Only route by which parties can see sunrise from Pikes Peak. Only proper route for ladies." Another news item explained that Fairley Brothers of Cripple Creek had loaded a pack train of twenty burros with furniture and were lugging it up to the hotel. Everybody, it seemed, had a plan for Seven Lakes. In 1887, Harvard University thought of building an observatory there, but the plans fell through. Unsatisfied with Smith's original land patent, the government required the former owner to set the record straight by filing a second patent in 1888.[69] Meanwhile, Curtis and Stevens continued advertising the hotel in Colorado Springs.[70]

The improvements were actually of little use, for other trails were being built to access the top of Pikes Peak from Colorado Springs. Slowly but surely, Seven Lakes lost its appeal. The hotel was ultimately closed sometime after 1890. A slight shadow fell over the once classy place in 1892, when a Detective Sawyer alleged that J.A. Cross, accused of robbing David H. Moffat's First National Bank in Denver and a Wells Fargo Express Company in California, had hidden his loot near Seven Lakes. Nothing came of Sawyer's story, however, which was "regarded with considerable doubt."[71]

By 1895, Seven Lakes had shifted from renowned resort to a utility capable of supplying not only water but also power. In November, there was talk of erecting a power plant to service a new electric railroad for the Cripple Creek District. Plans for this project fell through, but in 1901, after years of arguing over water rights and wanting to access the water at Seven Lakes, the City of Colorado Springs purchased the parcel from owner Edgar E. Wade. The sale price was a whopping $69,000.[72]

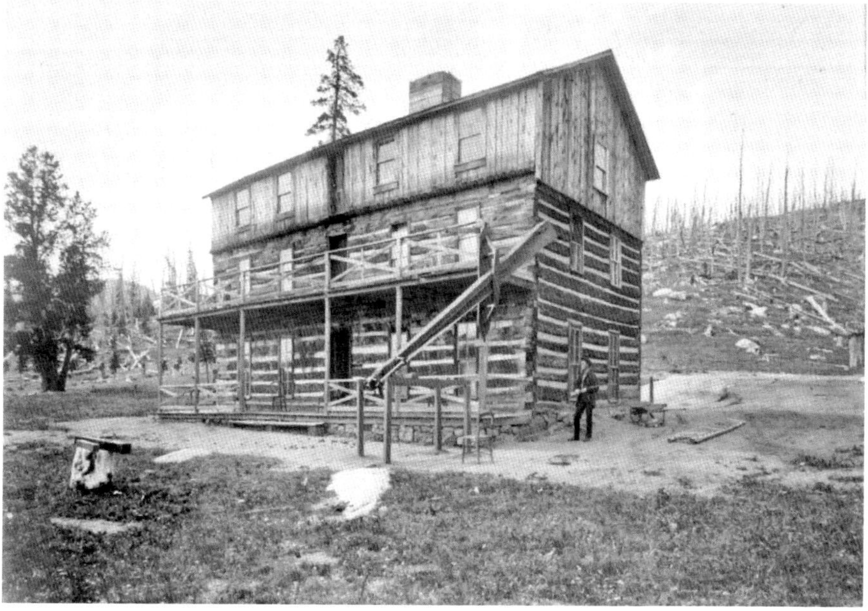

This image of the magnificent Seven Lakes Hotel was taken in 1887 after the third floor was added. *Courtesy Harvard University, W431903L.*

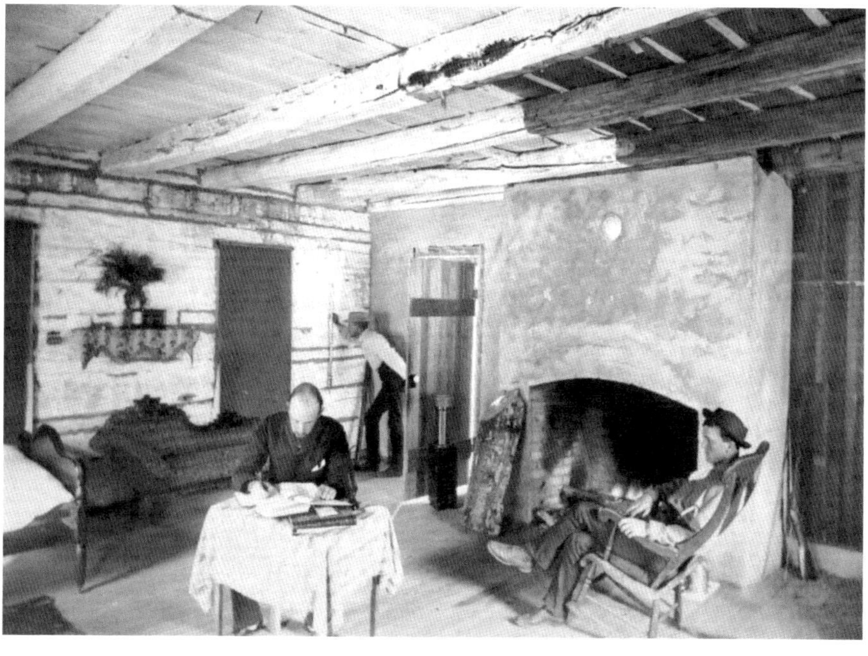

Visitors to Seven Lakes Hotel enjoyed a rustic but very comfortable setting. *Courtesy Harvard University, W431903L.*

The sale to Colorado Springs was soon under fire as the cities of Cripple Creek and Victor objected on the grounds that allowing Colorado Springs to access the water would endanger the Cripple Creek District's own water supply. Ultimately, it took an act of Congress for Colorado Springs to gain full and sole access to Seven Lakes. Construction on a new pipeline began in 1904. Within a year, the landscape had been changed considerably, and the original seven lakes were no longer visible. Today, Seven Lakes remains remote and inaccessible, although new regulations beginning in 2015 allow limited access with required permits.[73]

8
SPRING CREEK
A Suburb of Cripple Creek

Located on the outskirts of today's Cripple Creek Mountain Estates west of Cripple Creek, Spring Creek had its beginnings with several area mining claims. The hamlet was located along its namesake creek in a pleasant and quiet valley. The main drag skirting the creek was dotted with tidy little houses. A wagon road cut through the valley between Copper Mountain and Mineral Hill, providing easy access to Cripple Creek.

Spring Creek's beginnings can be dated to 1893, the year its little cemetery was established. Fourteen to sixteen people were entombed there over time. Longtime locals remembered seeing five or six wooden grave markers and a wrought-iron fence surrounding the graveyard.[74] The first mention of Spring Creek in newspapers was in the *Cripple Creek Morning Times* of December 6, 1895. A small article mentioned that the Modoc Mine sold a mining deed to the Spring Creek Gold Mining and Milling Company the previous November. There was little other news, as Spring Creek never grew large or prominent. The community never had a post office or even a newspaper.[75]

Although there were many settlers at Spring Creek, it is Jacob Abby who is most often mentioned in a handful of notes about the town. Abby first dabbled in mining and with good reason. In January 1896, the *Morning Times* revealed that the Mineral Hill Tunnel Company was "quietly" digging a tunnel from Spring Creek, through Mineral Hill and "directly to the new Midland Terminal depot in Cripple Creek." Work had just started, but "solid formation has not been reached."[76] The tunnel never materialized. A short time later, two of Abby's children—three-year-old Clare "Nugget" and

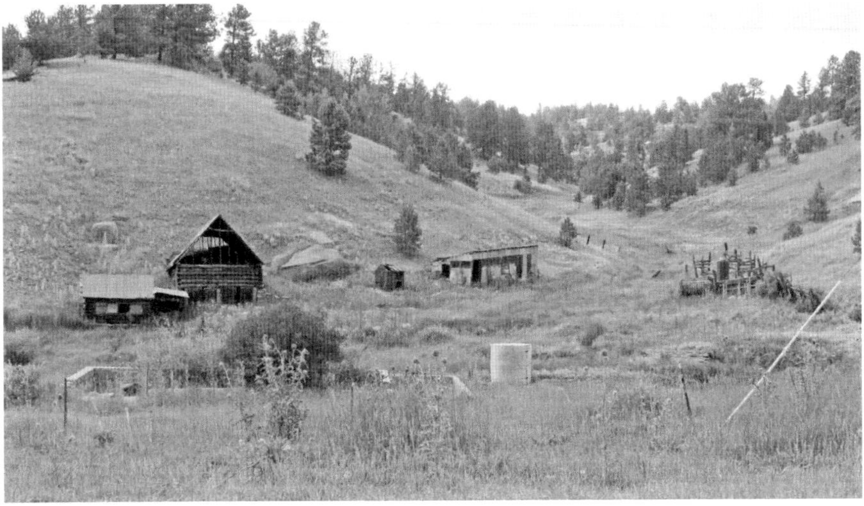

A road at Spring Creek, seen here, led to Cripple Creek via Mineral Hill and Copper Mountain. The land is privately owned. *Jan MacKell Collins.*

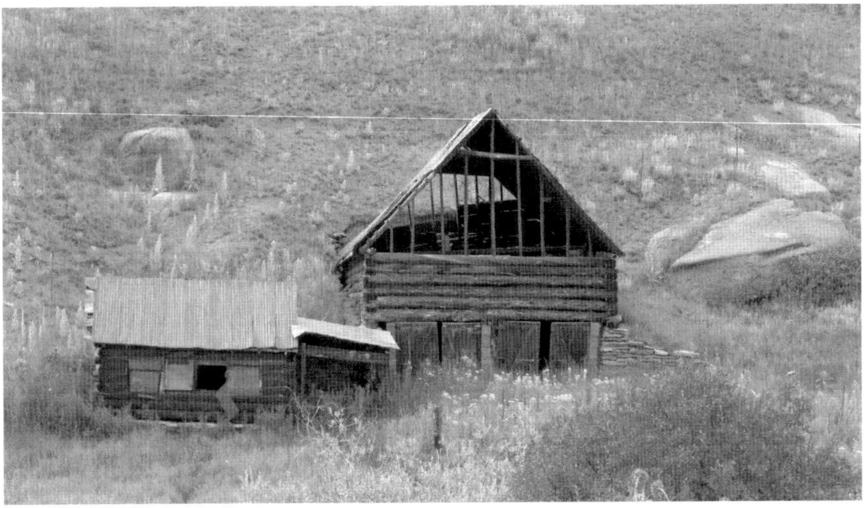

One of the last standing buildings at Spring Creek as it appeared in 2015. *Jan MacKell Collins.*

five-year-old Lloyd—died on January 18 and 25, respectively. The children were buried in the cemetery alongside another sibling named Hazel (died 1894). Later, Jacob named the Little Lloyd mining claim after his son. Other claims filed by Abby include the Little Annie, Little Ellen, Little Emma, Little Jessie and the Little Mary.[77]

Spring Creek was just far enough away from law enforcement authorities in Cripple Creek for some rather odd crimes to occur. On New Year's Day 1898, a most gruesome discovery was made at the home of Annie Robinson on Spring Creek. Robinson's large log house, occupied by herself and two young children, had burned to the ground. A *Morning Times* reporter and neighbor W.S. Carmele investigated and found charred bones among the ruins. Then in June, the *Times* reported, "Officers last night effected the capture of the man who has been deranged for some days, and has eluded capture, staying in the country near Spring Creek. He was brought to this city and locked up, charged with insanity."[78]

Last, in August, stolen goods were recovered from the Spring Creek cabin of Sherman Crumley, one of three bad men "who have been responsible for many a depredation in this district for the past two years." Crumley's cohorts, a man named Purdy and one Charley Ripley, had already been apprehended following the theft of some saddles and harnesses from a Mr. Harker. Three days later, it was reported that Cripple Creek sheriffs Frank Boynton and Tom McMahon had found more stolen goods in a cabin near Crumley's home, known to be one of his "hiding places."[79]

In 1900, the census reported the Abbys and forty other people still living at Spring Creek. Abby is listed as a carpenter. There were also two dairies—the Union, run by Fred Desplaines, and the Midway, owned by Charles Warner. Twenty-three miners lived at Spring Creek, too. Their children attended a schoolhouse on the south slope of Copper Mountain, taught by Alberta Smith, who lived in Cripple Creek. There were also Edward Tealon and his nineteen-year-old wife, Belle, who ran a saloon. Tealon employed his brother-in-law, John Parr, as bartender. Ten years later, the census notes that Abby was a farmer. The total population was around eighty people, but folks gradually began moving away as the Cripple Creek District's mines began playing out. In the 1920 census, the Abbys were living at the town of Gillett, where Jacob had once again returned to carpentry. Abby's wife, Mary, died in 1927, and Jacob died in 1934.[80]

Throughout the 1930s and '40s, Spring Creek continued to shrink, although there were still several occupied cabins as late as the 1960s. During the last half century or so, many of the buildings were dismantled or moved into Cripple Creek.[81] The remaining buildings at Spring Creek have silently sunk into the grass, and a few modern homes have appeared in the area since the 1990s.

9

SUMMIT PARK

HOSPITALITY AND A STRANGE RELIGION

There are many references to Summit Park, located between today's Woodland Park and Divide. The area was first surveyed between 1872 and 1877 by D.C. Oaks, who recorded a handful of miners working their claims. Summit Park's post office was among the earliest in Teller County, opening on September 1, 1873. Great things were in store for the young community. On January 11, 1874, a letter to the editor of Denver's *Rocky Mountain News* recommended opening the "West Plum Creek Trail" from Denver. The proposed road would run from Denver to West Plum Creek Canyon, on to Bergen's Park and finally to the Summit Park post office. The letter was signed "El Paso." A hotel already existed at Summit Park as well. In August, it was noted the hotel had "been enlarged, and the proprietor, Mr. W.S. Nichols, intends to have it kept in first class style."[82]

In June 1875, the Summit Park post office was noted as being "kept by the gentlemanly proprietor of the Summit Park House, located on the Fairplay road." Compliments were further extended to Nichols, who "keeps a fine assortment of groceries, which he sells at bed-rock prices." Another article in August described him as "one of the best landlords in the interior of the state. He keeps a store and the post office, and his hotel is a popular stopping place." Rave reviews of Summit Park House continued into 1876, this time describing proprietor E.D. Nicholas as "an old Topeka (Kansas) man, and one of the most obliging gentlemen." The hotel rooms and their beds were "nice and clean, and the table is loaded with the best in the market." Notably, a Mr. J.A. Nichols ran a stage line between Colorado Springs and Fairplay.

The trip included staying overnight at Summit Park House. The fact that proprietors of Summit Park House and the stage lines it accommodated were named Nichols seems to indicate the men were somehow related.[83]

A second survey of Summit Park was conducted during 1876 and 1877 by E.H. Kellog and Albinus Z. Sheldon. Area residents included Ed Humphrey, who "occupied himself with the counterfeiting of half-dollars until apprehended"; the Moody family; and three others identified as Drader, Kule and Nichols. In 1877, a Mrs. Edwards, identified as the "first settler," sold "squatter rights" to John H. Himebaugh and E.E. Nichols for $625. This Nichols was perhaps the same man who made history at Manitou Springs, El Paso County. He had come to Colorado looking for a cure for his tuberculosis and became a prominent businessman and real estate investor. He was also an early mayor of Manitou Springs, a position he held for eight years. Himebaugh, meanwhile, took over both Summit Park House and the post office.[84]

Crime at Summit Park first reared its ugly head in September 1877, when "Oregon Bill" left the town for Lake City in Hinsdale County to receive treatment for a bad foot injury. Bill returned to find that A.A. Desrosiea had "jumped" his place. A gunfight over the matter resulted in the death of Desrosiea. Then in November, a couple horse thieves were reported as having abandoned their horses at Summit Park while being pursued. A Colorado Springs posse was hunting for them.[85]

Three months later, two men, Klawen and Miller, were apprehended after arousing the suspicion of a rancher named Tubbs and breaking into the home of Judge Castello, who had founded the town of Florissant up the road. A posse formed at Tubbs's ranch, found the outlaws' camp and closed in. Klawen and Miller "sprang for their rifles, when the order to fire was immediately given, upon which a volley was poured in upon them." Klawen was wounded and Miller surrendered. The men were taken to Colorado Springs, where it was learned they had several warrants out for them in numerous counties.[86]

In 1882, the first two homestead claims in Summit Park were filed by Benjamin B. Logan and Wesley C. Wheeler.[87] Three years later, Summit Park was noted as being on Post Road Number 38 between Manitou and Florissant. Travel writer George Crofutt described the community as

> *a ranche* [sic] *post office, in a beautiful little park, away up in the mountains, via Ute Pass wagon road, 17 miles northwest from Colorado Springs. It is surrounded by magnificent mountain scenery, abundance of*

game, plenty of trout in the streams, petrified trees not far distant, and a lovely place to sojourn for a season.[88]

Within a year, there were thirty people at Summit Park, a number expected to rise as the Colorado Midland Railroad began laying tracks up Ute Pass. One thousand railroad workers converged on the area. One of them, a subcontractor named Arbuckle, hit foreman George Richardson over the head with an axe handle at Summit Park and killed him.[89]

Wheeler and fellow pioneer Frederick Bacon had partnered by 1887 to officially plat Summit Park in hopes the railroad would run through their combined properties. The race to compete for the attentions of the railroad escalated. Newspapers throughout 1887 record men filing land claims all around Summit Park, yet the post office closed in March 1888 and was moved to Manitou Park, which was later renamed Woodland Park. Although Wheeler and Bacon specifically laid out the town so the railroad would run through the center, they neglected to pay the recording fee to file their plat in 1889, and it was subsequently never registered. Bacon eventually sold his property to Edward Moore.[90]

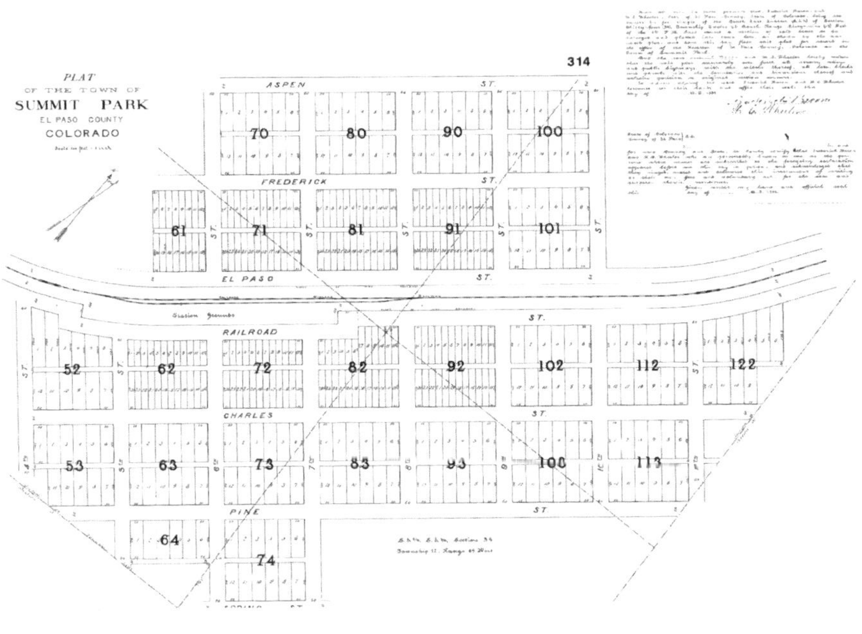

The plat map for Summit Park shows the Colorado Midland Railroad running through the middle of town. *El Paso County Clerk and Recorder.*

Although there was no depot at Summit Park, the train did stop there to unload "helper" engines, which assisted the cars up the steep grades of Ute Pass. There were only two railroad buildings and a few houses, and things were fairly quiet. A Mrs. Hays remembered that "there was a lot of travel through the pass. We never locked our doors, even when the railroad came through, until a group of unsavory characters moved in from Kansas."[91]

Hays might have been recalling a religious sect called the Williamites, who moved to the area beginning in the early 1890s. The group was led by Henry Truman Williams, the son of a Chicago minister and former editor for the *Horticulturist* magazine. He also freelanced as a travel agent for railroads in Colorado, Texas and the "Mormon Territory." In 1870, Williams gave General William Jackson Palmer a tour of the area east of Colorado City in El Paso County, where the latter later founded the city of Colorado Springs. In gratuity, Palmer's fiancée, Queen Mellen, named Williams Canyon in Ute Pass after their guide.[92]

In 1872, Williams published two booklets: *A Tourist Guide and Map of the San Juan Mines* and *The Pacific Tourist*. But his career took a strange turn when he established—or joined—a religious cult in Brooklyn, New York, in about 1879. Soon he was the leader of the group, which he named the Williamites, and the bunch migrated to Chicago. In time, lurid details of Williams's religious sect emerged. Although he himself was married, Williams's followers were not allowed to marry. Some of those who joined the group abandoned their spouses and children. Everyone was required to surrender their money and worldly possessions to Williams, who used the money for clothing and food "as needed."[93]

The Williamites also had a fondness for taking in orphans, especially infants. Rumors of abuse and "dead infants" were soon circulating. Some of the group had left with Williams for Denver when Chicago authorities raided the headquarters, arrested the adults and took the children to orphanages. The adults were later released, but eight of the children were kept by authorities, who apparently feared for their welfare.

Upon arriving in Denver, Williams discovered the authorities had been contacted by those in Chicago. The group, consisting of three men, ten women and a dozen children, moved on once more, this time to Colorado Springs. There, the bunch took up quarters at various houses in town for a few years. One day, a Mr. Riley appeared from Denver looking for his wife, who had left him to join the Williamites. Williams defended her actions, assuring authorities that the woman "came here through no persuasion of mine, but was sent through Divine influence." Mrs. Riley was judged insane and taken back to Denver.[94]

Then in 1889, James and William Campbell went to court in Colorado Springs to have their sisters, aged eleven and fourteen years, "removed from the guardianship" of the Williamites. Authorities investigated and found Williams unfit as a guardian, having neglected the girls "morally, mentally and physically."[95] Shortly afterward, Williams purchased 480 acres near Summit Park with money from his followers and established a new camp for "wayward youths."

The place was situated on either side of the wagon road to Leadville. Williams segregated the men and boys on the north side of the road and the women and girls on the south. But the group once again drew suspicion when it was discovered that Williams was the only man allowed in the female quarters, and several women from the group were getting pregnant. Williams and his followers left Colorado shortly after these claims came out and finally settled in Arkansas. Williams died in 1915. In 1956, Williams's descendants had a plaque commemorating him placed in Williams Canyon below Cave of the Winds on Ute Pass. The plaque was stolen in 2010.[96]

Summit Park survived the Williamites and continued to progress. The post office reopened in March 1890, perhaps in hopes that Summit Park would become a regular stop on the railroad someday. It didn't, but at least the community was included in a "Grand Excursion" hosted by the Colorado Midland in 1891. The trip ran from Colorado Springs to Salt Lake City and Ogden, Utah. The fare for those at Summit Park was $20.

By 1892, there were still not enough people to support the post office, which closed a final time in July. One last effort was made to revive the area in April 1896, when five hundred miners from Summit Park and Divide gathered at the latter town's school and organized the Pikes Peak Mining District.[97] By then, however, the nearby Cripple Creek District had its own mining boom going on. Summit Park evolved into a mere place name with several ranches. In a few years, however, the village would find new life as the town of Edlowe.

PART II

MINING CAMPS AND TOWNS

10

THE MINING CAMPS

Where Miners Worked and Lived

The typical mining booms of the West began with surveyors, mineralogists and miners exploring for signs of rich minerals. If the finds were promising, a mining claim was staked. Miners generally camped at their claims and hoped for the best. Sometimes nothing was found and the men moved on. Other times, the findings realized a small profit. The best claims resulted in mining companies big enough to merit establishing a town or city nearby.

Teller County was the scene of numerous camps throughout the late 1880s and well into the twentieth century. Most were in the Cripple Creek District, but many others could be found in the hills north of Divide and Woodland Park. Some of these places have quite literally been lost to history, with no documentation or other sign they ever existed. Still others have been documented to some degree, and it is these that are listed here.

Beacon

Beacon's name was applied not only to a mine but also a hill and even a park—the latter term being assigned to any grassy or open area. All of these names in the Cripple Creek District appear to refer to the same place, which was located near the town of Arequa and later absorbed by the larger town of Elkton. The earliest reference to Beacon comes from the 1893 *Cripple Creek Complete Directory*, which identifies the Beacon Mine as being on Beacon Hill.

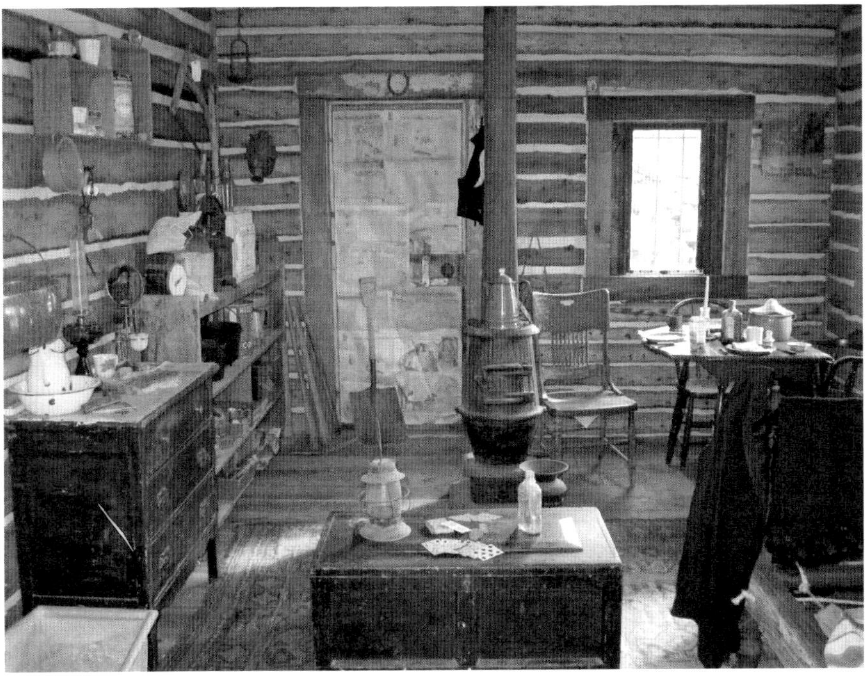

A miner's cabin display at the Cripple Creek District Museum accurately depicts how men lived during the gold rush. *Jan MacKell Collins.*

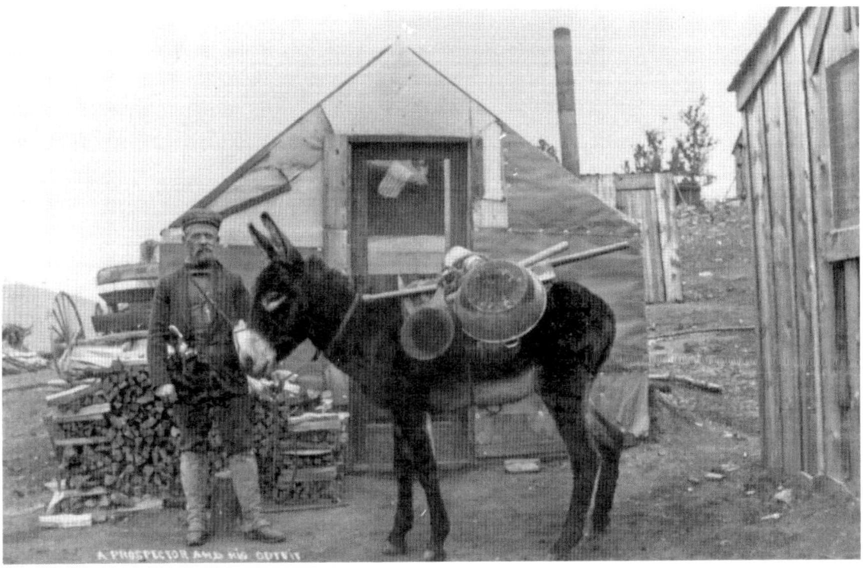

Mining camps like Beacon were populated by men from different backgrounds and nationalities. *Cripple Creek District Museum.*

In 1900, W.N. Bainbridge, superintendent of the El Paso Mine, was living at Beacon Park on the west side of Beacon Hill. Also present were numerous miners, including W.L. Daniel, who resided at Beacon Hill House.[98] By 1902, residents of Beacon were listed under Elkton in the *Cripple Creek District Directory*. When the Beacon Mine played out, the miners simply packed their belongings and moved on.

CAMP HOVER

Camp Hover was located two miles southeast of Gillett. The camp was named for William Maxin Hover, a former photographer who had come to the Cripple Creek District from Nebraska with his wife, Addie.[99] By 1900, Hover was secretary of a mining company at his namesake camp, although the Cripple Creek District directory for that year does not say which one. Neighbors included miner Rich Harris and blacksmith Fred Schenkel. Also at Camp Hover was Andrew Wharton, vice-president of an unidentified mining company. Wharton's family at Camp Hover included his wife, Martha, and five children, who were attending school. Another neighbor was Bonar Martin, a widower who was raising stock near Camp Hover with his three grown children. Others lived in the area, too, but whether they were in Camp Hover proper is unknown. Like many other places, Camp Hover eventually faded into history. By 1910, Hover had returned to Nebraska to farm. He died in 1914 and was buried in Iowa. Addie died in 1932 and shares a tombstone with her husband.[100]

DUTCHTOWN

Dutchtown was south of Victor and founded by Scottish miners who were originally unwelcome in other parts of the Cripple Creek District. Such racism was not unusual in the district, whose residents were predominantly white, Irish and Catholic. "Foreigners," including African Americans, Chinese, Italians, Greeks, Mexicans and other nationalities, were often not afforded much respect. Immigrants and people with different ethnic backgrounds tried their luck in the district anyway, keeping to themselves and establishing their own neighborhoods.[101]

The population of Dutchtown numbered over one hundred Scotsmen. One family, the McCormacks, changed the spelling of their name to

McCormick in order to pass themselves off as Irishmen.[102] The community appears in area newspapers only a few times. One article in 1898 reported a tragedy near the settlement:

> *A Little Boy Killed—A frightful accident occurred at 10:30 yesterday morning on Straub mountain, resulting in the death of the 10-year-old son of Amos Aspey. Mr. Aspey, accompanied by the boy, Harry, went after a load of wood. While coming down the steep grade near Dutchtown Mr. Aspey got off the wagon to clear some obstructions out of the road. The team took fright and ran away. The boy was thrown from the wagon bed and the hind wheel passed over his head, crushing his skull in a horrible manner.*[103]

The 1910 census reflected only a few residents at Dutchtown, who were actually counted as part of the town of Lawrence. They were Carrie and John Pearson, locomotive engineer Charles Bauel and John D. Myers, who ran a dairy. Three men—Simon Peterson, Dan Gleason and Randal Percy—worked for Myers. In time, the residents of Dutchtown moved to other parts of the Cripple Creek District, and the tiny settlement was forgotten about.

EAGLE JUNCTION

Eagle Junction was the name given to a camp near the Eagle Sampler Mine in the Cripple Creek District. The mining camp was located just above and in between the towns of Goldfield and Independence.[104] When the Eagle Sampler closed, the miners moved on to other camps.

EMPIRE

Empire was a mining camp near Empire Mine west of Victor. All that is known about the camp was that when it was established in 1900, the population was 276.[105]

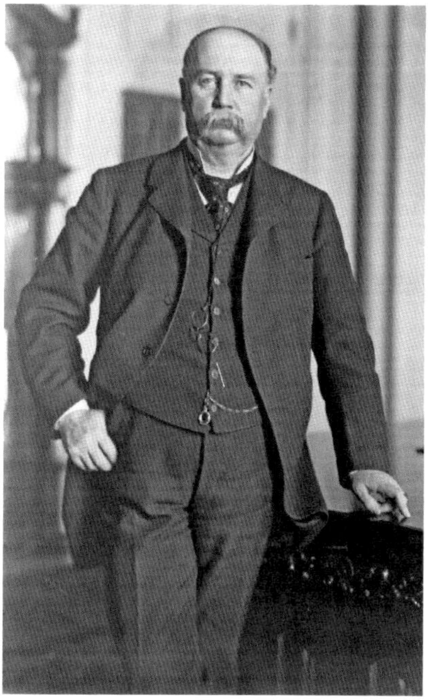

U.S. vice president Garret Hobart, for whom the mining camp of Hobart was named. Hobart died in 1899. *Library of Congress.*

HOBART

The tiny mining camp of Hobart owed its existence to the Hobart Gold Mining Company, sometimes known as the McKinley-Hobart Gold Mining Company, in the Cripple Creek District. News of the mine first appeared in the February 16, 1896 issue of the *Cripple Creek Morning Times*. The corporate office was located in Colorado Springs. Principle officers were G. Miller, William Hohnes and E.B. Simonson.[106]

Both the mine and the camp were named for Garret Hobart, who was nominated for U.S. vice president in 1896 and elected in 1897 under President William McKinley. Hobart died in 1899 but his namesake mine lived on, and on February 6, 1900, the Hobart post office opened. That year, the mining company owned three claims: the Last Dollar, the Nancy Hanks and the Wild Cat. All of the claims were located on Trachyte Mountain in the heart of the mining district. Stock, however, was selling for a mere penny. Little of note happened at Hobart, and the post office closed quietly in February 1902.[107]

HOOSIER

Both the camp of Hoosier and nearby Hoosier Pass were named after the Hoosier Mine. All three were located along an electric railroad known as the High Line in the Cripple Creek District. All three places also are mentioned in newspapers and other sources, but nothing of note happened to miners at the camp.[108]

HORACE

Horace was named for the Horace Clark Mine, located between the settlement of Signal Butte and the Fisher Lumber Company's narrow-gauge railroad leading to Manitou Park. A post office opened there on June 5, 1896. Horace would have been located in Teller County when the latter was officially formed on March 23, 1899, but the post office had already closed just two weeks earlier, on March 8.[109]

HULL CITY

With the establishment of the Cripple Creek District, an old trail called Shelf Road, which ran between today's Cripple Creek and Cañon City in Fremont County, was developed for ease of access to the district. Part of the trail ran from the head of Wilson Creek all the way to Hull City in the district, where a mine of that name had been staked. Shelf Road was incorporated as the Cañon City and Cripple Creek Toll Road in November 1891 by Cañon City entrepreneurs.[110]

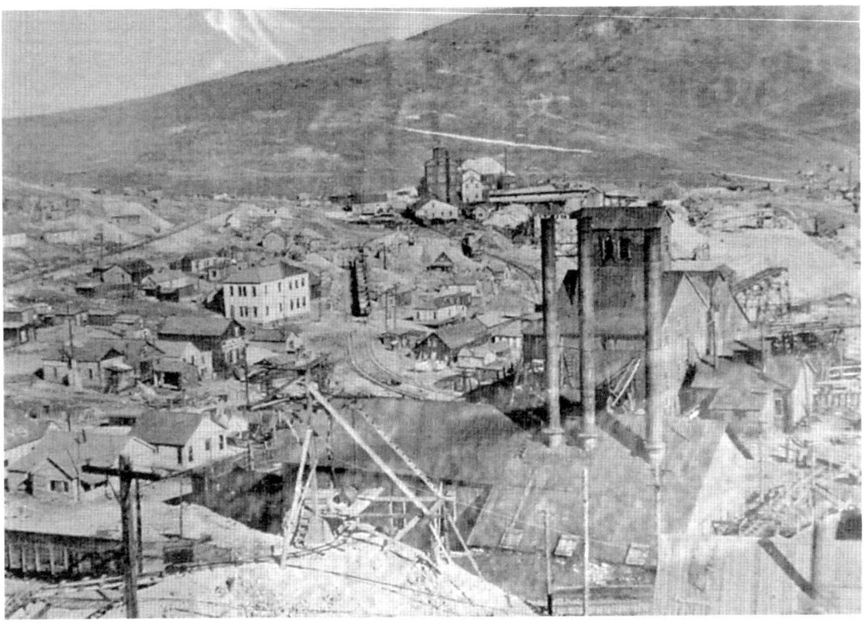

The Hull City Mine's three smokestacks can be seen here in the Vindicator Valley. *Jan MacKell Collins.*

There was never an actual "city" at the Hull City Mine. When the nearby town of Independence was platted in 1894, the mine was located at the very northwest corner of the town. Notable miners at the camp included at least one colorful character, A.G. "Smitty" Smith. Formerly a Missouri farmer, it is said Smith had more tobacco stains than buttons on his shirt. Those tobacco stains must have been lucky; Smith hit a rich vein and made $750,000 almost overnight.[111]

One early source notes that when Willis S. Montgomery platted Hull City Placer in 1895, the survey included forty acres around the mine that might have included a portion of Independence. But by 1896, when "Hull's Camp" had formed at the mine, its residents were still included as part of Independence. Miners at the camp remained as such, and by 1902, both the camp and its citizens had officially been absorbed by the town.[112]

JACKPOT

Jackpot was a small camp at the Jackpot Mine northwest of Elkton. In 1905, the camp was identified as being about half a mile from the town of Anaconda on the way to Victor.[113]

LOS ANGELES

The Los Angeles Mine had a small population of miners living around it but was eventually absorbed by the City of Victor.[114] Coincidentally, the mine was located close to the tiny mining town of Hollywood, but there appears to be no link to those same two iconic names in California.

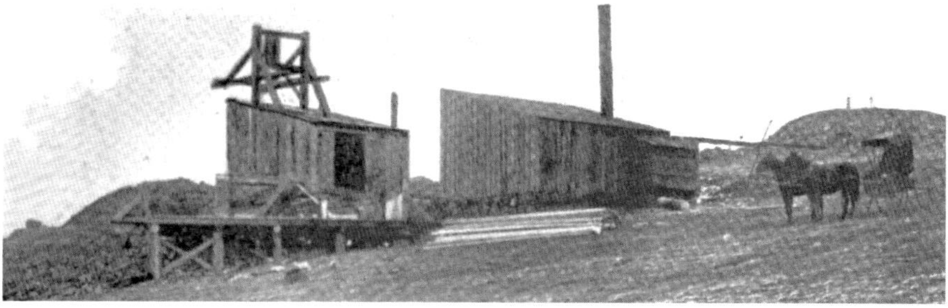

The Los Angeles Mine was one of many homes to a small miners camp. *From Henry Lee Jacques Warren and Robert Stride,* Cripple Creek and Colorado Springs: A Review and Panaroma of an Unique Gold Field, with Geological Features and Achievements of Five Eventful Years, Including Outlines of Numerous Companies *(Colorado Springs, CO: Warren & Stride, 1896).*

NEWPORT

The short-lived camp of Newport was located near the Newport Mine on Four Mile Creek, roughly two miles northeast of the whistle-stop of Midland.[115]

PECK'S CAMP

Although some limited prospecting surely took place there, very little is known about Peck's Camp except that it was in place by 1909. The settlement was located near Rosemont on East Beaver Creek. The only reference to it comes from Victor resident Ken Lorenz. In 1944, Lorenz remembered, Peck's Camp was in the heart of some rough country that was barely accessible by vehicle when he and his school chums took a hunting trip to the place. The weather was too warm for good hunting, but the boys did encounter a small herd of wild donkeys.

In lieu of hunting, the boys spent the rest of their week wrangling and playing with the donkeys. "The first jack ate nearly all our cookies," Lorenz remembered. "They threw us off so many times that if we did manage to stay on one a short time, we would reward him with a cookie. After awhile they learned that if they were to get any more cookies, they would have to let us ride. They sure learned fast. Those were good cookies, and those donkeys just loved them."[116]

PORTLAND STATION

Portland Station came about primarily because of the Portland Mine, situated on Battle Mountain outside of Victor beginning in 1893. In 1900, the Cripple Creek District directory described the camp as "a small town on the south slope of Battle Mountain comprised for the most part of people working on the famous Portland mine." To wit, the population, according to the directory, consisted of nine miners and their families, as well as the miner's bookkeeper B.F. Starr, tracklayer W.L. Lavery, assayer John Staats, two civil engineers and Thomas Fitzmaurice, a bartender at Victor's Silver Dollar Saloon. By 1902, Portland Station was considered part of Victor, surviving just a few more years before fading into the past.[117]

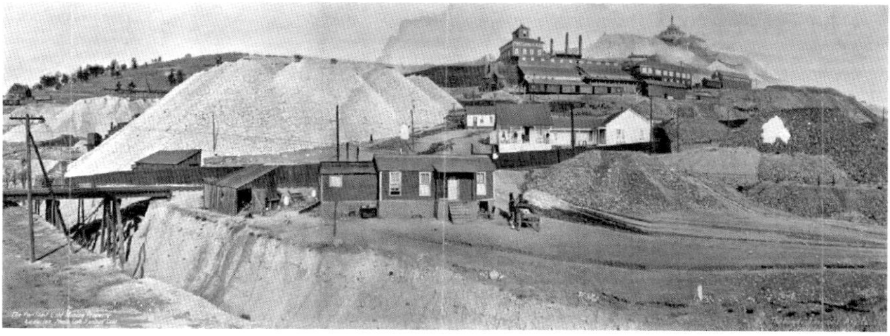

Tidy cabins and a nice white Victorian home provided shelter for mine workers below the Portland Mine. *Mining History Association.*

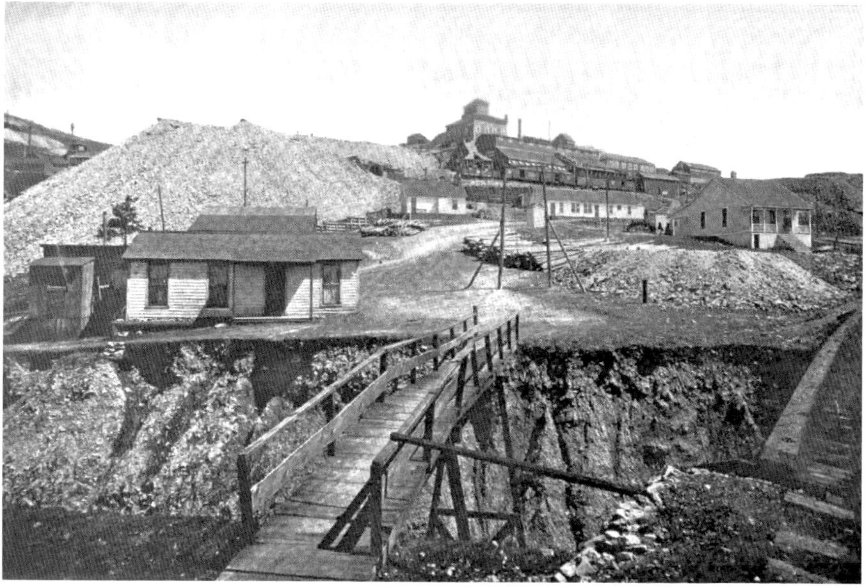

The main buildings of the Portland Gold Mine Company are in the background. *From Hills,* Official Manual of the Cripple Creek District.

REIGERVILLE

Reigerville was quite the enigmatic little community. Located in Wilson Creek Gulch south of Victor, the place was so called because a family named Reiger lived there beginning in the mid-1890s. When the place first appeared in the 1896 *Cripple Creek District Directory*, the inhabitants were listed as citizens of Victor. Members of the Reiger family included Antone Sr. and his sons, Antone Jr., Charles and George. Everyone worked as teamsters hauling freight except George, who was employed as an engineer. The Reigers were a hardworking family with many children. Antone Sr. was born in Germany in 1927; immigrated to America in 1854; married his wife, Mary, in 1867; and was manufacturing pottery in Missouri by 1880. By 1899, he had relocated to the future site of Reigerville, applying for a mineral patent for his Bell Donna lode.[118]

Reigerville was also sometimes listed as "Riggertown" in the 1900 district directory. For unknown reasons, the place was also sometimes called "Kellerville."[119] The 1900 census gives a good indication of how fast Reigerville was growing. Residents included numerous members of the Reiger family, all of whom lived within proximity of one another. Their neighbors included miners Randolph Erickson and Fred Hand; miller Edward Rust and his wife, Mary; and brick maker John Ward and his family. Antone Reiger Jr. boarded two men, a seventy-year-old brick maker named Osker Pistle and teamster George Winters. Most of the residents had children, who presumably attended school at the nearby town of Lawrence. The 1900 directory also lists several miners, along with J.A. Stull and John W. Ward's Stull & Ward Assay Office and Ed Rust's Oneida Mill. Also present was Lamb & Sprague Brick Manufacturers and the Stull, Ward & Reiger Brick Yard. Antone Sr. was employed as a janitor at the school nearby Lawrence. He remained there through at least 1902 before retiring and died in 1907.[120]

Reiger's job gives at least a little credence to the local rumor that Reigerville had an orphanage. When the 1910 census was taken, fourteen-year-old Wilbur Rayland is listed as working as a "milker" for dairyman Arthur Stearns. Also, Christine and Antone Reiger Jr. had two children living with them who were listed as lodgers. They were Lawrence Pell, age nine, and Herman Pell, age five. How the Pell boys came to live with the Reigers is truly a mystery. Lawrence Edward Pell was born to Maud and John Pell on April 19, 1900, in Nevadaville, west of Denver. His brother, John Herman, was born around 1905. That same year, Maud Pell is thought to have died. What became of John Pell is also a mystery, as is the fate of Herman, who apparently died sometime before the 1920 census was taken.[121]

Another intriguing rumor about Reigerville is that there was once a "pest house" there for confining people with contagious diseases that had burned by 1917. What is known for sure is that Edward Pell stated he was employed by Antone Reiger Jr. as a farmer in 1918. By 1920, Antone and Christina Reiger appear to be the only family members left at Reigerville; Edward Pell appeared in the census as their "foster son."[122]

As of the 1930 census, the Reigers were living on Alamo Street in the southern section of Victor. Pell may have returned on at least one occasion; one source recalls that "Eddie Reiger" once got drunk and decided to shoot up his own town. Victor chief of police Armour Olson was summoned to quiet things down, only to be shot by Reiger. Olson was seriously injured but lived. This would have happened during the 1930s or early 1940s since Olson is listed as police chief in the 1940 census. That same year, Antone Jr. died and was buried in Pueblo. Edward Pell died in Seattle, Washington, in 1958, and that was the end of Reigerville.[123]

Spinney Mill

The ill-fated town of Beaver Park at the edge of the Cripple Creek District had barely been platted in 1892 when reports came that a new mill, erected by "Mssrs. Spinney," was due to be built nearby.[124] "The Spinney Stamp Mill at Cripple Creek has been started and is a complete success," announced the *Fairplay Flume* newspaper in its August 31, 1893 issue. Accordingly, the 1893 *Cripple Creek District Directory* listed the mill as being located on Beaver Creek. Over time, the mill would also be known as Spinney's Mill and Spinney Mills.

The first real news about the mill came during the district's tumultuous labor war of 1894, when angry miners kidnapped Isabella Mine manager D.E. Locke in January. The *Buena Vista Herald* in Chaffee County reported:

> *D.E. Locke, manager of the Isabella Mining Company, which property is located on Bull Hill, was met at or near the Taylor boardinghouse a few minutes after 10 o'clock Saturday morning, while on his way to the property, by about 100 miners, quickly taken from his cart, relieved of his side arms and walked down to the Spinney mill, where he was told to get down on his knees and solemnly declare that never, so long as he lived, would he again put foot on Bull Hill.*

Locke started to protest, but upon being shown a rope fashioned into a hangman's noose, he agreed to the demand. The manager was then escorted "down the Cañon [*sic*] several miles" and released.[125]

In fact, Spinney Mill became quite the hangout for outlaws. On a July evening in 1896, three masked men stopped the Kuykendall stage just a quarter mile from the mill. Fourteen men, four women and driver

George Worden were aboard when a man accosted the coach with a Winchester, telling Worden to stop and warning him, "If you pull a line, I will shoot you." Two other men then appeared, brandishing revolvers. The passengers were made to exit the coach and line up, whereupon the men's pockets were emptied.

The women might have been robbed as well, but Mrs. Joseph Gandolfo of Cripple Creek fainted. The robbers instead turned their attentions to the coach, overlooking two pocketbooks hidden under the seat by their owners. The thieves allowed their victims to "go ahead," and the coach resumed its trip to Cripple Creek—although two of the men actually remained behind to look for money they had discreetly tossed out the window upon seeing the masked men. The thieves, who came away with about $500 and ten watches, were believed to be three escaped prisoners from the Victor jail.[126]

A third lawless, yet puzzling, incident occurred in 1900. Ed Ash and J. Kirk were working at a pumping station when seven mounted masked men suddenly appeared. The group ordered Ash and Kirk to quit working and marched them to Spinney's Mill. Five of the men rode off toward Cripple Creek, but the remaining two escorted Ash and Kirk to "the half way house." There, the kidnappers called their victims a couple of "lying scamps" and ordered them not to return. Ash and Kirk continued on to Colorado Springs to report the incident. They were "beaten up some" but otherwise unharmed, and the mystery of why they were kidnapped remained unknown.[127]

Only a few miners and blacksmith James Wells were living at Spinney Mill in 1900.[128] Further evidence that someone still lived there came in 1901, when a sudden ferocious cloudburst broke the reservoirs of the Victor waterworks. "The great wave of water rolled down the gulch, wiping out three dwelling houses near the Spinney mill and breaking against the new steel concrete dam of the Pikes Peak Power Company two miles below," stated the *Golden (Colorado) Transcript* newspaper in its May 22 issue. That was the last mention of Spinney Mill.

STRONG'S CAMP

Grocer and lumber hauler Sam Strong was but a tenderfoot when his Strong Mine hit it big in 1892. The mine was located on Bull Hill directly above Victor—in fact, almost in Victor. Yet, in time, the mine actually grew large enough to merit a small camp around its perimeter. By 1900, Strong's Camp was referred to as a "residence town only, being a suburb of Goldfield and

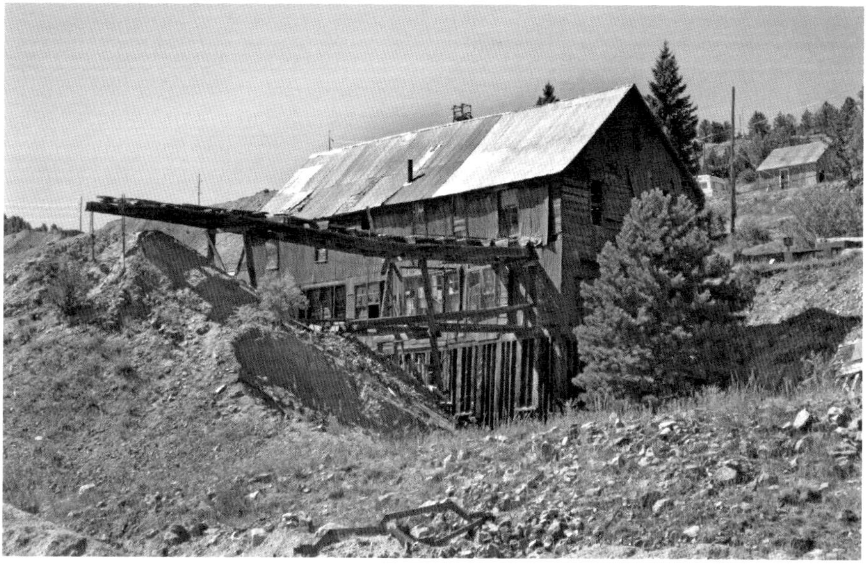

The Strong Mine as it appears today above Victor. Strong's Camp was likely represented by shacks and tents around the mine. *Jan MacKell Collins.*

using that post office for mails." Notably, the 1900 census shows that nearly every male resident was a miner. Some of them lodged at Mrs. A.L. Pierce's boardinghouse.[129]

Sam Strong, described as a heavy drinker and gambler, likely spent little time at his mine. Upon marrying Miss Regina Neville of Altman in early 1900, Strong was almost immediately sued by Luella Vance of Goldfield and Nellie Lewis of Cripple Creek, both of whom claimed he had promised to marry them. "Sam Strong, the millionaire miner of Cripple Creek, has two breach-of-promise suits on his hands," tattled the *Aspen Daily Times* in February, "and that during his honeymoon."[130]

Strong settled those suits and others that were lodged against him concerning his mine, but trouble seemed to follow him. On an August night in 1901, he got into a gambling brawl at the Newport Saloon in Cripple Creek. Bartender Grant Crumley, who was on the receiving end of accusations that the roulette wheel was crooked, ultimately shot Strong to death. Crumley was acquitted in 1902 and moved to Nevada. That same year, Strong's Camp was absorbed by Victor.[131]

11

ALTMAN

A Rough and Tumble Town

Nobody seems to agree about the exact altitude of Altman, one of the most notorious towns in the Cripple Creek District. The elevation was first reported in the 1894 *Cripple Creek District Directory* as 10,500 feet. Other sources have claimed altitudes ranging anywhere from 10,700 to 11,650 feet. At the very least, everyone agrees that during its heyday, Altman was the highest incorporated city in the United States.

Situated at the top of the Cripple Creek District with a clear view of Pikes Peak, Altman was platted on September 25, 1893, by Samuel Altman. In its infancy, the town grew very quickly. Along the main thoroughfares of Main, Baldwin and Brown Streets were wooden, false-fronted buildings. Four restaurants, six saloons, six grocery stores, a schoolhouse and two hundred homes already dotted the hillside by the time the town was platted.[132]

Almost immediately, a few roughnecks moved into town. On October 10, 1893, Felix Parrow, Robert McCullough, Harry Cavanaugh and Jim McDonald showed up at W.R. Goodey's saloon. The men spent the entire night and early morning playing cards for drinks. Around 1:00 a.m., the men suddenly broke into a fight as a ruse to rob the place. Barkeeper John Ashby was whacked in the head with a gun and "laid out," while faro dealer J.S. Bush was disarmed. In all, the robbers took $610 in cash and another $350 in checks, along with five gold watches and a pair of bracelets. Then in November, ex-prizefighter George Lear was labeled a "Green Monster" when he shot and killed a dance hall girl named Irene Goode during a jealous rage. A short time later, Altman bartender Sam Jones killed Lear at Kilday & Sullivan's Saloon.[133]

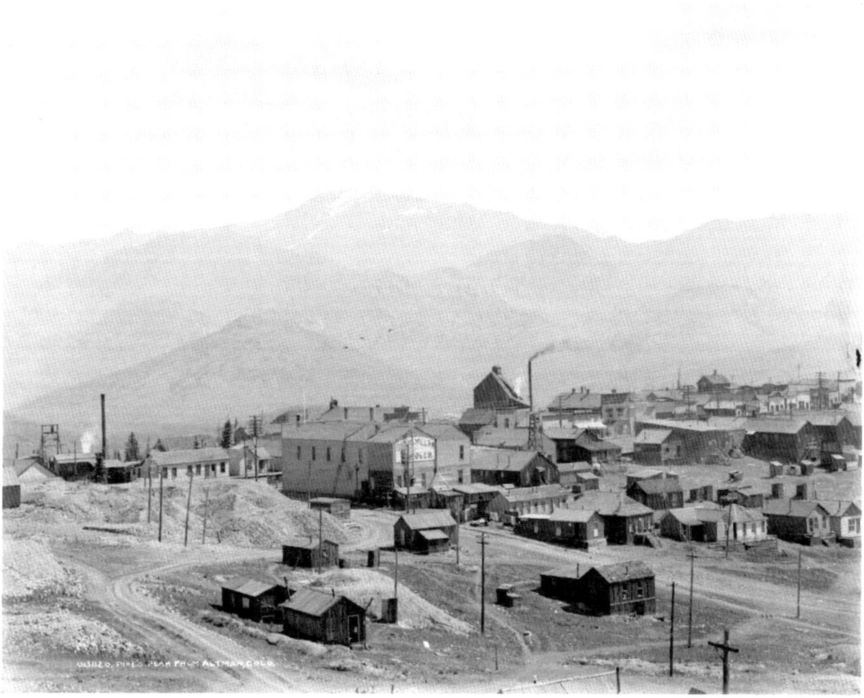

In this image by renowned photographer William Henry Jackson, Pikes Peak is clearly visible from Altman, the highest incorporated city in America. *Library of Congress.*

As of January 1894, Altman's population was guessed to be around two thousand residents. The post office opened on January 18.[134] Shortly afterward, the town unwittingly became a major player in the labor war of 1893–94. Beginning on February 1, local mine owners, including Sam Altman, changed their employees' workday from eight to nine hours per day—for the same daily wage of three dollars. Rather than bow down, the miners took matters into their own hands and simply walked off the job on February 2. Residents of Altman decided to further drive their point home by leaving town altogether. "The entire population of the camp packed up their effects," reported the *Aspen Daily Times* on February 7, "and a motley procession was formed, including miners, saloonkeepers and their outfits, merchants with their stocks and the denizens of the brothels. The hilarious cavalcade moved to Cripple Creek and within a few hours the camp was deserted."

Failing to get a proper response to their actions, the population of Altman was soon back and openly declaring their hometown a union town. Most of the residents were pro-union anyway and before long, the Free

Coinage Union Local No. 19 plopped down in the midst of the town. In the meantime, mine owners succeeded in procuring court orders to cease striking, but to no avail. As the highest town in the district, Altman afforded views in all directions and offered relative security from invading forces. The Western Federation of Miners, led by John Calderwood, soon found a home in town and successfully closed Altman to all but union men. Union membership cards were required of anyone wishing to enter town.[135]

Angered mine owners next hired deputies to disperse the miners at Altman. During one encounter in March, six deputies on their way to Altman were accosted by the town's own police staff. A fistfight broke out, and shots were fired. One deputy was wounded, and two others were arrested for carrying concealed weapons. Then El Paso County sheriff Frank Bowers sent a message to Colorado governor Davis Waite. He claimed a deputy was actually killed, Waite later said; hence, the governor allowed fifty special sheriffs to be deputized and sent up from Colorado Springs. Adjutant General Thomas J. Tarsney, who received similar embellished reports, hurried to Altman but encountered only "disheartened but dedicated miners."

Tarsney was ready to rescind his offer of assistance by the time Bowers secured numerous warrants against the miners. In the end, only one of them was tried and acquitted; the others were released without going to trial. In June, another scuffle broke out as deputies cut the telegraph wires at Altman, arrested reporters who were covering the event and were exchanging gunfire with miners on Bull Hill when a fresh militia was sent by Governor Waite. But so many lies were being told by men on either side of the war that Waite ultimately visited Altman himself and called for a civil mediation in Colorado Springs. On June 11, the strike was finally settled.[136]

Altman recovered nicely from the labor war. By late 1894, businesses were flourishing. They included the Hill Top Hotel, the Altman Oyster and Chop House, the Belmont Restaurant and other eateries, as well as stores, laundries, bakeries, liveries and boardinghouses. There were also six saloons where hardworking miners toasted their town on a regular basis.[137] They also supported their town with vigor. In 1895, postal authorities announced plans to move the post office down the mountain to the town of Independence. The problem, they explained, was that Altman was simply too darn high to be lugging mail up and down Bull Hill. When Altman's citizens protested at an "indignation meeting," it was agreed that the mail would temporarily be directed to Cripple Creek and delivered to town by Faharbeck Brothers express company until an investigation could be held. A month later, the post office was reestablished at Altman.[138]

Meanwhile, the crime sprees continued. In March 1895, a four-horse stage was coming down the hill from town when three men jumped out of nowhere and tried to stop the vehicle. One of the robbers grabbed the lead horse's bridle. Instead of slowing down, however, the stage driver simply snapped his whip. The horses "made a jump and rushed down the road, throwing the would-be robber to the ground and apparently running over him."[139] While Altman did gain a reputation for being a rough town, history buffs, over time, have sometimes stretched the truth. Miner, poet and *Colorado Springs Gazette-Telegraph* columnist Rufus Porter (aka the "Hard Rock Poet") once wrote a ballad about the town's first marshal, Mike McKinnon. The honorable lawman died following a gunfight with six Texans (but not, allegedly, before he killed all six outlaws).[140]

Porter may have actually been recounting an incident from May 1895, when outlaw "General" Jack Smith dueled it out with Marshal Jack Kelley. Smith had been running amuck for some time and had been warned by Kelley to stop trying "to run the town in his usual style." On May 14, Smith wrapped up a night of drinking by shooting the locks off the Altman jail, thereby freeing two of his buddies, who were already incarcerated for drunkenness. Smith wisely left town, but the next day, a constable named Lupton and one Frank Vanneck located him in a Victor saloon. "I want you, Jack," Lupton said, to which Smith replied, "If you want me, then read your warrant."

Lupton began reading the warrant, but Smith appeared to go for his gun. The constable quickly pinned the outlaw's arms while Vanneck shoved a gun to Smith's chest. Smith was arrested with a bond of $300. He managed to pay the bond quickly, however, and was next seen riding toward Altman "with the open declaration of doing up the marshal who swore the complaint." Altman authorities were notified as Lupton and Victor deputy sheriff Benton headed for the town. By then, Smith had already gathered a small force of men, including one named George Popst. The bunch headed to Gavin and Toohey's Saloon, where Smith started ordering one drink after another.

Outside, Lupton and Benton met up with Marshal Kelley and set out in search of the "General." Kelley "had just lifted the latch of Lavine and Touhey's [*sic*] saloon, when 'crack' went a gun from the inside. The ball struck the latch and glanced off." Kelley threw the door open and shot Smith just below the heart. From the floor, Smith fired and emptied his own gun as Kelley continued shooting him. Outside, Benton fired a shot through the window that hit Popst. "The latter may recover," predicted the newspaper, "but Smith is certain to die." Popst also died, about a week later.[141]

Next, a bartender at another saloon was killed and robbed in early September. This time, two men entered the place, which was occupied by the barkeep and two other men. One of them shouted, "Throw up your hands!" and the bartender was shot three times. "And this is after he had thrown up his hands," it was noted, "a signal which even bandits respect." The bandits got only seventy dollars because the bartender had wisely hidden the bulk of his nightly proceeds. The robbers remained elusive to authorities until two men fitting their descriptions turned up in the El Paso County jail for robbing a Wells Fargo Express coach. They were identified as Lloyd Marye and Pete Wilson. Marshal Kelley went to have a look at them, concluding they were the men he was looking for.[142]

The gritty events at Altman were not enough to deter the Denver Chamber of Commerce from visiting Altman later that month. And when the Miners Union Ball was hosted in Altman in December, an advertisement promised the dance would "be the event of the season." Residents of Altman learned to work around the rowdy outbursts of certain citizens. In January 1896, Mr. and Mrs. H. Wolf were driving to Altman from Goldfield when two men stopped them. The gentlemen bandits relieved Mr. Wolf of his valuables but let Mrs. Wolf keep hers. A short time later, the men, identified as Mike McMillan and Jack Haggerty, were arrested in Goldfield.[143]

By 1896, every business imaginable was available at Altman, including several stores and groceries, as well as two physicians and four barbershops. Six saloons served thirsty miners at all hours of the day and night. They included the Thirst Parlor, the Mint, the Silver Dollar and the Monte Carlo. Newcomers and visitors to town could choose from eight boardinghouses and two restaurants. Around the town, about thirty-seven mines employed miners. Their children attended the Altman School, overseen by schoolmaster Thomas Roundtree. Altman's *Weekly Champion* newspaper reported the goings-on around town.[144]

Altman's founder, meanwhile, was suffering financial woes by June. Sam Altman eventually moved to Colorado Springs, and his town carried on without him. In October, the Florence & Cripple Creek Railroad announced plans to build a spur to Altman.[145] Growth beget more crime, however, and another shooting occurred in April 1897. The perpetrator in this case was Jack Cox, a pardoned murder convict who had been in Cripple Creek since 1895. Cox had been gambling and drinking all night at McElroy and Coll's Saloon. With him were his best friend, Bob Daily, and another friend, Sam Loshey. At 10:00 a.m. the next morning, Cox and his friends were still at it when a fight broke out. Said to be "crazed with liquor," Cox opened fire and

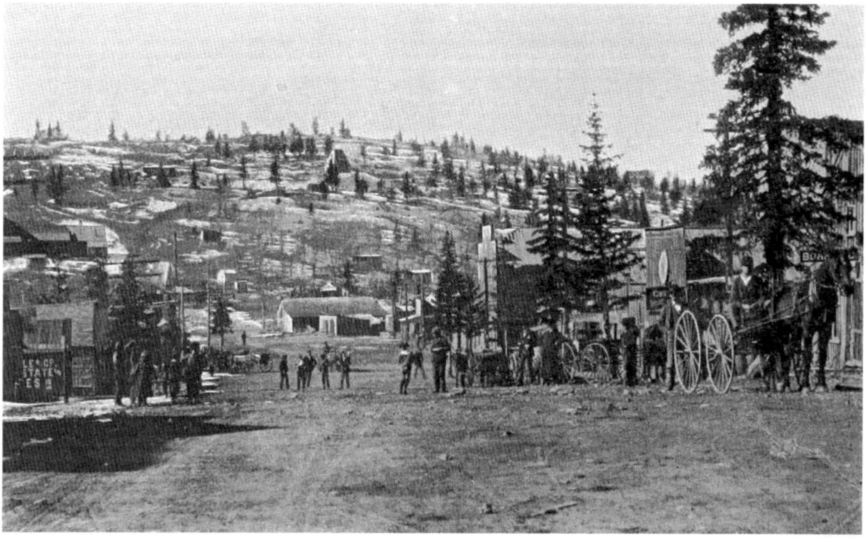

Altman appeared quite busy when this picture was taken around 1896. *From C.J. Kelly,* Cripple Creek Illustrated *(Chicago: Poole Bros., 1896).*

killed Daily. He shot at bartender J.C. McElroy, too, but missed. Next, he fired at Loshey, killing him, also.

Running out the door, Cox encountered Harry Miner, whose mother ran the boardinghouse where Cox lived. Miner was shot in the arm. Out on the street, Cox saw town marshal Ed O'Brien coming and fired yet again. The marshal returned fire, seriously wounding the man. Cox lived to stand trial, but three key witnesses on the stand played dumb. Finally, Cox explained the "witnesses" were actually his gang members, and the fight had been over stolen goods. The witnesses were arrested, and Cox was once again found guilty of murder.[146]

Violence broke out yet again in September. This time, miners Pat Gildea and Jerry O'Donnell had a round at Goodley's Saloon. The two had been enemies since an altercation during the Corbett-Fitzsimmons boxing match back in March. At Goodley's, Gildea was arguing with saloon manager George Savadge when O'Donnell decided to chime in. "Maybe you want some of this yourself," sneered Gildea, striking O'Donnell twice in the face and knocking him down. Then he gave him a kick for good measure.

O'Donnell rose to his feet. "You wouldn't do this if I hadn't been drinking, and I don't believe you can whip me anyway!" he retorted. The fight was on. When Gildea hit O'Donnell in the face again, the latter pulled a knife and sliced his opponent right across the stomach. Gildea was able to run outside, bring in a rock, and clobber O'Donnell again before onlookers broke up the fight. By the next day, Gildea was suffering terribly and died soon after. O'Donnell was arrested.[147]

In spite of the violence at Altman, the 1898 New Year's Day edition of the *Cripple Creek Morning Times* noted that "South" Altman was "a place worthy of commendation" and explained that "more miners make their home in Altman than any other town in the district." The town appeared to be doing just fine with a population of two thousand, electric lights and both a telephone and telegraph company. The Florence & Cripple Creek Railroad declined to build tracks to Altman, but residents were hoping that David Moffatt's Golden Circle railway would come there instead.[148]

Altman continued living up to the newspaper's expectations. By February, the city had its own Bull Hill Literary Society, a French club and a Ladies' Aid Society. Crimes were still being committed, but they were half-hearted efforts at best. When two men robbed Mutterer and Blass's Saloon, they got only four dollars, and nobody was even hurt.[149] One rather odd incident of note occurred in October, when Edward Callahan appeared at the Cripple Creek police department. Callahan told officers he was turning himself in for shooting two men at Altman. He was out of breath, he said, because "he had started to this city on horseback but could not ride fast enough, so he had jumped off the horse and run (it was very evident that he had run)." It took some time for Marshal O'Brien to find a witness, who stated he had seen Callahan fire his Winchester twice at a hillside, but not *at* anybody. Meanwhile, Callahan "told a marvelously bloody tale of how he had shot the two men all to pieces, but every time he told it, the story took on new phases, until it was clear that he was *non compos mentis*." The police put him in jail until they could take him to Colorado Springs and "care for him."[150]

Another event of interest took place in December 1899. The *Denver Times* reported that Mayor Thomas Ferroll decided the people of Altman had no need for that newfangled contraption called a telephone. When the Colorado Telephone Company attempted to install poles in town, Ferroll retaliated by chopping two of them down. The mayor was made to pay for the poles, as well as the wages of the telephone workers. Ultimately, Altman succeeded in obtaining a single telephone located at Morrison & McMillan's store.[151]

Although the population had dropped in half by 1900, Altman still retained its school, city hall and several businesses, as well as a justice of the peace and a volunteer fire department. The Golden Circle railway was

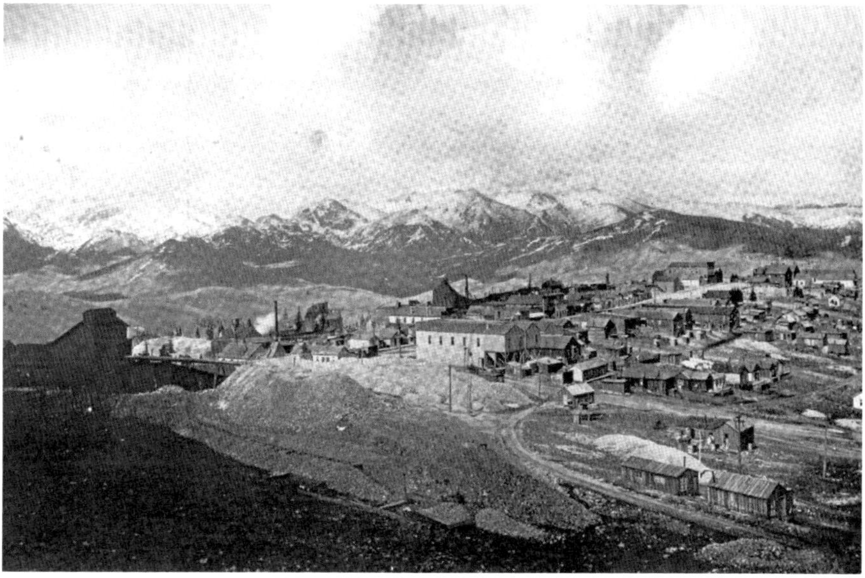

Another view of Altman as it appeared in 1900. *From Hills,* Official Manual of the Cripple Creek District.

providing transportation just west of town. Citizens could also frequent a number of clubs and unions. There also were still four saloons in which to whoop it up. Two years later, Altman gained more notoriety when the 1902 *Cripple Creek District Directory* boasted that the community was the highest incorporated city in the world. The population of 1,500 was composed of local residents, as well as those "who have no regular post office address, giving locations where possible." Businesses in town had dwindled to about seventeen but still included a physician.[152]

In May 1903, Altman's business district burned in its entirety. The fire had actually been burning for some time before it was discovered in the early morning hours at Mrs. Ollie Davisson's Altman Hotel. Firemen attempting to hook their hoses to the hydrants found they had been "tampered with." It took four hours to fix the hydrants, during which time some buildings were dynamited in an attempt to keep the fire from spreading. By the time surrounding fire departments had arrived to help, the entire business district and numerous homes were in ashes. It was noted that this was the second time someone tried to set fire to Mrs. Davisson's hotel, also that red pepper had been spread around the scene to deter bloodhounds. Investigations soon led to the arrest of Davisson, along with her housemaid, three men and even

Altman Water Company manager J.W. Dumpee. Davisson, it was alleged, set the fire herself to gain insurance money.[153]

Further news of the fire was lost in the shuffle as the Cripple Creek District launched into a second labor strike in 1903–04. Altman had no time to set up a fortress like before, and the militia plopped down in the middle of town before anyone could do anything. Eventually, the miners' union lost the war, and their members were forced to leave town at gunpoint.[154] Altman's population continued to fall, totaling only 900 people by 1907. "While many of the rich mining properties of the District are located in the neighborhood," explained the *Cripple Creek District Directory* that year, "the facilities for reaching the valley towns are so excellent that many of the miners prefer to travel back and forth rather than to reside at so high an altitude." Only a dozen businesses remained. A year later, the population was reported at 150 residents, with only 8 businessmen and women appearing in the *Colorado State Business Directory*. The post office closed on May 20, 1911.[155]

By 1915, those left at Altman were considered residents of Independence. The town was eventually vacated. Most of the buildings were gone by 1937 although the city hall, with its safe, still stood as late as the 1960s.[156] A few buildings even survived into the 1980s, when the road to Altman was closed by a modern mining interest. Finding Altman is literally impossible today, for even the mountain where the town once stood no longer exists.

12

ANACONDA

A Rival to Cripple Creek

Anaconda was named for the Anaconda Mine, which, in 1892, was already producing $50,000 in gold each month. David Moffat, the famed Colorado railroad tycoon, was president. Around the Anaconda, other good producing mines also were staked and grew rapidly. These included the Mary McKinny in 1892, and the Doctor Jack Pot and the Morning Glory in 1893.[157] Without much aplomb, the *Aspen Daily Times* of May 20, 1893, simply mentioned that the "town of Anaconda, near Cripple Creek, has taken out incorporation papers." The *Daily Times* was equally impressed by the town newspaper, which began two months later. "The *Anaconda Herald* is a new candidate for newspaper favors at Cripple Creek. It is very ably edited by A.J. McNasser."[158]

The Cripple Creek District's first directory in 1893 lists Anaconda's first mayor as Dr. A.A. Smith, with trustees consisting of U.G. McCrackin, James A. Doyle, Chas. A. Keith, J.C. McKenney, F.C. Hathaway and W.M. Armstrong. A second newspaper, the weekly *Mining Standard* run by W.A. Bray, soon replaced the *Herald*. Hotels, drugstores, groceries, physicians and lawyers put out their shingles. There were churches, a school and a jail. There were even a music teacher and dressmaker. Three saloons—Good's Place, Mayer & Cook and Page & Allen's "X 10 U 8" sample room—kept miners happy. The Anaconda Dance Hall and the Barry Club also provided entertainment—not bad for a town of only two hundred people. Later that year, Anaconda managed to snatch the post office from, and absorb, the smaller nearby towns of Barry and Mound City. Anaconda's post office officially opened on December 7. M. Lehman, who also ran a "gent's furnishings" store, was postmaster.[159]

Leslie Doyle Spell, who moved to Barry as a young boy, remembered the small jail at Anaconda. The building was a simple two-room affair built of rock. One night, Marshal Tom Flanagan jailed a miner known as "Big Kelly" for being drunk. Flanagan was next playing poker in a local saloon when Big Kelly suddenly appeared at his elbow. "Tom whirled and said: 'I thought I put you in jail,' whereat Kelly answered: 'You didn't expect to keep a hardrock miner in a jail like that, did you?'" It turned out that Spell and some other local children had found an old knife and given it to Kelly, who had then dug his way out through a weak place in the mortar. Flanagan duly marched Kelly back to the jail and made him crawl through the hole, telling him to stay put or the marshal "would come back and give him a good licking." Kelly stayed put for the rest of the night. Spell recalled that many years later he was telling this story in Bisbee, Arizona. "An elderly man spoke up," he remembered, "and said, 'That's a true story, men. I was playing poker with Tom at the time.'"[160]

During the labor strike of 1893–94, miners at the Anaconda Mine acquiesced to working an extra hour for the same pay. In March 1894, it was announced that the Anaconda Mine was one of the few that would reopen and hire anti-union employees to work there. The strike was close to being settled when the town's plat map was finally filed in May. The population consisted of about one thousand people, "who enjoy their cosy [*sic*] life snug in the embrace of the hills." Billiard halls and saloons were present, but there also were more respectable businesses, such as the Delmonico and Keystone Restaurants, hardware stores, attorneys, doctors and more.[161]

As Anaconda grew, both the Midland Terminal Railroad (MTRR) and the Florence & Cripple Creek Railroad (F&CC) were running a most heated race to reach the Cripple Creek District. The F&CC won, with a passenger train chugging into nearby Cripple Creek on July 1, 1894. The next day, the train was returning through Anaconda when two passenger coaches and the baggage car went over the edge of a trestle. Twenty-one people were injured, and W.G. Milner of Leadville was killed. The F&CC recovered, and by 1895, upward of two thousand train passengers and visitors were passing through Anaconda daily.[162] Jimmy Doyle, soon to strike it rich at the famed Portland Mine and a future mayor of nearby Victor, advertised his assaying services in newspapers throughout 1895. Anaconda even had a baseball team. The town rounded out its prosperous year with the MTRR finally rolling through in November.[163]

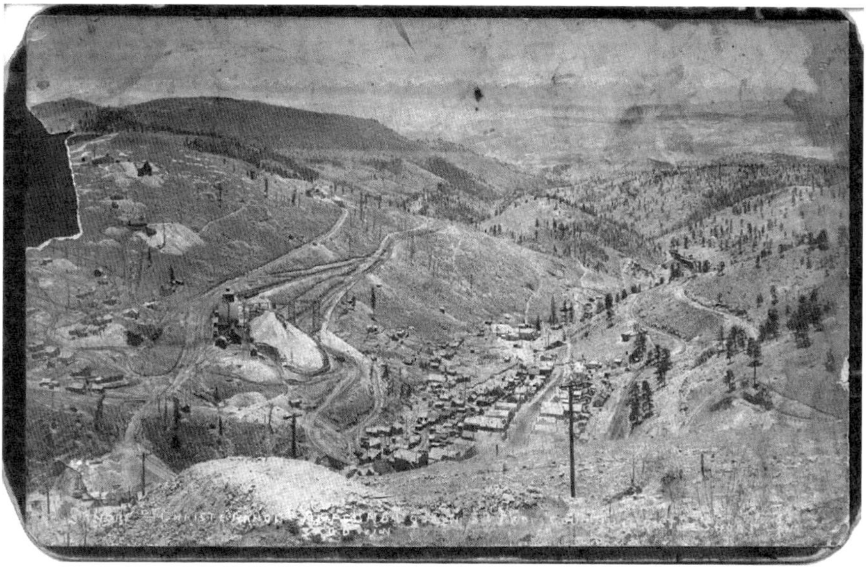

An early image shows Anaconda spilling down Squaw Gulch below the Mary McKinney Mine. *Library of Congress.*

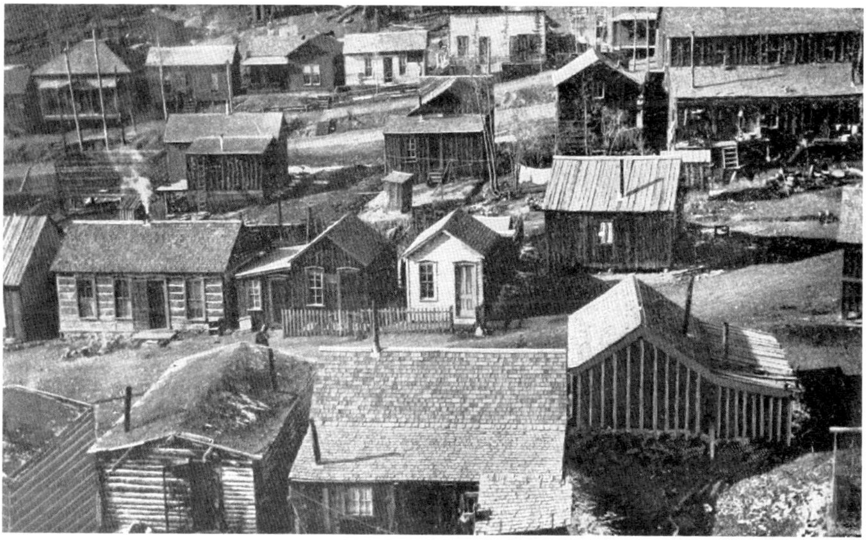

The identical homes in this Anaconda neighborhood were probably ordered from a catalogue. *From C.J. Kelly,* Cripple Creek Illustrated.

When the city of Cripple Creek suffered two devastating fires in April 1896, its displaced citizens crowded into Anaconda, tripling business at the post office for a couple months.[164] The *Cripple Creek District Directory* of 1896 guessed there were roughly 1,800 people living in Anaconda and forty-one businesses in operation. A new newspaper, the *Assayer*, met with approval. Charles P. Brooks was editor. "Mr. Brooks, it is needless to say, knows how to make a bright and newsy paper," commented the *Leadville Herald Democrat*, in its May 27 issue.

Indeed, Brooks kept the readers of the *Assayer* and several other newspapers entertained with plenty of news and a good dose of sensationalism to boot. On January 13, 1898, Brooks's former hometown newspaper, the *Greeley Tribune*, noted that "Charles P. Brooks, who was reported a few weeks ago to be in a dying condition at Anaconda" had just become editor of the *Cripple Creek Prospector* newspaper in nearby Cripple Creek. The irrepressible Brooks also continued working for the *Assayer*. "The editor of the *Anaconda Assayer* has been having a high old time with the mayor and town board of that camp," reported the *Elbert County Banner* on January 14, 1898. "But he seems to be plenty for them even when they do pummel him around and draw guns on him when he attends town council."

The *Cripple Creek Morning Times* New Year's Day edition of 1899 had much good to say about Anaconda, calling it "a well governed little city with no debt and where the people are prosperous and happy." The writer went on to claim that "there is no place in the state more picturesque, and as a 'summer camp' it has no equal." Compliments were showered upon the peaceable population as well. "The old-time notion that a mining city must in the nature of things be 'tough' does not obtain in Anaconda," the paper went on, emphasizing the point by mentioning a "splendid" school system with over four hundred students.

By 1900 Anaconda was the fourth largest town in the Cripple Creek District. The downtown area spanned two blocks with false-fronted buildings housing businesses and three churches. At the school, Principal E.E. Morris oversaw teachers Nellie Riggs, Maud Sheldon and Alida Colwell. There was also a volunteer fire department at the town hall. Irving Douglas was postmaster. Even telephone service was available.[165]

Anaconda also unwittingly became home to a handful of people who eventually became famous in their own right. One of them was Josiah Roberts, who was ten years old when his family lived in town in 1900. During the 1920s and 1930s, Roberts worked for motion picture companies in Los Angeles. Most notably, he was a cinematographer who had worked on the films *White Shadows in the South Seas* in 1928 and *Eskimo* in 1933.[166]

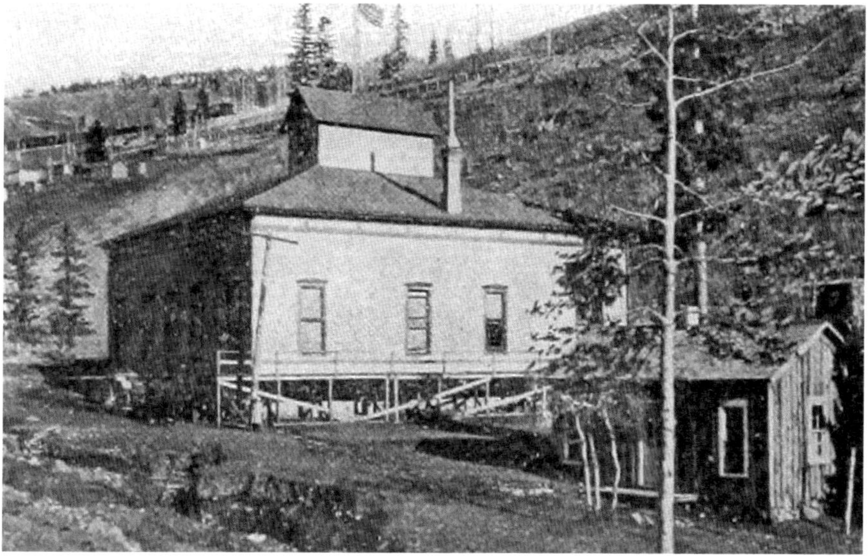

Anaconda's schoolhouse once employed upward of three teachers and a principal. *From Kelly,* Cripple Creek Illustrated.

Another famous resident was the later-known speakeasy queen Mary Louise Cecelia "Tex" Guinan, who came to Anaconda on a visit with her mother in 1902. During her extended stay, Tex began playing the organ for the local Sunday school. But she also began dressing a little too modern for the standards of the young ladies at Anaconda. Not only were her outfits a bit too revealing, but she also wore rouge and makeup. Undaunted by gossip, Tex lined up a series of suitors whom she would date once or twice before casting them aside. Those who complained were given the same response that would soon be Tex's trademark saying: "Oh, you poor sucker."[167]

In 1904, Tex wed John Joseph Moynahan, whose uncle lived in Anaconda. The couple left Colorado and later divorced, but Tex soon made her way to New York, where she found work as a chorus girl. By 1917, she was appearing in short films. During Prohibition, she ran a series of successful nightclubs and speakeasies. The name of one of them, the Culture Club, was later used by the popular British band of the same name during the 1980s. Tex appeared in more than thirty films before she died in 1933. A film, *Incendiary Blonde*, profiled her lively and interesting life in 1945.[168]

Its colorful characters aside, Anaconda boasted "good schools and several churches" in 1902. A fire in 1904, however, was almost the town's undoing.

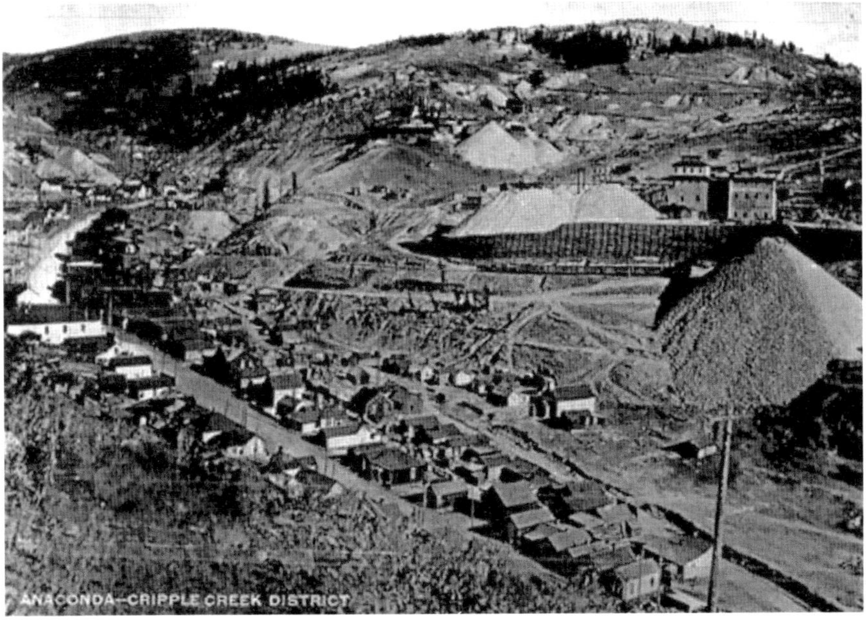

A later view of Anaconda, taken from the bottom of Squaw Gulch, shows how much the Mary McKinney Mine had grown. *Cripple Creek District Museum.*

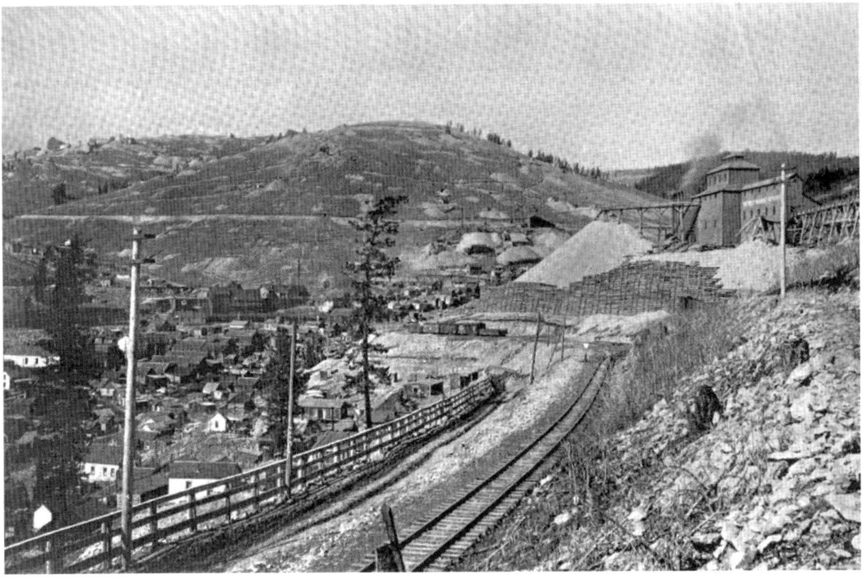

This striking image shows the MTRR leading into Anaconda. *From Hills,* Official Manual of the Cripple Creek District.

On November 11, Edwin Irwin noticed flames coming from Nelson's Grocery at 11:30 p.m. News of the conflagration was reported as far away as Los Angeles, where the *Los Angeles Herald* warned the town was "in danger of total destruction by fire." One block of the downtown had already burned, the article said, with many others in danger. Lack of water pressure combined with strong winds spelled disaster, even after a bucket brigade was formed. Many buildings, including the city hall, were dynamited in a vain effort to stop the flames. In the end, every building south of the railroad tracks through town burned. Only one was insured. Newspapers guessed the damage to be between $50,000 and $60,000.[169]

Many thought the fire was the end of Anaconda. The 1905 *Cripple Creek District Directory* offered the disclaimer that "a large portion of the business section of Anaconda was recently burned and owing to its nearness to the city of Cripple Creek there is considerable doubt of its being rebuilt." In preparation for the town's eventual demise, the MTRR depot was moved to Bull Hill near Victor. By 1907, only 700 people remained along with a mere four business houses. A year later, there were only 250 people left in town.[170]

Anaconda's post office closed in 1909. There were still 130 residents, however, so postal authorities allowed the post office to reopen in 1911. In fact, the population of Anaconda looked to be on the rise by 1912, when 200

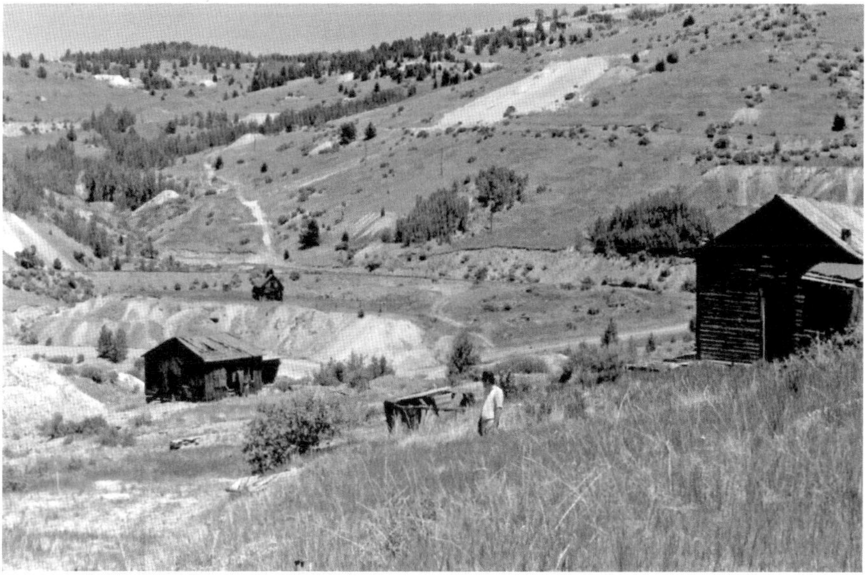

Anaconda in 1985. The town was razed by mining operations in 2012, except for the blacksmith shop (background), which was moved. *Jan MacKell Collins.*

citizens were calling the town home again. The business district was gone, but folks simply did their shopping in nearby Cripple Creek. The population remained steady until the post office closed a final time in 1917.[171] By 1920, the remaining residents of Anaconda were included as citizens of Victor in the census. The Mary McKinney Mine finally closed in 1953 after producing $11 million in gold. For years, the main road through Anaconda, Barry and Mound City contained only a few buildings scattered about. In 1967, the Cripple Creek & Victor Narrow Gauge Railroad in Cripple Creek opened to take visitors on a scenic four-mile tour to the ghost buildings of Anaconda.[172]

Anaconda made the news one last time in 1984, when Wayne Tease of Colorado Springs fell down a one-thousand-foot-deep mine shaft at the Mary McKinney. Authorities could do little to retrieve the body. Tease's family erected a memorial to him at the shaft, but it took Tease's mother fourteen years to obtain a death certificate for her son. Then in 2011, it was discovered that modern mining operations were slated to cover the shaft. Although Tease's family objected on the grounds that the shaft constituted the boy's grave, the mine proceeded with their plans.[173] Today, Anaconda has gone the way of Wayne Tease, most of the town being buried under tailings piles and totally unrecognizable.

13

AREQUA

One of the Earliest Gold Camps

Arequa's beginnings date back to when "Uncle Ben" Requa had a general store down at Fountain, south of Colorado Springs. Born in 1835 in New York, Requa had fought for the Union during the Civil War in California and Arizona before coming to Colorado. He was active in local affairs, investing in much property during the 1870s. His store and eatery served as a gathering place for locals. His company, Requa, Croft & Co. was a frequent advertiser in local newspapers.[174]

South of Fountain, near Rock Creek along today's Highway 115, was the Womack family and their Sunview Ranch. Sam and Corella Womack had settled there in 1867. One day in 1873, their son, Bob, happened into Requa's store. There he ran into a distant cousin, who told him that a group of men in the store were with Ferdinand Hayden's U.S. Geological and Geographical Survey. Womack, who was sure that gold abounded on the backside of Pikes Peak, approached the group.[175]

Requa listened as Womack described the area to Hayden's men, who seemed only vaguely interested. The group did visit what would become the Cripple Creek District but found only signs of volcanic activity and some "dirty-gray rock," which would later turn out to be hardrock gold ore. Requa, however, was more optimistic and rounded up one hundred "argonauts" to follow Womack to the area he described. The group blasted a tunnel near Eclipse Gulch, located roughly halfway between today's Victor and Cripple Creek. They christened the area the Mount Pisgah Mining District even as little hope was held for finding anything of real value. Just in case, Requa filed a claim in September and called it Requa & Brown Mining Company. A nearby gulch was subsequently named Requa Gulch. Although Requa dabbled in mining endeavors throughout Colorado and even South Dakota's Black Hills, nothing seemed to come of his claim in the Mount Pisgah district.[176]

As others discovered there really was gold around Requa Gulch, a small settlement grew up there. Historian Robert L. Brown theorized that Requa, who was Italian, had such a thick accent that people thought he pronounced his name "Arequa." Thus, when real estate investors Horace Bennett and Julius Myers officially platted a town in February 1892, the name stuck. Bennett and Myers named the streets after past U.S. presidents and began selling lots. In all, the partners made a profit of $320,000.[177] Later, Arequa was credited as the place where both the stream near town and later the city of Cripple Creek were named. An article in the 1896 *Quarterly Sentinel*, while admitting confusion as to the origins of Cripple Creek's name, offered this story:

> *A little old house, still to be seen in Arequa…was occupied by a family from Posey County, Indiana, who were one day invited to a dance by some distant neighbors. The Posey County lady answered that "We kain't go; all broke up; Sam's down with th' rumatiz; Betsy's got th' fever; Jake's got 'is arm broke; old Pied (the cow) broke 'er laig, and the hosses is run off…But if you all 'ill come over to Cripple Creek, we'll he'p ye out th' best we can fur yer hoedown."*[178]

Much discussion has occurred among local historians as to whether Arequa had a cemetery. A GAR cemetery is thought to have been established in 1892 on a hillside between Arequa and Victor before the latter town was founded. However, Victor's newspaper, the *Victor Daily Record*, verified that the graveyard was new when it was dedicated in 1909. All forty-six burials were exhumed in the 1920s at the direction of the man who owned the land on which the graveyard was located. The bodies were moved to both Victor's Sunnyside Cemetery and Cripple Creek's Mount Pisgah Cemetery. Some have surmised the cemetery might have been part of Arequa. What is known for sure was that there were fifty people living at Arequa by 1893. Businesses included W.G. Nichols's Assay Office; the Arequa House; Booher Bros. Groceries and Supplies; the Kassar Hotel; the Miners' Home boardinghouse, run by Caroline Lark; and the Prince Albert saloon.[179]

The pioneers kept coming, and in June 1894, a post office opened. Unfortunately, it was soon apparent that Arequa's hilly terrain was too

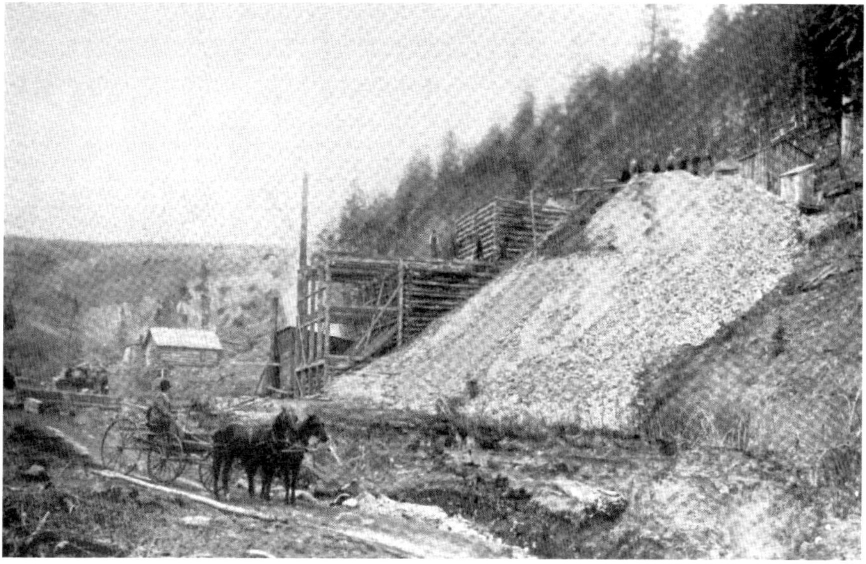

This image by Henry Lee Jacques Warren depicts a rare view of Arequa Gulch. *From Warren and Stride,* Cripple Creek and Colorado Springs.

rough to really build much, and the town was a bit too far from the bigger producing mines of the district. Other communities were being formed, and residents of Arequa began moving away. By September, it was clear that a post office would not be needed, and the designation was rescinded. As of December 1895, the ninety acres containing Arequa's town site were pretty much considered a part of Elkton, one of the new communities just up the gulch. On the eighteenth of that month, a portion of the town was vacated as mining operations closed in.[180]

Arequa did continue to survive on a small scale, if only because the Arequa Gold Mining Company was formed in January 1896 on the edge of town. The Arequa Mill was constructed in 1898 to serve as a chlorination plant for the nearby Cresson Mine. Other mines established in the old part of town were the Common-Wealth Mining and Milling Company in 1899, and the Cable Consolidated and Little Nell in 1900.[181] The Midland Terminal and Florence & Cripple Creek railways were still servicing Arequa in 1900. Most of the few businesses left were proudly called the "Arequa" something-or-other—the Arequa Club, Arequa Grocery, Arequa Barbershop, Arequa Saloon, etc. There also were still three hotels: the Arequa, the Palmer and the Cantlon.[182] These places were patronized by residents not just of Arequa, but also the nearby communities of Beacon, Eclipse and Elkton.

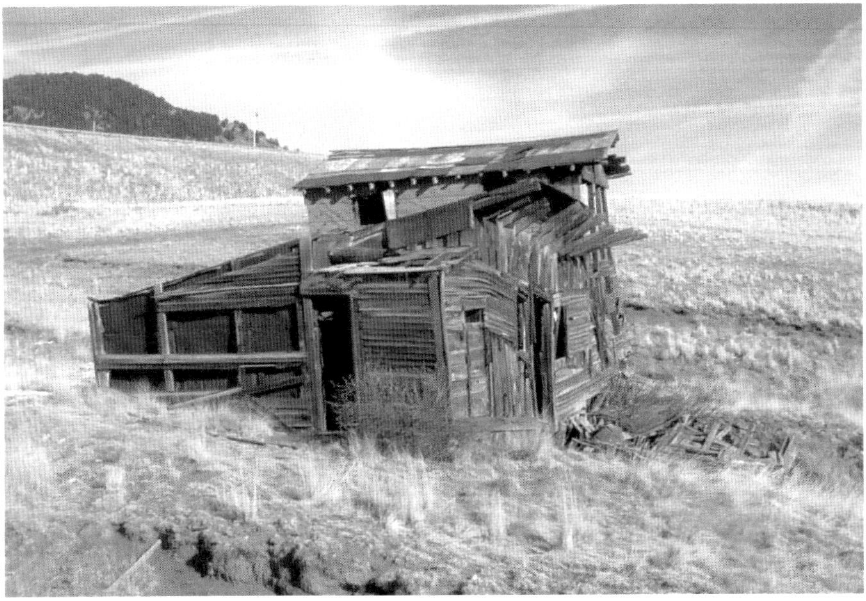

A lone building is the only one left representing Arequa. Most of the town was buried under mine tailings decades ago. *Jan MacKell Collins.*

The 1900 census combined the population of these towns and camps, which numbered 2,500 people.

Four years later, much of Arequa was owned by the Beacon Hill Mining & Townsite Company. The company was owned by Warren Woods and his son, Frank. The Woodses, along with Warren's other son Harry, also owned the controlling interests in the city of Victor, as well as the town of Cameron. In 1904, the company vacated even more of Arequa in favor of mining interests. There were still almost one hundred people living at Arequa as of the 1910 census. Most of the men were miners, but there were also two dairymen, two carpenters, three teamsters and a twenty-one-year-old actress named Maud Palmer who lived with her family. Still the mines continued encroaching, and within four years, the Gold Dollar Mine owned more than half the town.[183]

By 1918, those remaining at Arequa were listed as residents of Victor. What little was left of the town slowly decayed, and by the 1990s, nearly all of it was already covered by mine tailings. In 2001, the Cripple Creek/Victor Mine constructed a new bridge over Arequa Gulch. The cost was $8 million, with the behemoth stretch of steel and pavement towering 250 feet high. To date, this is the tallest non-suspension bridge in Colorado.[184] As for the town itself, Arequa is simply no more.

14

BARRY

A Bountiful Little Town

As the Cripple Creek District developed and hundreds of prospect holes dotted the landscape, a "female aborigine" was unearthed in a gulch located roughly halfway between Cripple Creek and Victor. The remains were most likely those of a Ute Indian, since those Native Americans once favored the area as a summer hunting ground. The area where the woman was found became known as Squaw Gulch.[185]

Leslie Doyle Spell recalled moving with his family from Florissant to Squaw Gulch in 1891. "This was a two-room cabin," he remembered, "with one room used for eating, sleeping and general use while the other was to serve as sleeping quarters for the men." Spell also remembered a young woman, Emma Rickett of Florissant, who had been hired to help his mother. After Emma died "an agonizing death from blood poisoning," she became the first woman buried in what was later Mount Pisgah Cemetery in Cripple Creek. Spell also remembered that two small children were killed by a bear shortly after his family arrived. "Quite often," he said, "while sitting on the porch of our cabin or playing nearby, we would be startled almost out of our wits by the screams of panthers, or mountain lions, in the nearby forests."[186]

The first Christmas at Squaw Gulch was reported on by a correspondent for the *Colorado Springs Daily Gazette*: "Christmas passed very quickly up here and, indeed it seemed hard to realize that it was Christmas. In the evening a dance was held in the loft over Sills & Mills grocery store in Squaw Gulch…a very pleasant evening and their first in Cripple Creek." The school at Squaw Gulch was a log house, built by and lived in by cobbler Fred Hackey. In

1892, Spell's father, William, donated a lot and building materials for a proper school, on the condition that should the school be moved elsewhere, the building was to be used for "inter-denominational church services." William Spell was eventually appointed marshal of Fremont and Hayden Placer (both towns later became Cripple Creek), Mound City and Squaw Gulch. Squaw Gulch soon had a small jail, built primarily for the son of a prominent rancher who often came home drunk from the saloons and dance halls in nearby Cripple Creek.[187]

Spell remembered brothers Bill and Vint Barry coming to Squaw Gulch and renaming the town for themselves. While laying out their town, the Barry brothers encountered Andy Frazier, whose cabin sat right in the path of the new main road. Frazier refused to move, explaining his wife was expecting a baby at any moment and that, besides, he had squatter's rights. The Barrys built a new house along the proposed street and presented it to Frazier as a gift. But Spell's account of the Barry brothers is confusing, since other sources show that Barry was named for prospector Horace Barry. Upon founding his namesake town, Horace Barry told others he believed the little village would become the "cultural center" of the district.[188]

Barry's post office opened on March 1, 1892. Surrounding mines did well; many residents were employed by the nearby Blue Bell Mine. Shops, restaurants and two or three neat rows of homes lined the road up Squaw Gulch. New residents included H. Susan Anderson and her family. "Doc Susie," as Susan was later known, was born in Indiana in 1870. When her parents divorced in 1875, Susan's father William took custody of Susan and her younger brother, John. By the early 1880s, the family was living on a farm in Kansas, where Susan learned to "doctor" the animals around the homestead.[189]

In 1892, William Anderson married Minnie Croy. Soon afterward the family moved to Barry, where William pursued mining interests. Susan and John were sent off to college in 1893. Susan's chosen field was medicine, and she began her studies at the University of Michigan. Midway through her classes, however, Susan's father cut off her financial support. Susan persevered, borrowing money from a classmate and finishing her schooling. Despite contracting tuberculosis during her internship, she graduated in 1897.

Upon her return, Anderson opened an office in Cripple Creek. She almost married in 1900, but her fiancé and father had some sort of falling out; the engagement was broken off. A few days later, Susan's brother, John, died from pneumonia at Anaconda. The heartbroken doctor left the Cripple

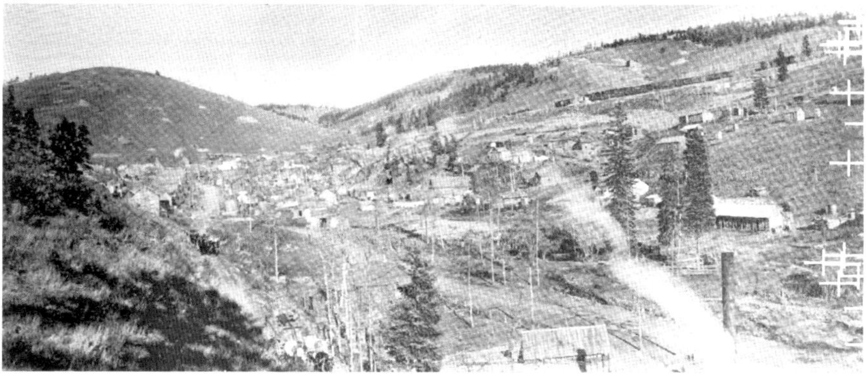

Barry's Blue Bell Mine (foreground). *From Warren and Stride,* Cripple Creek and Colorado Springs.

Creek District and eventually settled at Fraser in northern Colorado, where she became well known and well loved. She died in Denver in 1960 and was buried in Cripple Creek. The popular television show *Dr. Quinn: Medicine Woman* was based on her life.[190]

Another well-known citizen of Barry at the time was Judge M.B. Gerry, the man who sentenced Colorado cannibal Alfred Packer to hang in 1883. Gerry was a member of Horace Barry's Squaw Gulch Amusement Club, as were prominent ranchers George Carr and Bob Womack. Advertisements for the club boasted "a membership of 400, of which 399 are from the high-toned aristocratic circles of Squaw Gulch." Not surprisingly, the Squaw Gulch Amusement Club proved lucrative for the soiled doves who eventually flew into town. Les Spell remembered a prostitute who worked next door and had a little boy who often played alone in his backyard. One day, Spell's brother asked the boy to come over. The child replied, "No, my mother is a whore and says I am to stay home." Another time, a cowboy was sleeping off a drunk at the house of his favorite call girl. As he slept, the gentleman's mischievous companion donned his overalls and rode down Main Street on his horse.[191]

Barry had other amusements, too. There were two newspapers, *Write Up the Camp* and the *Squaw Gulch Nugget*. The articles might have included news on Horace Barry, who was investing in various mine interests and was an officer at Sam Altman's Free Coinage Mine above Victor. By 1893, Horace Barry was suffering some financial setbacks. In addition, his namesake town was being swallowed up by the new town of Anaconda at the head of Squaw Gulch. The town newspapers went out of business, and in December 1893, the post office was moved to Anaconda.[192]

Horace Barry eventually left town, but he did continue dabbling in mining even after he moved to Denver in 1899. In 1903, the *Iowa Press-Citizen* newspaper in his home state of Iowa reported:

> *The Valley Mining company today sued its general manager, H.W. Barry, M.I. Barry and Laura Barry Elmendorf, for $2,000 in damages, and asked for writ of attachment against Mr. Barry's property and against certain shares of stock, now held by the other defendants. The petition avers that Barry made misrepresentations as to the title of certain property, and that he misused funds entrusted to him. The plaintiff further declares that Mr. Barry has disappeared from Silver Cliff* [Colorado].

Barry later surfaced in Denver and California before disappearing altogether.[193]

15

BEAVER PARK

A SHORT-LIVED DREAM

There were actually two places known as Beaver Park in Teller County. The first was a place name of sorts near Clyde. The second Beaver Park, located some miles away, was platted in 1892 by a man named Forney and his partner, A. Hawkins, both of the Beaver Park Land & Water Company. City blocks were laid out along the curves of West Beaver Creek. Beaver Street ran along the actual stream, while Main Street paralleled one block north and eventually turned into Junction Street as it left town.[194]

Forney and Hawkins originally intended Beaver Park as a resort. By November it was reported that a

> *fine hotel and summer resort are to be built at the head of Beaver Park near Cripple Creek by a syndicate of Texas capitalists. A lake which will cover thirty acres of ground is also to be created and the contract has been let. A new townsite will probably arise in this location which is at present occupied by Hancock's halfway house and ranch, which is one of the most beautiful in the district.*

Mining investors and budding millionaires Spencer Penrose and Charles Tutt were among the few to buy lots at Beaver Park. Everybody was hopeful, however, that others would purchase more land as the gold boom in the Cripple Creek District developed. In June, the Beaver Park Stamp Mill opened. By 1894, it was said that "a mill operating as cleanly and successfully as the Beaver Park does is a great necessity."[195]

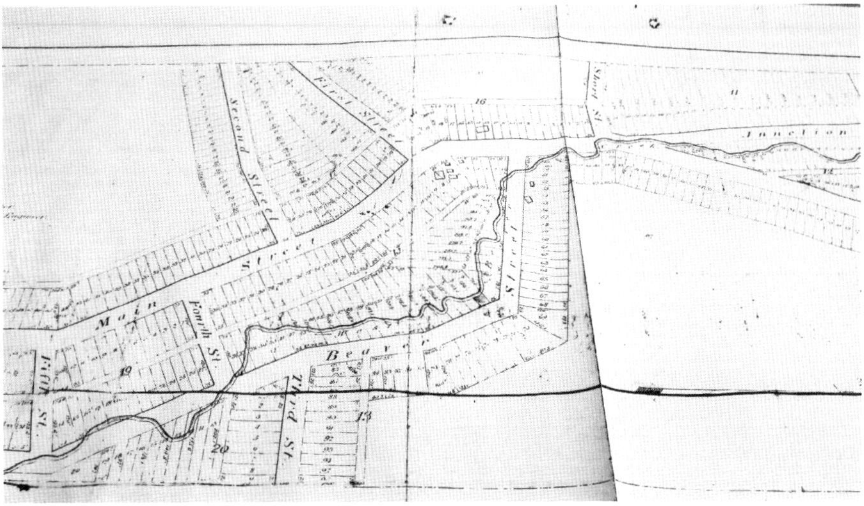

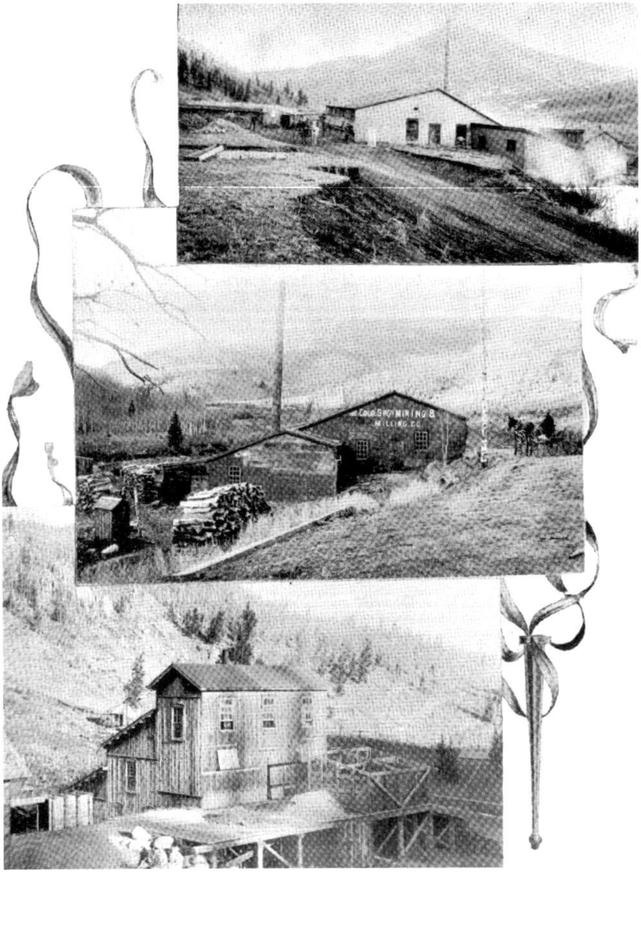

Above: The Beaver Park plat map of 1892 shows the town meandering along its namesake stream. Little interest was taken in the town. *Teller County Assessor.*

Left: Henry Warren recorded this image of three stamp mills along Beaver Creek. Two of them are probably the Beaver Park and Spinney Mills. *From Warren and Stride,* Cripple Creek and Colorado Springs.

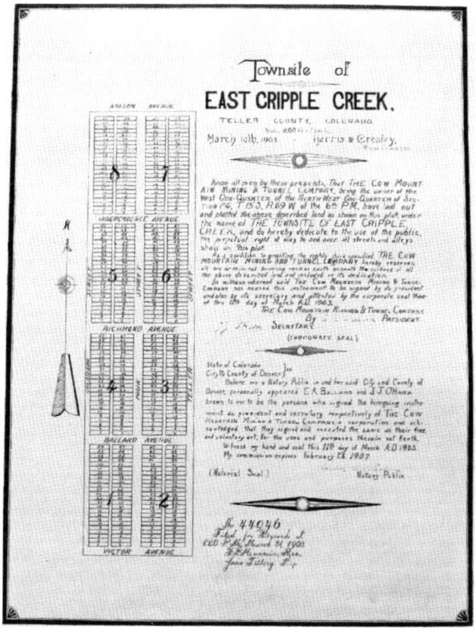

In 1903, East Cripple Creek East was platted next to the original Beaver Park, but potential investors soon lost interest. *Teller County Assessor.*

The stamp mill aside, Beaver Park first gained notoriety when the town served as the temporary quarters of troops sent to quell the 1893–94 miners' strike in the Cripple Creek District. The men were led by Winfield Scott Boynton, a county commissioner who decided on his own to gather a force of men and break the strike. Boynton initially gathered an impressive group of 1,200 men in Colorado Springs, and "made stirring orations and lectured the deputies on tactics and held drills and song-fests." The group marched to Divide, where Boynton next "locked up the newspaper reporters" and cut all telephone and telegraph wires. When Governor Davis Waite heard of Boynton's antics, he immediately ordered a militia to go to Divide. Boynton heard about it and quickly began marching his men toward the Cripple Creek District on June 6. Boynton's "troops" got as far as Beaver Park, where they set up a post that even included quarters for a hospital.[196]

From Beaver Park, Boynton tried to stage a couple attacks on Altman but failed. In the meantime, Adjutant General Thomas Tarsney arrived ahead of the militia and ordered Boynton's troops to disperse. Boynton refused, stationing his men instead near Bull Hill and below Altman. When the militia arrived, El Paso County sheriff Frank Bowers ordered the men back to Beaver Park. This time, they obeyed, and the strike was settled soon afterward. Later, Boynton was elected sheriff of El Paso County in Colorado Springs.[197]

Boynton's men composed the largest population Beaver Park would ever see. The town never grew, mostly because the larger railroad town of Gillett was founded in 1894 just up the road. Miners from Gillett could easily access the Beaver Park Stamp Mill, and between 1895 and 1897, the Beaver Park Land & Water Company remained the largest property owner in Beaver

Park. In 1900, Beaver Park's population numbered only seventy-five. The town was later vacated. For some reason, in 1903, a new town was platted one section over from Beaver Park. This was East Cripple Creek, created by the Cow Mountain Mining & Tunnel Company. East Cripple Creek was quite small and, like Beaver Park, was eventually abandoned.[198]

16

CAMERON

An Eventual Playground for the Cripple Creek District

Cameron was very nearly named Cripple Creek when it was first founded. This was back when today's Cripple Creek was divided by two separate towns, Fremont and Hayden Placer. The towns were in a heated battle over who would be first to secure a post office. Hayden Placer even took the name "Moreland" as a marketing ploy to imply there was "more land." When the post office accepted Moreland's name, Fremont founders Horace Bennett and Julius Myers platted an all new town northeast of Moreland and called it Cripple Creek. A short time later, however, the post office combined Fremont and Moreland into one city and designated the post office name as Cripple Creek.[199]

Bennett and Myers changed the name of their town to Grassy, although it was sometimes misspelled on various maps as "Gassy" and "Gassey." True to its name, Grassy was located in a wide, grass-filled meadow at the edge of a forest. Bennett and Myers saw potential in Grassy as an eventual mining and railroad hub. The town was officially platted on October 29, 1894. The Midland Terminal Railroad intersected the east half of the town, with a tidy depot built on the southeast corner of Teller Avenue and Third Street.[200] Soon, however, it was apparent that Grassy would not develop very fast, for it was a tad too far from other towns in the district. A portion of the town was vacated in August 1895, and by 1899, the whole place was up for sale.

Enter the Woods Investment Company, which had already built much of the nearby town of Victor (and would build it again after a devastating

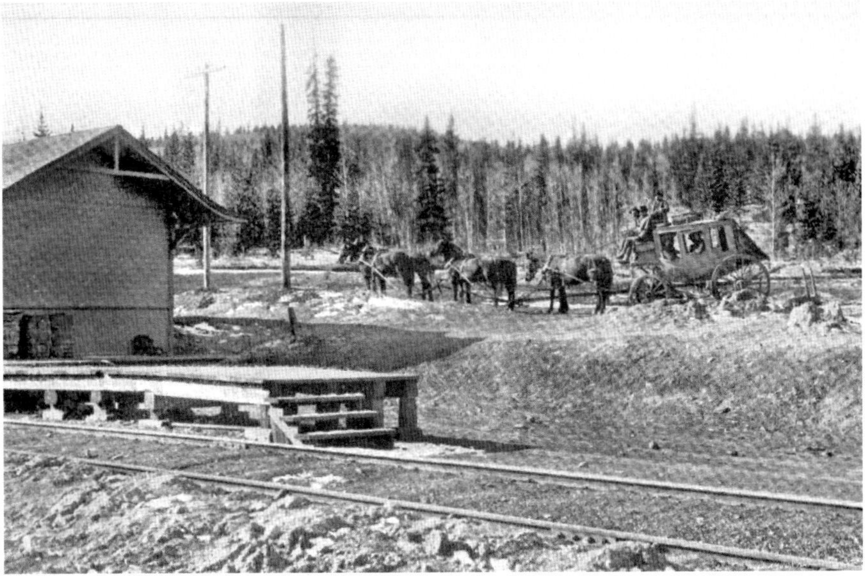

A portion of the depot is visible to the left of a stagecoach at early Grassy. *From Warren and Stride,* Cripple Creek and Colorado Springs.

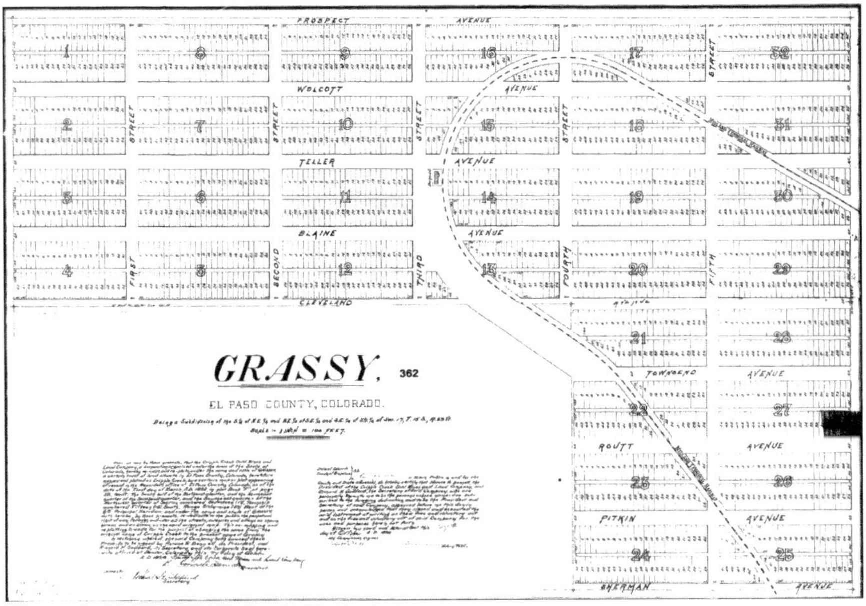

The name of Grassy, platted in 1892, was changed to Cameron when the Woods brothers purchased the town in 1899. *El Paso County Clerk and Recorder.*

fire in August 1899). The Woods Company purchased the Grassy town site at a cost of $123,000 for 183 acres. The investment was solid enough; surrounding mines had produced $250,000 in gold ore just that year. On July 25, 1899, the *Cripple Creek Morning Times* reported that the "Cameron Company that now owns the Grassy townsite has changed the name of the place to Cameron. Several new houses are now in the course of construction there." Beginning on August 3, Cameron began appearing on the timetables of the Midland Terminal Railroad. Nice brick structures now lined Cameron Avenue, housing several businesses, including three saloons and a newspaper, the *Golden Crescent*.[201]

On August 10, readers of the *Cripple Creek Morning Times* saw a most interesting article. "Sunday an excursion will be run from this city to Cameron, formerly Grassy," reported the paper. "Pinnacle Park, at Cameron, promises to be a very attractive pleasure resort." Learning from old Grassy's uncertain fate, the Woodses had come up with a fabulous idea to draw folks to Cameron. They built a giant amusement park for the people of the Cripple Creek District to enjoy. The park spanned thirty acres and cost $32,500 to build. Architect Matthew Lockwood McBird, who had designed numerous buildings in Victor, was hired to draw plans for the park. McBird was perfect for the job, being "a bit of a visionary, a dreamer and creator."[202]

Images of the park show that McBird's designs gave the place a rustic look. Pinnacle Park afforded the amenities of any great amusement park: a large wooden dance pavilion and bandstand, a picnic area, restaurants and an athletic field with seating for up to one thousand spectators. Football and baseball games were the main attraction. Nearby, a zoo exhibited native animals. There was also a playground with assorted popular rides of the day. Entrance was gained via Acacia Avenue, and the Midland Terminal Railroad tracks cut directly through the middle of the park with elaborate wooden arches spanning over the tracks.[203]

Pinnacle Park's first Labor Day in 1899 was amazing indeed. Although plans were already in the works for a great festival with a "grand picnic," the event was turned into a "benefit of the families of Coeur d'Alene miners" who were suffering through violent labor strikes in Idaho. Activities featured a baseball game among Cripple Creek district teams and other events, including greased-pole climbing, burro and horse races, a sack race, a fifty-yard "Fat Man's" race and a dance. The celebration was deemed a great success, from the giant parade that made its way from Cripple Creek to the games, craft booths and lemonade and cigar stands at the park. "The outgoing trains from Cripple Creek to Pinnacle Park were so crowded,"

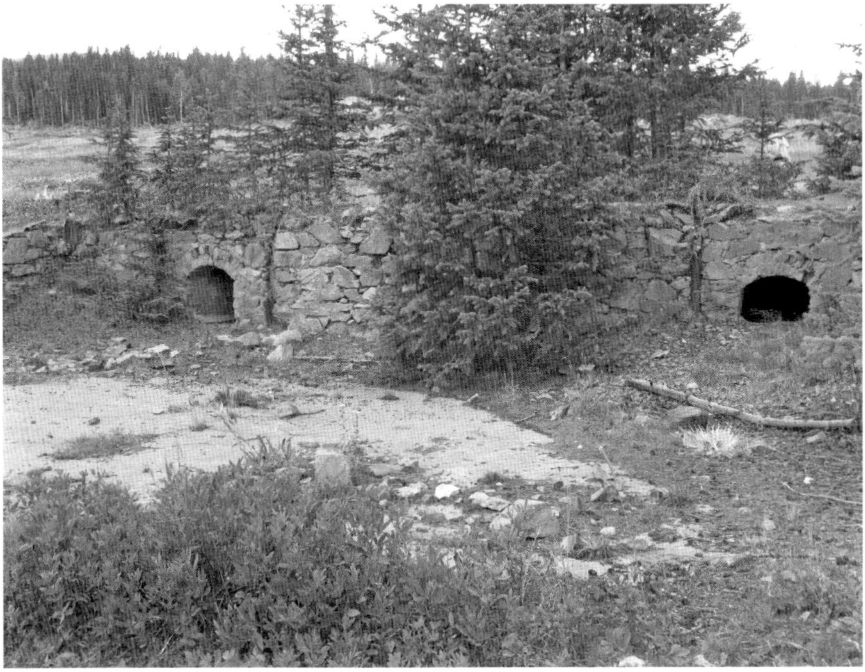

The bear caves from Pinnacle Park's zoo were dismantled in 2010 but are now on display at the Cripple Creek District Museum. *Jan MacKell Collins.*

reported the *Cripple Creek Morning Times* on September 3, "that people hung on the sides and scrambled all over the tops of the coaches to get a place to sit." Furthermore, a "solid stream" of wagons stretched from Tenderfoot Hill above Cripple Creek all the way to Cameron. In all, over $6,000 was raised for those at Coeur d'Alene. "It is doubtful if the people of the district ever appreciated before yesterday's parade what a host of organized working men there are here," concluded the *Morning Times* on September 5, "or how many different trades and crafts are in the camp."

On September 30 an announcement was made that a new "broad gauge" railroad was planned from Colorado Springs to Cameron. The project was led by Irving Howbert and E.W. Giddings of the Cripple Creek District Electric Railway. By October, the school at Cameron had fifty-two pupils. On December 8, a new post office was established. The name of the office was Touraine, however, "there being a Cameron in another portion of the state." The Woods Investment Company closed the year by announcing plans for the Gillett Light & Power Company, which would supply light to both the town of Gillett and Cameron.[204]

Both Grassy and Cameron were listed in the Cripple Creek District directory in 1900. The Woodses had not yet filed a new plat map for the latter town. The Cameron School operated in the town proper, but a Lower Grassy School also appears in the directory, indicating that a portion of old Grassy now functioned as a suburb of Cameron. The downtown area offered an exciting array of business houses. The Arcade Saloon and the Cameron Club Saloon and Barber Shop attracted miners, while the more domestic could choose from numerous stores and services. As promised, water was furnished to both Cameron and Gillett from Woods Lake. Finally, Cameron was officially platted on April 14, 1900.[205]

Labor Day 1900 at Pinnacle Park was even larger than the year before. Nine thousand people attended the festivities at ten cents per head. For a few more glorious years, thousands of visitors came to Pinnacle Park every weekend and holiday during the summer. Meanwhile, the April 18 issue of the *Aspen Daily Times* announced that the "continued discovery of gold in the vicinity of Gillett and Cameron confirm the theory so long urged that the Cripple Creek veins extend to an unknown distance to the north." Mines around Cameron included the Elsmere, Lansing and Wild Horse. The Colorado Springs & Cripple Creek District Railroad, aka "the Short Line," reached Cameron in March 1901. A month later, the Touraine post office name was officially changed to Cameron.[206]

Beginning in about 1902, Cameron's popularity began fading as rumors began that the Woods boys were in financial trouble. Lot sales came to a stop. By the time of the 1902–03 directory, Cameron's population had shrunk to around three hundred. There was still an Episcopal church, a city hall, Kings Hall and three other clubs, but the business district consisted of only a boardinghouse, a grocery, one doctor and the *Cameron Crescent* newspaper. Nearby labor wars in 1903–04 took a further toll on Cameron, which was located dangerously close to the mining strikes. Just five days into the strike, "Big Bill" Haywood gave a rousing speech to a group of union men at a Pinnacle Park picnic. Haywood urged the miners "to stand with" the Western Federation of Miners until the strikers won.[207]

By 1905, neither of Cameron's two churches had a permanent pastor, and both congregations met at town hall. There was still a boardinghouse, general merchandise, grocery, hotel and shoe store, but the town was suffering a slow death. The population was only two hundred in 1907 and one hundred in 1908, although the *Colorado State Business Directory* did list Pinnacle Park as being managed by Thomas Morris. The park closed shortly afterward, and the post office closed in August 1909. Only fifty residents

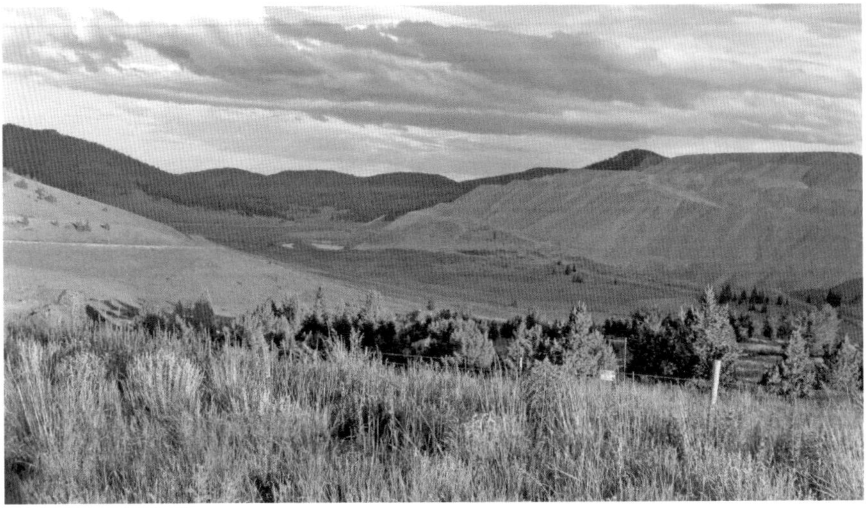

The expansive town site of Cameron as it appeared in 2015. The land is now owned by Newmont Mining Corporation. *Jan MacKell Collins.*

remained at Cameron by 1910. Two years later, they were being counted as part of Cripple Creek. Finally, in 1917, Cameron was vacated altogether. The school officially closed in 1921, when only six pupils, taught by Miss Mannering, were left.[208]

The quaint buildings and fancy log fence at Pinnacle Park were eventually torn down. For years, the logs lay in a heap in the woods just off the former rail bed of the Midland Terminal. Brick and rock enclosures built to house bears and wildcats at the zoo were the only remnants left until 2010, when they were dismantled in the wake of mining operations. In 2014, the City of Cripple Creek assisted in reconstructing the "caves" at the Cripple Creek District Museum. A small portion of Cameron's grassy meadow survives at this writing, but it is fast being encroached on as mining in the area progresses.

17

ECLIPSE

Small Town in a Big Mining District

For a small town with a short life, Eclipse was once an important facet in the Cripple Creek District's growth. The town actually owed its existence to the nearby town of Victor, where J.R. McKinnie of the famed Mary McKinnie Mine was building a new hotel in 1894. When the construction crew struck a vein of gold, plans for the hotel were quickly thrown over and the Gold Coin Mine was born. During the next several years, the Gold Coin would pay out over $1 million in dividends. But having a monstrous mine smack-dab in the middle of town posed a serious problem as the mine's waste tailings built up. McKinnie solved the problem by drilling a tunnel through Squaw Mountain between Victor and Eclipse Gulch to transport and process the gold ore.[209]

As the tunnel progressed, a small camp developed in Eclipse Gulch. Both Eclipse and its namesake gulch were named for the Eclipse Mine in nearby Arequa Gulch. Although residents of Eclipse were initially counted as part of Elkton up the road, the camp was soon a regular stop on the Midland Terminal Railroad. During fare wars between railroads in 1898, one could ride between Cripple Creek and Eclipse for just ten cents. McKinnie's tunnel was finally completed in about 1899 and extended some 3,700 feet through Squaw Mountain. The new tunnel was alternately called the United Mine Tunnel and the Columbine–Victor Tunnel. Next, Victor founders Harry and Frank Woods financed the construction of a huge mill, the Economic Gold Extraction Company, at Eclipse. The Economic quickly gained notoriety as one of the very first mills of its kind, using a chlorination process to refine gold. Furnaces at the mill were fired by crude oil brought up on the Florence & Cripple Creek Railroad.[210]

By 1901, Eclipse had become a semi-official town in its own right. The Economic's employees lived just below the mill. Electric cars from the Low Line also offered transportation to Cripple Creek and Victor. Also nearby was an even smaller camp referred to as Economic Junction. At Eclipse, business houses mingled comfortably with the suitably large homes around the mill. Residents could walk a short distance up to Elkton to shop or receive mail. Victor was just on the other side of Squaw Mountain, and the communities of Barry, Mound City and Anaconda were not far away.[211] Eclipse never did have a post office or newspaper, even though the 1900 *Cripple Creek District Directory* records that the town stretched for one full mile up and down Eclipse Gulch. Still, not much in the way of amenities were available aside from the Uintah Roominghouse, Jennie Doyle's boardinghouse and Mrs. Rose Ellebrecht's dressmaking parlor. Eclipse was about the only town in the Cripple Creek District without a saloon of its own.

At its peak, the Economic Mill was processing three hundred tons of ore daily, and the Gold Coin Mine in Victor yielded thirty thousand tons of ore in one year. In 1908, however, the Economic Mill caught fire, and the flames engulfed much of Eclipse. By this time the chlorination process was being surpassed by more feasible mining processes, so there was no real reason to rebuild Eclipse or the mill. The last newsworthy event occurred in 1915, when someone leased one of the old mining dumps below the mill, yielding $10,000 in gold. After the excitement subsided, what was left of Eclipse faded quietly back into the hills. The empty foundations of the Economic remained on the hillside below Highway 67 for decades, long after Elkton and other district towns were abandoned. From the 1940s to the 1980s, the ruins remained only as points of interest to sightseers. In the fall of 1994, the remains of both were razed by current mining endeavors.[212]

18

ELKTON

A Pleasant Mining Town

The story goes that William Shemwell, an amateur prospector and former blacksmith, partnered with two other men on a mine. Shemwell remembered seeing some elk antlers near the dig and named his stake the Elkton Mine. Next, he talked Colorado Springs grocers George and Sam Bernard into grubstaking him in exchange for $36.50 worth of groceries. Later, the Bernards bought Shemwell and his partners out, hired a respected mining man named Ed DeLaVergne to run the mine, and made millions.[213]

In 1894, the town of Elkton was founded near the mine. The post office opened on April 2, 1895. The town was very fortunate to be served by all three railroads in the Cripple Creek District: the Florence & Cripple Creek, the Midland Terminal and, later, the Colorado Springs & Cripple Creek District Railway. The Low Line Interurban System also ran through town, with a station house and telegraph office below the Elkton Mine. Soon, the Midland Terminal was the chief shipper for the Elkton Mine. In 1896, the railroad built a siding on the outskirts of town, just to pick up the ore.

The population of Elkton was about eight hundred at the time. There were several businesses, and thirty mines around the town provided work. The only news of note happened in 1897 when "fusionists" were discovered padding voter registrations with fake names in an attempt to throw an election in Elkton. Marshal Hunter said upward of two hundred names were faked, some by registering people whose headstones could be found in local cemeteries.[214] Other frauds popped up in Elkton from time to time. In March 1898, Mrs. Carrie Berry accused Cripple Creek District School

Board president McKelvey of accepting bribes and placing a $2,400 insurance policy on the Elkton school without approval.

Otherwise, Elkton's residential areas appeared downright neighborly. Neat rows of roads were built along the hillside, with modest miners' cabins lined up beside one another. Two rooms were added on to the school, and the *Cripple Creek Morning Times* was riddled with pleasant news about the town such as this one from November 1898: "A dance at the hospitable home of Mrs. Bolton, at the Elkton Hotel Friday evening, was well attended and highly enjoyable." And in December, the Midland Terminal built a new depot for the town.[215]

Elkton continued growing and eventually absorbed the nearby hamlets of Arequa and Eclipse. Prominent residents of Elkton included Father Victor, who served the catholic churches at the towns of Anaconda and Gillett. Several businesses proudly put "Elkton" before their names, and there was even a justice court in town. Notably, there was only one saloon. By 1902, Elkton's combined population with the smaller surrounding towns was around 2,500. Two thousand people still lived there in 1905, although the directory that year noted that the property was "owned by various mining companies and there are no city lots." The business district saw its ups and downs through 1912, when the population had downsized to 900 people.[216]

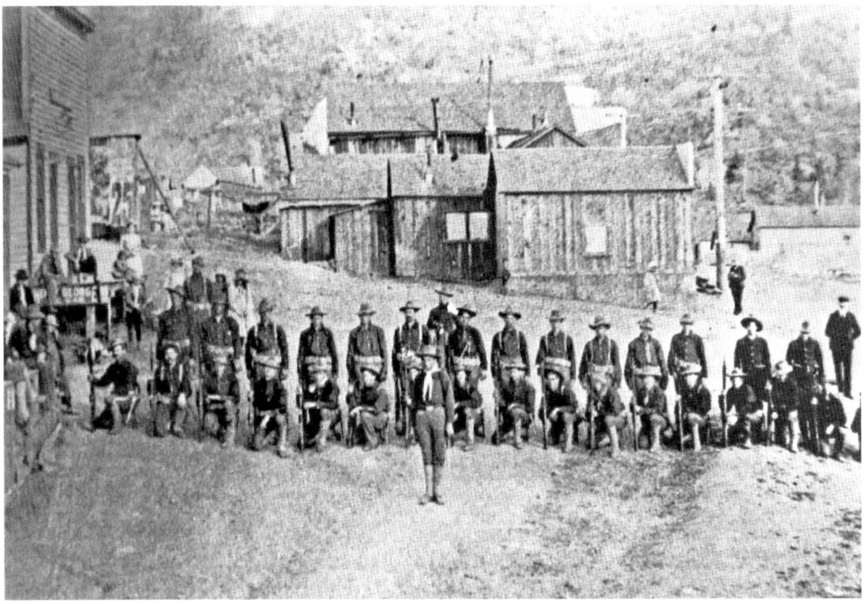

State militia troops pose at Elkton during 1904 labor wars. *Cripple Creek District Museum.*

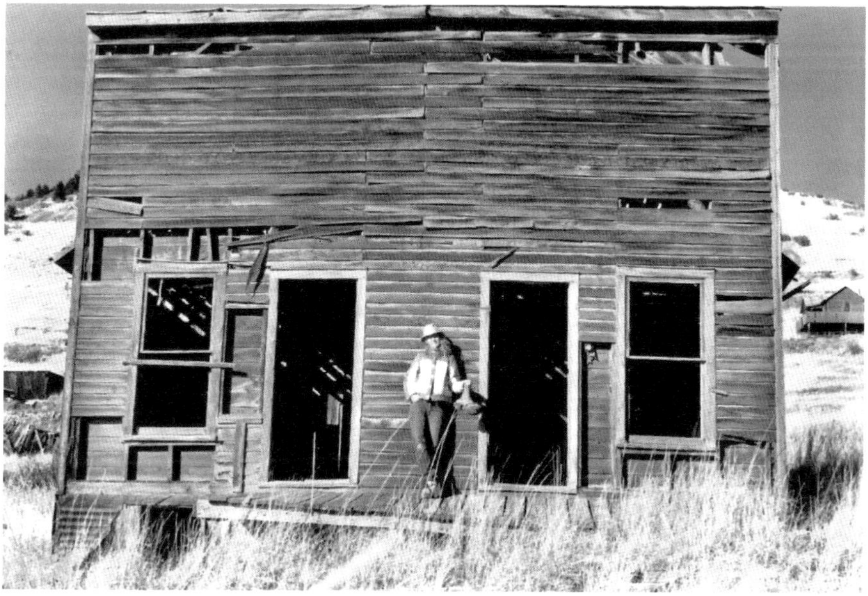

The author at Elkton in 1985. In the historic image of the town on page 108, this building can be seen on the left. *Jan MacKell Collins.*

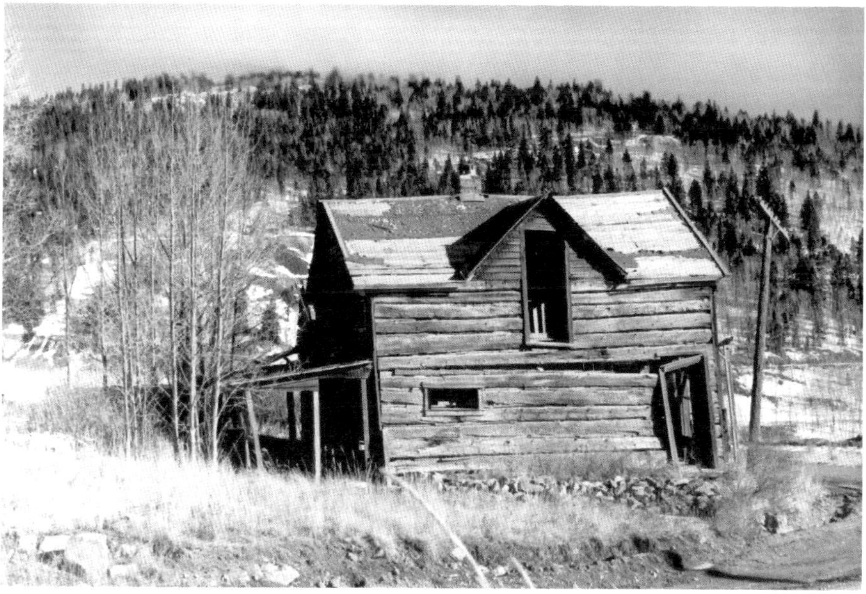

Another abandoned building of Elkton in 1985. People continued living in town off and on as late as the 1970s. *Jan MacKell Collins.*

Elkton's dwindling population was largely due to the mines in the Cripple Creek District playing out. A brief reprieve came in 1914 when mining engineer Richard Roelofs discovered a gigantic "vug" filled with gold flakes and nuggets at the Cresson Mine about a mile above town. Miners from all over the district were summoned to work on the Cresson, and Roelofs built an overhead tram that extended down through Elkton and ended at Eclipse. By 1916, the Elkton Mine had produced $16.2 million in gold but, like the Cresson vug, was producing less and less. The Cripple Creek District continued its downward spiral. When the station house below the Elkton Mine closed in 1919, only 350 people remained at Elkton. The school closed a year later.[217]

Elkton's post office was the next to close, in 1926.[218] During the next few decades, both before and after the Cresson Mine closed in 1959, a few people still called Elkton home. Throughout the 1980s many homes remained, but in 1994, modern mining operations bulldozed the entire town. Even the hill on which Elkton sat is long gone today.

19

GILLETT

A Gambling Man's Town

Shortly after the town of Beaver Park was platted in 1892, a nearby suburb became known as West Beaver Park. Later, the name was changed to Cripple City. As the Midland Terminal Railroad built tracks from Divide, the name was changed again to Gillett. The new city was renamed for railroad man W.K. Gillett, who, along with Henry Collbran, Irving Howbert and Harlan Lillibridge, was making big plans. The partners created the Midland Terminal Railroad, a spur of the Colorado Midland Railroad that would turn at Divide and head toward the Cripple Creek District (Gillett wanted to name the new railroad the "Cripple Creek and Gold Gulch Railroad," but when the directors of the Colorado Midland objected to such a whimsical name, the moniker was changed to the Midland Terminal). The new company was officially formed in October 1893.[219]

Early buildings at Gillett included log cabins but also hewn wood structures. The new town attracted such influential men as Albert E. Carlton, who had designs on a new freight company in Cripple Creek, as well as Charles Tutt and Spencer Penrose. Gillett was the perfect place for two young wealthy bachelors to build an entertainment mecca. Accordingly, Tutt and Penrose built an exclusive horse track and casino and called it "Sportsman's Park." The town was platted on January 19, 1894.

"A site with more picturesque surroundings could not have been chosen," crowed the 1894 *Cripple Creek District Directory* about Gillett. Located in a vast meadow with stunning views all around, Gillett would be the first town reached by the Midland Terminal on its way into the Cripple Creek District.

Plans were underway to build a $150,000 "railway hotel station," meant to be a "resort hotel adapted for the comfort and enjoyment of leisure seekers and tourists, and for the residents of the district."[220] The main drag through Gillett was named Parker Street after First National Bank president J.M. Parker. The avenue was soon lined with tidy, false-fronted buildings and aspen trees, which had been planted for accent. In anticipation of the railroad, a nice wood depot and telegraph office were built.

The Midland Terminal reached Gillett as planned, chugging gloriously through town on Independence Day 1894. A month later, the post office opened on August 29. Since the mountains between Gillett and Cripple Creek were too steep on which to build a railroad, a stage road led to the latter town instead as the Midland Terminal continued building through Beaver Park toward the city of Victor. On September 11, Pullman sleeper service began on the rail lines between Denver and Cripple Creek. Now, sleeper passengers could disembark at Gillett depot and catch a stage into Cripple Creek or stay the night in town.[221] Others also stayed the night in Gillett before traveling on, bringing extra commerce to town.

Gillett did suffer minor social issues. Tutt and Penrose soon realized that their wealthy friends were quite content patronizing the elite Broadmoor Casino in Colorado Springs rather than making the trek all the way to Gillett. Thus, the racetrack at Sportsman's Park never opened for more than two days a week and eventually scaled down to just a few Saturdays in the summer. The newly built Monte Carlo Casino suffered the same fate and was eventually converted to a school for the children of the town. Even budding madam Pearl DeVere purchased property in Gillett but soon moved to Cripple Creek, where she became the town's most famous harlot. Even so, a city jail was built to house lawbreakers. Outside town, the newly erected Beaver Park Stamp Mill processed ore from the Lincoln Mine (alternately known as the Lincoln & Gibbons), as well as the King of Diamonds. There was also the Gillett Reduction Works. Additional employment could be found at the shops for the railroad.[222]

In August 1895, the only "legal" bullfight in the United States took place at Gillett. The event was the brainchild of Joe Wolfe, owner of Cripple Creek's prestigious Palace Hotel and described as a "sometime confidence man." Wolfe partnered with Wild West performer and rodeo cowboy "Arizona Charlie" Meadows to form the "Joe Wolfe Grand National Spanish Bull Fight Company." As a means to secure the support of the town council, Wolfe appointed them as the board of directors of his company. But it was Charlie Meadows who was Wolfe's ace in the hole.

The six-foot-six, long-haired, mustachioed man from Arizona must have been startling to the citizens of Gillett. Meadows's career in rodeo began at Payson, Arizona, in 1884. In 1888, he hosted a "cowboy contest" in Prescott, where he earned a reputation as a "crack shot" and the "fastest man with a rope in the business." A few months later, he was a winning participant in Prescott's first rodeo.

Meadows used his skills and accompanying finesse to eventually turn from rodeo cowboy to showman. For seven years, he had toured several countries with a Wild West show, worked with Buffalo Bill's traveling troupe and eventually formed his own show. He was well known throughout the West by the time he hooked up with Joe Wolfe. Together the pair borrowed $5,000 to build a five-thousand-seat amphitheater at Gillett, print tickets and posters and secure real matadors and bulls from Mexico for the event. Wolfe's contribution to the town included the purchase of nine and a half blocks of real estate.[223]

Almost immediately, people began voicing their opposition to the upcoming event. The *Colorado Springs Gazette* in particular published several editorials. "If it be illegal to import bulls for fighting at the Atlanta Exposition, surely it must be illegal to import them across the border for fighting at the Gillett Exposition," argued one article. "Here is a chance for Francis Hill of the Humane Society to write to the Secretary of the Treasury, informing him that it is proposed to import bulls for the same purpose of fighting and 'keep them out of El Paso County.'"[224]

The authorities did ultimately stop the bulls and their keepers at the Texas border. But the matadors still came, and Wolfe and Meadows managed to wrangle some local bulls who were anything but fighting bulls. Things took an equally nasty turn when Wolfe invited renowned bunco artist Soapy Smith to set up his games of chance outside the entrance to the event. Soapy took so much money from his victims that some of them could not afford the $5 ticket to get in. Those who did gain admittance on the first day were shocked as the animals were led to a cruel death. Fewer than three hundred spectators attended on the second day. On the third day, Wolfe and Meadows folded the show and were promptly arrested for animal cruelty. In all, the total proceeds were a mere $2,600.[225]

Gillett citizens quickly overcame their embarrassment over the bullfights. By late 1895, two daily trains were still bringing plenty of passengers to town, and citizens had their choice of four newspapers to read on the trip. As of 1896, 1,500 residents had access to numerous businesses, including three doctors and an amazing nine saloons. Father Volpe's Catholic Church and a Congregational church were built in 1897. By 1899, the Golden Crescent Water and Light Company, owned by the Woods brothers in Victor, was servicing Gillett.[226]

Unfortunately, Gillett proved to be too far from the mines, and much of the town was eventually vacated. Even with eight trains passing through daily, the population in 1900 was only a little over five hundred people, including those living at nearby Monte Carlo Lakes. At least, there were still a few bars, and the school still supported a handful of students with Miss Mary A. Wilson as principal. The Co-Operative Brick Company on the outskirts of town was supplying bricks for surrounding businesses, homes and mines. Eventually, however, both the Lincoln and King of Diamonds mines played out, and the Beaver Park Stamp Mill became useless. The 1902 district directory commented that Gillett's "remoteness from the working mines has told against it, and at the present time its population is at a very low ebb." A hopeful endnote stated, "It is not at all improbable that something may occur at any time which will 'boom' the town and make it one of the largest in the District." But the numbers didn't lie; the directory reported Gillett's population at a mere three hundred people.[227]

Gillett's last newspaper, the *Forum* edited by Mayor James Parfet, closed in 1905. Now only 250 people remained, and neither church had a minister.

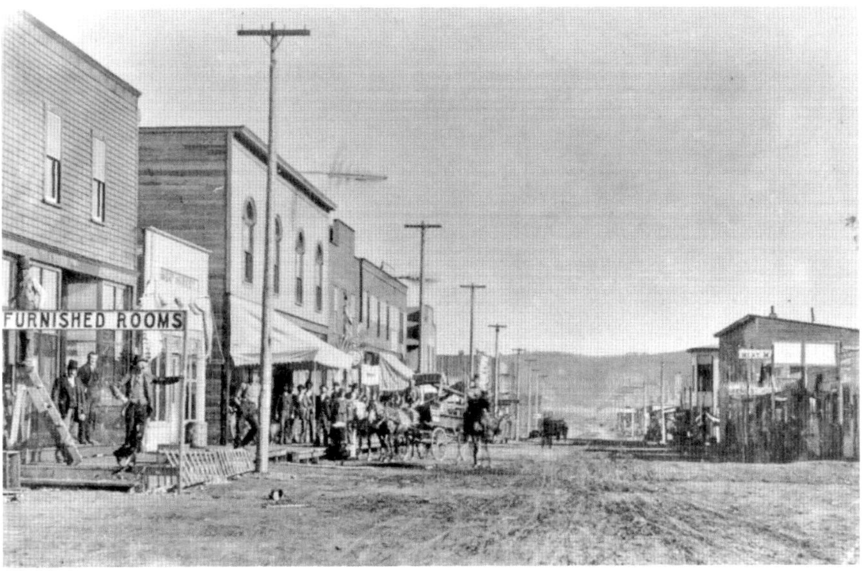

Downtown Gillett. *Cripple Creek District Museum.*

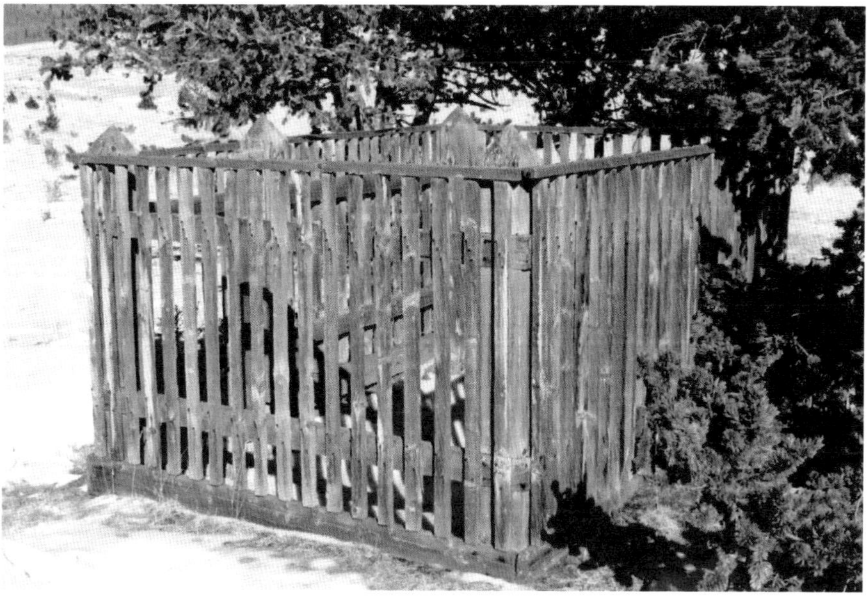

Only a few graves, such as this one, remain at Gillett's cemetery. The graveyard is now on private land. *Jan MacKell Collins.*

The post office, run by Charles Adams for many years, closed briefly in 1908 but reopened six months later. The reprieve was brief, for the 1910 census counted only forty-four people living in town. In 1911, the town entered a new era as a ranching community when the Vetter family purchased much of the land there, and the post office closed a final time in 1913. Gillett's once grand buildings sank into the ground, were torn down or burned. Rufus Porter remembered a man named Greasy Miller who lived at Gillett during its waning years. Greasy "burned down a score of houses by raking the ashes from the stove onto the floor. When the shack caught fire he'd simply move to another one."[228]

In time, some families moved their loved ones' graves from the cemetery to other local graveyards. The pews and the pulpit from Father Volpe's Catholic Church were moved to St. Peter's Church in Cripple Creek. The old church was used as a hay barn until it burned in 1949, and in 1965 a flood from a dam break above town washed away Gillett's remaining buildings.[229] Today, Gillett is known as Gillett Flats. The decaying ruins of the church, which sit on private land, can be spotted from the highway.

20

INDEPENDENCE

Victim of a Labor Strike

Named for the Independence Mine staked by Winfield Scott Stratton in 1891, the town of Independence was officially platted on November 11, 1894, next to the Hull City Mine. Other nearby mines included the Vindicator, the Teresa, the Portland Nos. 1 and 2, the Findley and, of course, the Independence. The Midland Terminal Railroad tracks divided Independence from the town of Goldfield, located across Montgomery Gulch. Because the two towns eventually grew to meet each other in the gulch, Independence was eventually ruled over by Goldfield's government. Also, there was already another Independence located near Aspen on Colorado's western slope. Thus, Independence's post office was called Macon when it first opened in February 1895. Soon the population numbered five hundred with a boardinghouse, two hotels and numerous business houses. The Midland Terminal provided passenger service at First and Montgomery Streets.[230]

In 1899, residents of Independence did succeed in renaming the Macon post office after their town. Not all of Independence's 1,500 people liked the arrangement with Goldfield. In late 1900, the Independence Mining & Townsite Company purchased a large plot of land and advertised the new town with vigor. "In twelve months, it will be the commercial center of the great Cripple Creek District," the town fathers declared. Despite their intentions, however, the men failed in their mission and Independence remained under Goldfield's shadow.[231]

Independence was not without some memorable residents. Among them was the so-called Queen of Independence, who was the toast of the town

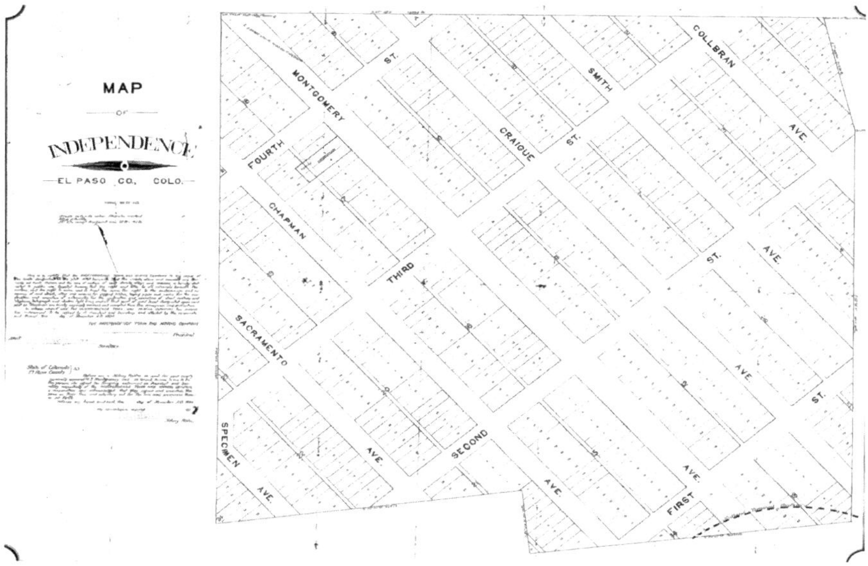

The town of Independence was laid out very neatly, with the Hull City Mine just outside of the city limits. *El Paso County Clerk and Recorder.*

according to Rufus Porter. Porter recalled the Queen's story of watching two gamblers resting on the sidewalk, each with a stack of gold pieces. The men were spitting at a crack in the sidewalk on twenty-dollar bets.

The town continued growing. Business houses of every kind were available in the downtown area. Among them was Mrs. Mamie Crooks's Hotel Montgomery, advertising a "nice home for miners. Good board and clean rooms at reasonable rates."[232] Independence made national news in 1903 when professional assassin Harry Orchard visited during the infamous Cripple Creek District labor strikes. Orchard began by bombing the Vindicator Mine above town, killing superintendent Charles H. McCormick and shift boss Malverne Beck. Next, in June 1904, Orchard bombed the Florence & Cripple Creek train depot in downtown Independence. Twenty-seven miners were standing on the depot platform when the bomb went off. Thirteen were killed instantly when "their dismembered bodies were blown 150 feet up the hillside." Orchard's actions were on behalf of the Western Federation of Miners, which was striking against unfair mine owners. His deeds, however, were so dastardly that they played a big part in the mine owners winning the strike.[233]

The strikes and subsequent bombings had an unfavorable affect on Independence. By 1905, many businesses had closed and the population

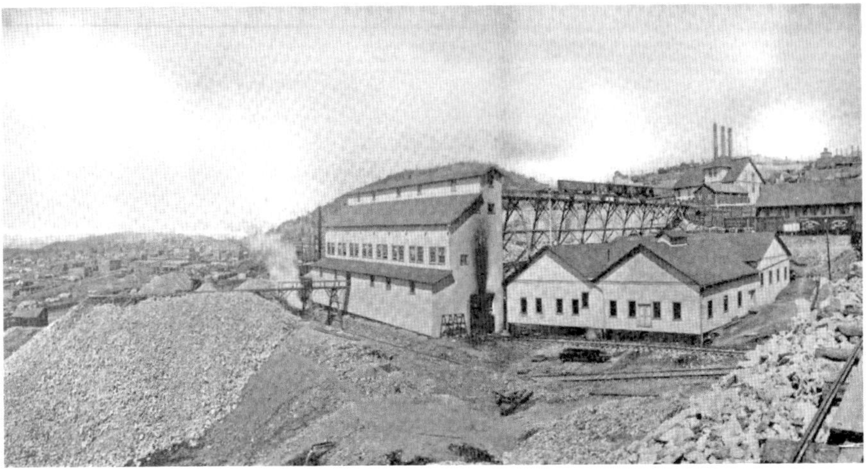

Stratton's Independence Mine. *From Hills,* Official Manual of the Cripple Creek District.

hovered around one thousand people. Things took an uglier turn when the Silver Bell Saloon was robbed in 1906. It was widely known that the Silver Bell cashed miners' paychecks, so there was money on hand at all times. At 10:00 p.m. on February 11, Eddie Foy, "Two-Gun Wild Bill" Gleason, Frank Drake, deputy marshals Hardy Potts and Cal Webster and several other men were in the bar when two masked robbers walked in and ordered everyone to put up their hands. Drake headed for a back room but was shot by one of the robbers, Harry Harris. Potts and Webster, along with Gleason, returned shots. More gunfire broke out. When it was all over, Drake and the second bandit, Fred Powell, were dead. Harris absconded with $1,800 in cash.[234]

The number of residents and businesses at Independence dwindled year by year, until there were only five hundred people left in 1919. Some of them, including Leslie Carlton and W.E. Ryan, were superintendents of area mines. Only a hardware store and two cigar stores were still open.[235] The town received a brief reprieve in 1921 when Carlton's brother, millionaire A.E. Carlton, purchased the old Vindicator Mine and tried to work it. Unfortunately, the mine was plagued by flooding. After Carlton's death in 1931, his wife, Ethel, successfully built the Carlton Tunnel to release the water from the Vindicator and other area mines. The Vindicator operated for nearly four more decades, even though the gold boom was long over.[236]

A few families continued living in Independence, including Mr. and Mrs. Alfred Bebee, who were there in 1939. Residents in the 1950s included a

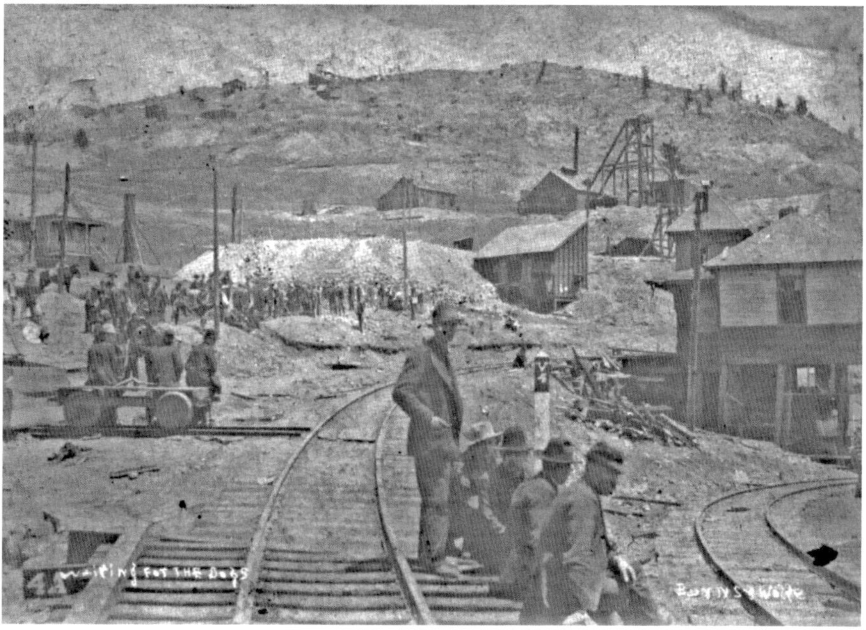

In this rare image, miners and other officials are awaiting deputies in the aftermath of the Independence depot explosion. *Cripple Creek District Museum.*

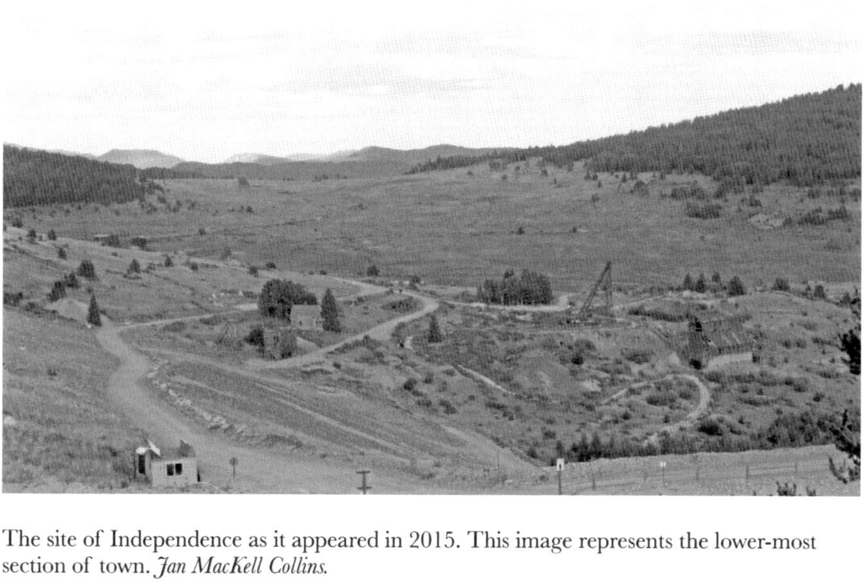

The site of Independence as it appeared in 2015. This image represents the lower-most section of town. *Jan MacKell Collins.*

man named Skinny Ward and the family of former Victor mayor Kathy Justice. Justice remembered her brothers finding sticks of dynamite at the Hull City Mine. "They brought it into town and sold it to the police chief for two cents a stick, and then we would buy candy at Harshie's [now the Fortune Club in Victor] with the money," she said. The post office closed in 1954, followed by the Hull City Mine in 1958 and the Vindicator Mine in 1959. A couple of homes were occupied as late as 1984, but most of the town was engulfed by modern mining efforts in 2004. Only a few structures at the very east end of town were preserved. The Hull City mine frame also was moved, and a hiking trail was installed.[237] Today, visitors can walk the Vindicator Valley trail and read interpretive signage about Independence and its surrounding mines.

21

LAWRENCE

First Official Town in the Cripple Creek District

The history of Lawrence has often taken a backseat to other historic towns around the Cripple Creek District. In its day, however, the town was among the most important communities in the area. Lawrence's history begins with Victor C. Adams's cattle ranch, established on the southeast slope of Squaw Mountain in 1888. In 1891, Mrs. Magdalene Raynolds, whose husband, Frank, had founded the Fremont County National Bank at Cañon City back in 1874, heard about the new gold boom. Mrs. Raynolds, along with her husband's business partner, Dana Lawrence, decided to visit the area. A good portion of Adams's ranch was flat and skirted by Wilson Creek. The area was ideal for a town.[238]

On January 4, 1892, Mrs. Raynolds purchased thirty acres of Adams's homestead. With Dana Lawrence, she platted the Cripple Creek District's first official town, Lawrence, on January 5. The town was laid out on a grid that was, appropriately, L shaped. The main streets included such presidential names as Lincoln and Cleveland but also Wilson Avenue for Wilson Creek, Raynolds Avenue for the Raynolds family and, of course, Lawrence Avenue. Shortly afterward, a stage stop was constructed at the new town so travelers could easily reach Lawrence from both Cañon City and Cripple Creek.[239]

Dana Lawrence appears to have been more than a business partner to the Raynolds family. In 1887, he was merely the secretary of the Raynolds Cattle Company, but when Mrs. Raynolds gave birth to a son just six months after the Lawrence plat was filed, the baby was named Dana Lawrence. The last reference to him appears in some 1894 court documents filed in

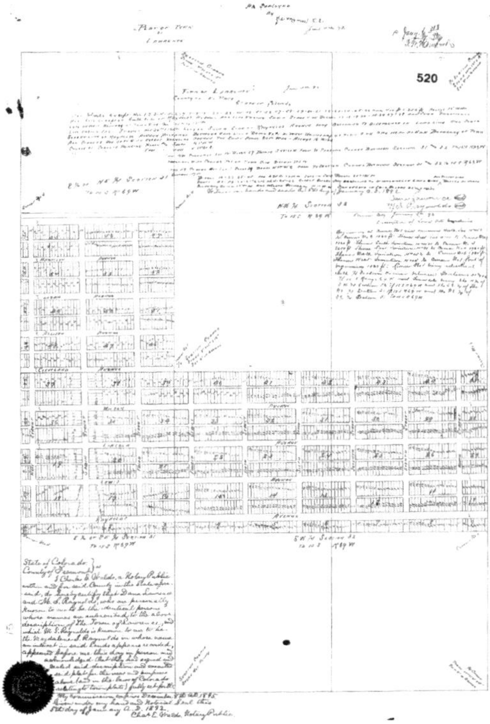

The plat map for Lawrence reveals its namesake, Dana Lawrence. Notably, the town was L shaped. *El Paso County Clerk and Recorder.*

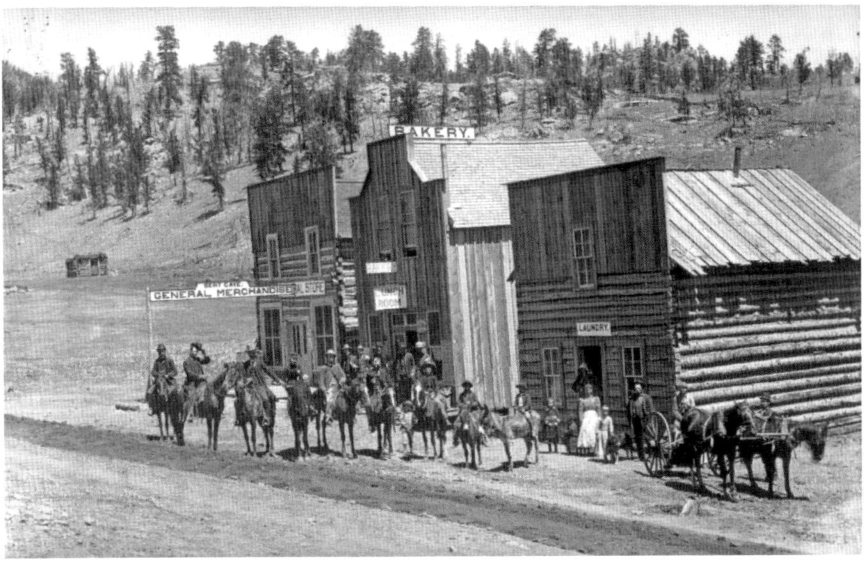

The best-known image of Lawrence shows three business houses. Only the lots on which they sat remain today. *Cripple Creek District Museum.*

Fremont County, which confirmed he still owned a portion of the Raynolds Cattle Company.[240]

There is nothing to suggest that the town founders ever lived at Lawrence. Being located along Wilson Creek, however, Lawrence proved an ideal place for all miners to live and work. Two early roads led there: the Cañon City Road along Wilson Creek, and the Florence Road, aka Shelf Road. Promoters of both roads also proposed building separate railroads: the Cañon City & Lawrence, and the Florence Railroad. Preliminary plans for the first railroad resulted in three studies to find the best route; in all three cases, surveyors of the hair-raising Shelf Road concluded that such a feat would be impossible. Even so, the post office at Lawrence opened on February 3, 1892. Before long, other amenities included Bert Cave's general merchandise store, a laundry and a restaurant. The short-lived *Lawrence Miner* newspaper reported the news. Early mines around town included the Florence E., the Gloriana, the Home Run, the London, the Lone Pine, the Lulu, the May Belle, the Monte Cristo, the St. Patrick, the Southern and the Tom Bigbee.[241]

Soon, the city of Victor above Lawrence was growing. Victor was larger and closer to the mines, and as more mines opened throughout the district their employees preferred to live closer to work. Miners did make social visits to Lawrence, gathering at the Eureka saloon to chat and drink. The saloon proved especially popular on Saturday nights. Lawrence's last hold out was the Lawrence Gold Extraction Company, an experimental chlorination plant for processing gold ore. The plant was the brainchild of Joseph R. DeLamar, a Utah mining man who partnered with mill expert Ed Holden to build the plant in 1893. Ads for the mill in 1894 promised the highest market price for Cripple Creek ores, and Lawrence was described as being "ribbed with gold bearing mineral veins."[242]

The 1894 district directory had much to say about the quality of life at Lawrence: "The numerous springs and flowing wells which came to the surface on the Lawrence townsite, together with its lively mountain brook, make it one of the most desirable residence spots of the entire district." A short time later, however, Victor's Sunnyside addition crossed into Lawrence. The new addition was the first sign that Victor would soon gobble up Lawrence. And when the chlorination plant burned during the winter of 1895–96, the town lost its only real claim to fame. Even so, Lawrence's population stayed steady at 250 through 1896 with a church, a school, a few businesses and the F&CC depot.[243]

By 1897, people were referring to Lawrence as "Oldtown." Those light in the wallet could still rent one of the rundown residences there, but the

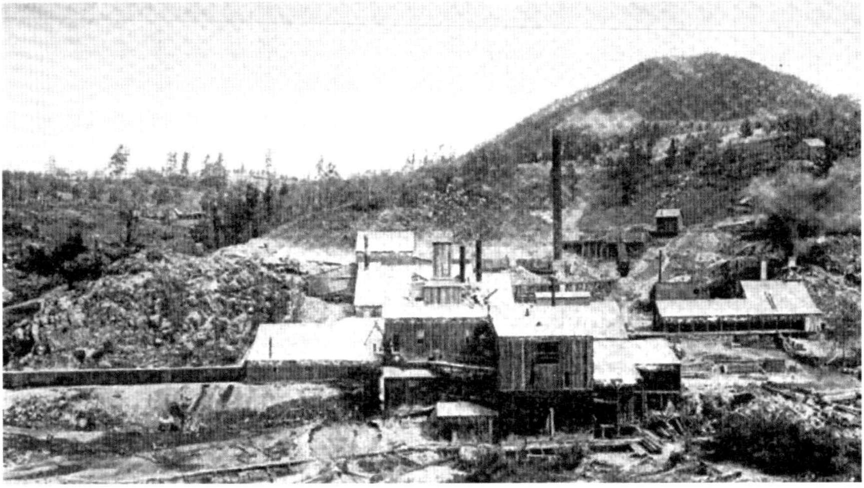

The Lawrence Gold Extraction Co. was an early chlorination processing plant. It burned in 1895. *From Warren and Stride,* Cripple Creek and Colorado Springs.

post office closed in April 1898. Although property transactions remained steady through 1899, the only one of note was a purchase by the Cripple Creek Gold Exploration Company. And there were still a few businesses as late as 1900, including the Lawrence School. Most of the three hundred residents were miners who lived in town or the nearby hamlet of Reigerville. Everyone got their mail from Victor.

City marshal George Cooper kept the peace at Lawrence, but even so, the town did see its fair share of lawlessness. Most of it was petty thievery, but there also was a September report that Henry Nelson had fired two shots at former miner Alec Carlson from the Pittsburgh claim. One of the bullets grazed Carlson's head just above the left eye. Carlson survived, and Nelson was arrested. Next, H.C. Rhien was found hiding at a Lawrence boardinghouse after bilking several merchants around Colorado out of $8,000 in general merchandise.[244]

By 1902, Lawrence had been officially absorbed by Victor, although folks did continue living there for a time. As of the 1920 census, ninety-five people were left in Lawrence proper. Ten years later, however, Lawrence no longer appeared in census records at all. Today, the town has settled back into the meadow, with only one private home from the old days left to prove it was there to begin with.[245]

22

MOUND CITY

A Quick Entrance and Exit

Established in 1891 on the lower end of Squaw Gulch, Mound City was one of the earliest settlements in the booming Cripple Creek District. The initial residents were primarily miners, but one citizen of note was Judge Melville B. Gerry. In 1883, Gerry presided over the trial of Colorado cannibal Alfred Packer at Lake City in Hinsdale County. Upon Packer's conviction, Gerry handed down his sentence for Packer to be hanged "until you are dead, dead, dead." Later, he moved to Barry and Anaconda, serving as a judge in both towns.[246]

The opening of Mound City's post office in March 1893 was quickly followed by other businesses. They included an ice cream shop run by Joseph Lesher, who would later move to Victor and make history by attempting to produce his own legal tender. J.L. Niebergall, who ran a store, would later open another one in Cripple Creek. On the bawdier side of life, there were five saloons. Interestingly, the large business district served a mere 116 residents who lived in rustic tents, log cabins and other small buildings made from rough wood planks. On one side of the fledgling town was the imposing Brodie Mill. Up the road a piece, the Rosebud Mill was also built. Mining millionaire Winfield Scott Stratton tried running some of his ore from the Washington Mine through the Rosebud, but when mill operators had a hard time processing the ore, Stratton turned his attentions elsewhere.[247]

By 1894, Mound City was competing with other new towns as more gold was discovered in the Cripple Creek District. "Anaconda, Mound City and Cripple Creek will soon grow together if building keeps on at the rate it has

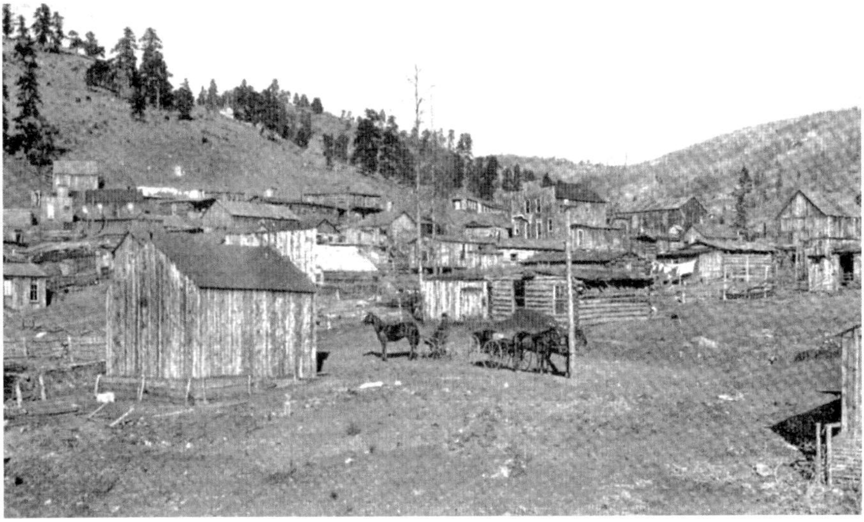

Mound City featured a large business district and several log homes. *From Warren and Stride,* Cripple Creek and Colorado Springs.

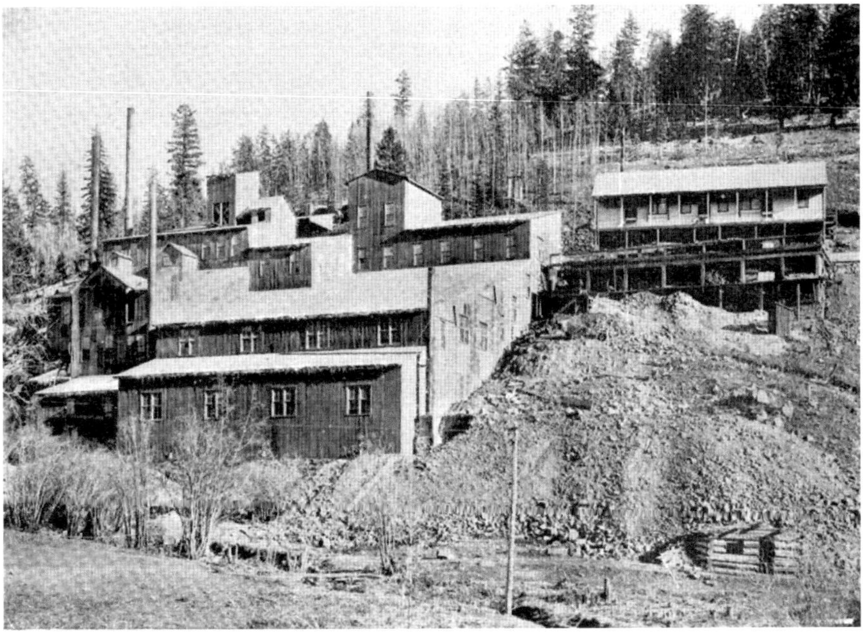

The Brodie Mill at Mound City, as photographed by Henry Lee Jacques Warren. *From Warren and Stride,* Cripple Creek and Colorado Springs.

Opposite, bottom: Ruins of the Brodie Mill are all that remain of Mound City today. *Jan MacKell Collins.*

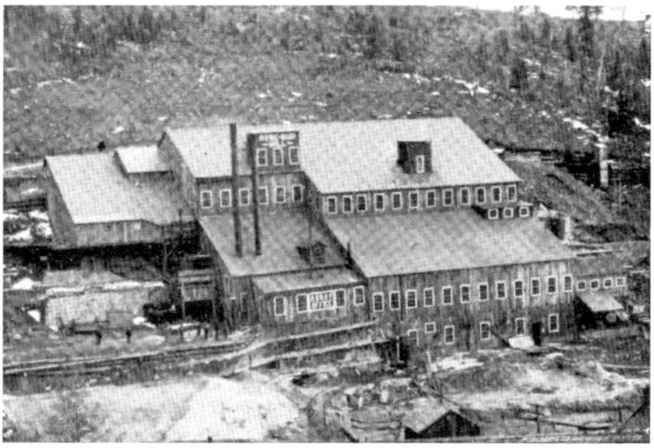

Left: Photographer Henry Lee Jacques Warren captured the Rosebud Mill at Mound City, circa 1893. *From Warren and Stride,* Cripple Creek and Colorado Springs.

Below: When Harry "Buck" Buckwalter captured this image of Mound City, the town was fading. *Cripple Creek District Museum.*

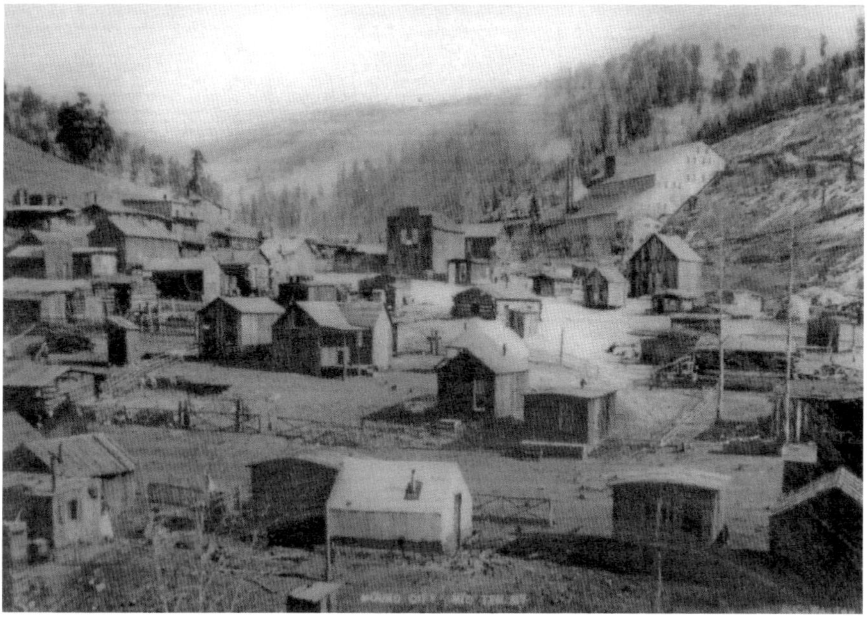

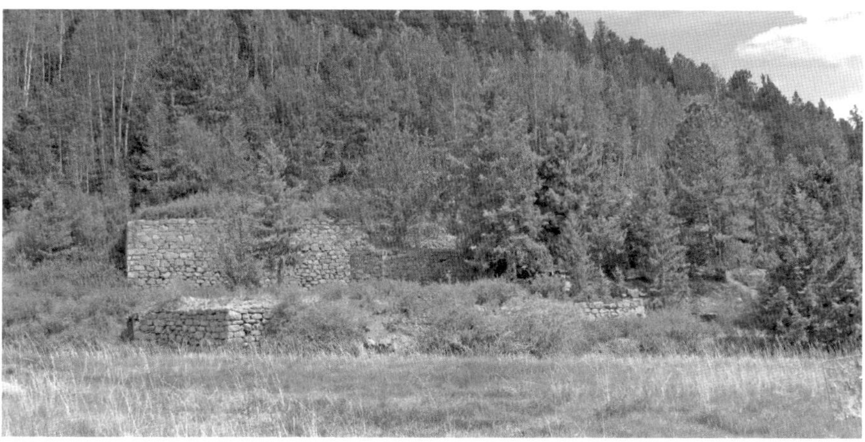

been going," predicted the *Cripple Creek District Directory* of 1894, "and there is now little vacant territory left between them." Mound City's population was about five hundred, but the business section suddenly stopped growing as larger towns offered better services. Throughout the year, there were only eight businesses in town.[248]

When the Rosebud Mill burned, it seemed to signify the end of Mound City. The post office closed in May, and by 1896, residents were considered part of nearby Anaconda. When photographer Harry Buckwalter of the William Selig's Denver film company captured images of Mound City during the late 1890s, the place looked almost deserted. By 1900, residents of Mound City were relying on Anaconda for their mail and groceries. The closure of the Brodie Mill just about did Mound City in for good. A mere thirty-eight residents composed the town, and the only local business was the Mound City Dairy.[249] Mound City slowly faded into dust, and only the ruins of the Brodie Mill remain today.

23

SIGNAL BUTTE

A LANDMARK FOR MINERS

For a short time, Signal Butte—sometimes referred to as just Signal—served as a small mining camp in the hills north of Divide. The camp was named for the small butte of the same name. Signal Butte is first mentioned in early 1896, when it was reported that "the greater part of the prospecting at the present time is being done in the lime belt east of Pemberton and in the porphyry belt west of West Creek." The article ended by noting that the area around Signal Butte "is not being neglected."[250]

To that effect, Signal Butte was platted on February 27, 1896, by M.E. Allen, M. Durocher, Minna Rische and Ernest L. Hall of Arapahoe County. Further news of Signal Butte's landmark knoll reported that it was "the highest mountain in the immediate vicinity," rising to an altitude of over ten thousand feet. Claims were being worked all around the butte. "There is very little patented land in this section," said Denver's *Rocky Mountain Sun*, "and while the available ground is rapidly being taken up, there is yet much land that has not been staked."[251]

News of Signal Butte eventually made its way across the region. In March, the *Castle Rock Journal* revealed that "eight miles south of Pemberton is the town of Signal Butte, being built by Dr. McHugh and others. A number of buildings are in course of erection and it is expected to make a separate mining district surrounding the town." As the excitement built, the town fathers were able to establish a post office, under the name Signal, on May 1.

Nothing more was published about Signal Butte until May 1898, when the *Mountain Echo* newspaper at the community of Nighthawk in Douglas

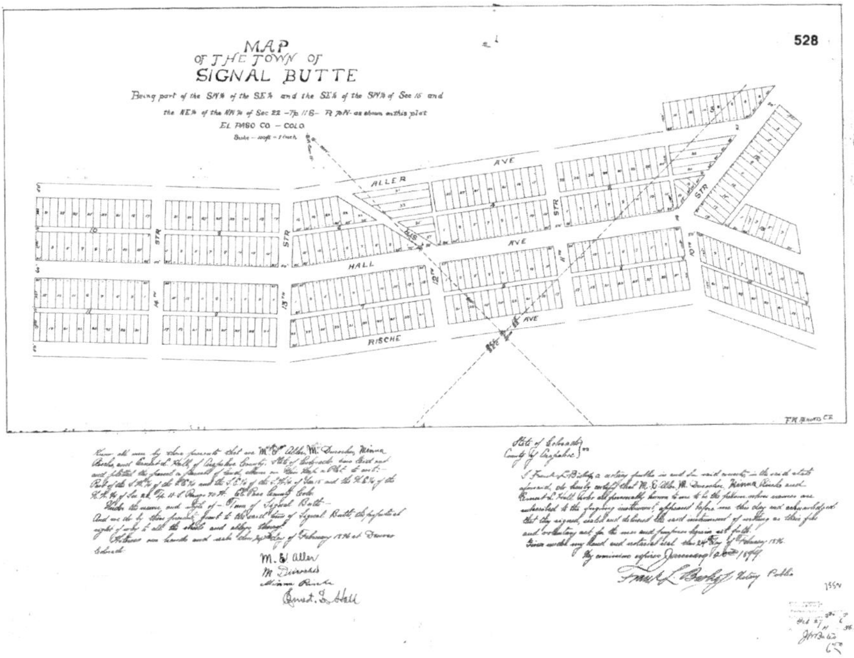

Signal Butte was platted twice, once in 1896 and again in 1899. *El Paso County Clerk and Recorder.*

County reported that editor Wilson of the *Woodland Park Times* ran into miner C.E. Auld at Pueblo. Auld was "holding down a job on the Gulf Road and earning enough to keep two men at work on his Friend lode at Signal Butte." There was also a note that "Signal Butte is preparing to be patented." The town of Signal Butte was indeed replatted in 1899, but not much came in the way of lot sales.[252]

Other newspapers reported regularly on several other claims around the settlement, but Signal Butte began fading rather quickly. The post office was closed on May 23. The last that was heard of Signal Butte was in 1906, when the U.S. Board on Geographic Names retained the name of Signal Butte instead of the suggested name of "Cheop's Pyramid."[253]

24

STRATTONVILLE

A Millionaire's Mining Town

Strattonville has proven confusing to historians because there were actually two towns known by that name in the Cripple Creek District. To add to the puzzle, one of them was located at the former mining camp of Summit. The latter place has sometimes been mistaken for Summit Park, the community located north of today's Woodland Park. Both places were named for Winfield Scott Stratton, a former carpenter from Indiana who came west and started dabbling in mining beginning in about 1874. By 1891, he had arrived in the budding Cripple Creek District. At the age of forty-two, Stratton was divorced, broke and tired, with little faith in this newest gold boom. Cowboy Bob Womack encouraged Stratton to stake a claim anyway. The chosen spot was calculated by Stratton to sit on the very edge of the giant volcano that encompassed the district. His formula worked, and Stratton's Independence Mine was staked on July 4, 1891. The Independence was yielding a whopping $50,000 to $100,000 per month by 1896.[254]

Initially, Stratton made his home just below the Independence Mine. The house was fine, with white clapboard siding and several outbuildings. Soon the area around Stratton's place was known as Strattonville and, sometimes, Stratton Junction. The community first appears in the 1900 *Cripple Creek District Directory*, which located it "on the hillside below Stratton's Independence and between Goldfield and Victor." There were about one hundred residents who used the post office at Victor. Most of them were miners, mixed in with a blacksmith or two, engineers, carpenters and firemen. But although the company town earned a reputation as a working miner's town, several women and children made their homes there as well.[255] Stratton eventually moved away, and Strattonville melded into a part of the nearby town of Goldfield.

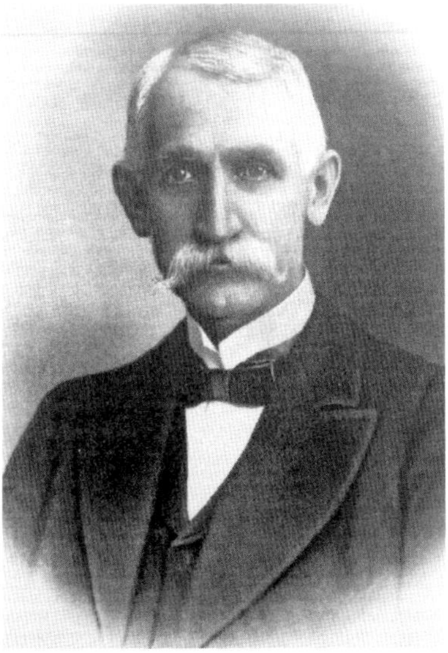

Winfield Scott Stratton was a generous but reclusive millionaire whose last name graced towns across Colorado. *Jan MacKell Collins.*

A few miles away from Strattonville was Summit, a mining camp that was almost certainly named for the Summit Mine located "on the very top of Squaw Mountain." More specifically, Summit was on Globe Hill a half mile north of the whistle-stop of Midway. First mention of Summit was made in 1895, when miner Barney McGiven left his home there to buy provisions in Cripple Creek. He was next found lying on the road in Cripple Creek's roughneck neighborhood, Poverty Gulch, "bruised from head to foot and unable to talk." Policemen, thinking him drunk, took him to Cripple Creek's jail. The next day, McGiven's friends took him to his home but soon realized his wounds were serious. A Dr. Knight was summoned and concluded McGiven had been "kicked severely in the stomach." McGiven could say only that he was attacked by two men before falling unconscious again and dying. An article the following day explained that McGiven had actually gotten into an argument in Poverty Gulch with another man that had escalated into a fight.[256]

In April 1899, Winfield Stratton purchased the Summit, Deerhorn and Plymouth Rock mining claims. Within a short time, he had taken over the Summit camp. The streets were made straight and clean and consisted of two or three main drags. Shanties were replaced with several fine brick buildings to house miners, dining halls, offices and assay laboratories. Power lines supplied electricity. There was also a clubhouse and one or two stores. A laundress was the only female inhabitant of the camp. Unlike other mining company towns that required their employees to shop on site, residents of the new Strattonville were welcome to do their business throughout the district. The population in 1900 included several miners who lived at the Stratton Boardinghouse, run by J.W. Blades. The

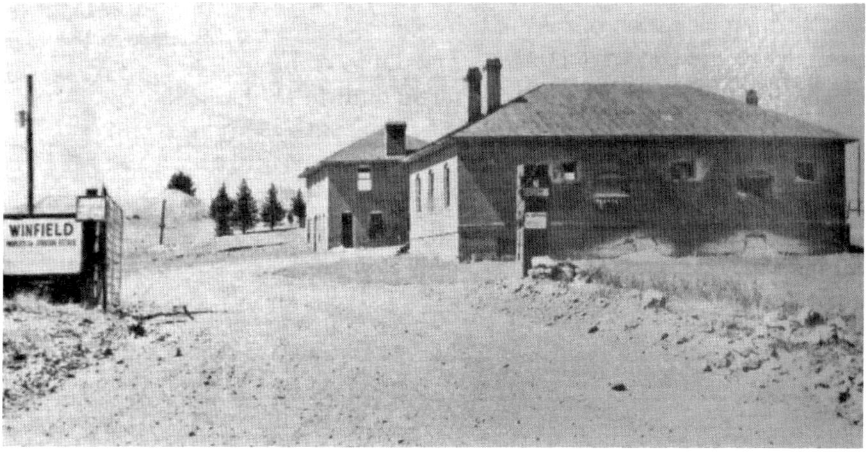

Strattonville as it appeared in 1976. Note the name on the sign identifies the town as Winfield. *Cripple Creek District Museum.*

men had easy access to such nearby mines as the Logan, Anchoria and American Eagles.[257]

Over time, Strattonville was known by many names. Later maps show the name of the town as Winfield, confusing it with another Winfield in Chaffee County. There was also another city called Stratton, located on Highway 24 in Kit Carson County. A third name, Strattonia, was applied in an article about a holdup at Strattonville in November 1900. The intended victims were assistant mine superintendent R.G. Grant and master mechanic Herbert Cramer, but the thieves were thwarted when "Grant gave the footpads the hot foot and Cramer gave up $5.00."

The town might have progressed a little more, but in 1902, Stratton died in Colorado Springs. Strattonville slowly faded away and was completely abandoned by 1913. The ghost town remained virtually undisturbed until about 1972, when it was razed in the wake of modern mining operations. One contractor recalled digging up a crystal chandelier at the old town. The once grand light fixture was the last remnant of what was once a dignified mining community.[258]

25

WEST CREEK AND PEMBERTON

Two Towns with the Same Name

During the frantic settlement of Teller County in the 1890s, one of the most enigmatic towns was surely West Creek. A town by that name still survives in Douglas County to the north. But there were actually two towns, both named West Creek, which were platted within five miles of one another: one in Douglas County and the other in what was then El Paso County and which later became part of Teller County.

The West Creek in Douglas County had just been platted in October 1895, when, barely two months later, the second West Creek in El Paso County was platted by John Dewese of the West Creek Town Site and Improvement Company. In the newer town, Midland, Santa Fe and West Creek Avenues were intersected by First through Fifth Streets. The creek of the same name bisected the town.

The founders of the new town immediately vexed the founders of the old town, although the latter acquiesced at first by renaming their town Pemberton. Not everyone received the news, however, and early writers and photographers continued calling both places West Creek. When H.S. Poley snapped several images of old West Creek in early 1896, he misidentified the town as the one lying in El Paso County.[259] At last, an explanation was offered in the March 11, 1896 issue of Douglas County's *Castle Rock Journal*:

> *Subsequent to the difficulty experienced by the new town of Pemberton in securing the name of West Creek, a new town was started four miles south and across the county line in El Paso County and the plat filed in that*

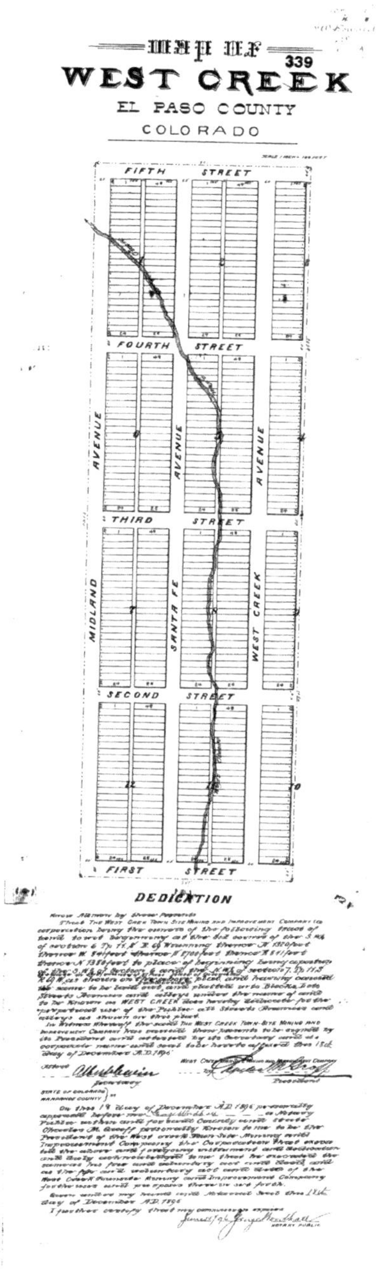

The plat map for West Creek, El Paso County, was platted two months after the West Creek of Douglas County. *El Paso County Clerk and Recorder.*

> *county as West Creek. Mssrs. Edward Lewin, C.M. Croff and G.W. Thornberg are meeting with success in this new departure, the town having already a number of very substantial buildings occupied by wide-awake enterprising business men. A fight is now on between Pemberton, the town originally applying for the name of West Creek, and the new town, as to which shall be known as the West Creek of the future.*[260]

Pemberton's town fathers were game for a war. "The fight between West Creek, El Paso County and Pemberton, Douglas County for the name of West Creek is getting very warm," reported the *Leadville Herald Democrat* on March 17. "This morning Judge Hubbard rode from Castle Rock to Denver on a bicycle to file preliminary paper for Pemberton with the secretary of state before the West Creek people could get there by rail. Both town corporations have been formally recognized by the respective counties as West Creek." The two municipalities went to court in Colorado Springs on March 30. The outcome of the trial escaped mention by newspapers, but in 1898, the *Mountain Echo* newspaper in Nighthawk, Douglas County, noted that West Creek's name in El Paso County had been changed to Stratton. No new plat was ever filed, however, and no post office opened under that name.

The final defeat against West Creek in El Paso County is evidenced only by a new newspaper, the *West Creek Mining News*, which was published in "West Creek, Douglas County," beginning in about 1899. By 1902 the West Creek of Teller County had been abandoned, and the post office at Pemberton was at last able to change its name to West Creek. Teller County's West Creek was so quickly forgotten that nobody even bothered to vacate the town until 1997.[261] Nothing remains of the community.

PART III

WHISTLE-STOPS

26

ALTA VISTA

A "Helper's" Town for the Railroad

As the Florence & Cripple Creek Railroad built its tracks up Eight Mile Canyon toward the Cripple Creek District in 1894, it was soon discovered that the last few miles into the district proved steeper than originally thought. There may have already been an old stage route in the high meadow where a "helper" town was built, wherein engines could travel down the canyon to the station at Adelaide in Fremont County and assist the trains in making it up the grade. By the time the railroad reached there, the place had already been named Alta Vista, Spanish for "high view." True to its name, Alta Vista, at 9,710 feet in altitude, afforded a beautiful view for miles around. From the whistle-stop's lofty location, passengers could see the district's working mines, as well as the budding city of Victor.[262]

Alta Vista was never platted and never had a post office, even after the railroad officially reached it on May 20, 1894. The settlement did, however, play a prominent role in the railroad history of the Cripple Creek District. Alta Vista served several purposes for the F&CC. A large station yard allowed for repair of both freight and passenger cars. A "classification yard" was also built, wherein freight cars could be sorted by content and destination.[263]

The founding of Alta Vista happened to coincide with the Cripple Creek District's labor war in 1894. The railroad had just reached town when miners of the district went on strike. On May 29, fifty picketing miners showed up at Alta Vista. Newspapers noted that "the entire four miles of winding track to Victor was picketed with sharpshooters." Denver deputies were present also and had a clear view of the nearby city of Victor. The deputies watched in horror as strikers blew up the Strong Mine above that town. Following the explosion, "the road supervisor accordingly required all trains to be searched."

After the labor war ended in June, coal, gold ore, mining equipment and supplies continued to be brought through Alta Vista regularly, as well as upward of six daily passenger trains. Alta Vista offered very few services, aside from a small one-room depot and some residences for railroad workers. For a mere whistle-stop, however, Alta Vista's presence was both necessary and important. Because the F&CC's early equipment often included the use of Denver & Rio Grande train cars, defective cars would be held at Alta Vista to await repair or maintenance.[264]

Perhaps the most exciting event to take place around Alta Vista was a flash flood that erupted just below the station on Eight Mile Creek on July 30, 1895. Water in the creek, which paralleled the F&CC tracks, reached speeds of thirty miles per hour as it swept down the canyon toward the next stop. A helper engine on the way back from Alta Vista made breakneck speed to outrun the flood until it reached Russell, another stop in Fremont County, at which point the tracks diverted away from the creek. But the flood caused much havoc, and some people were drowned.[265]

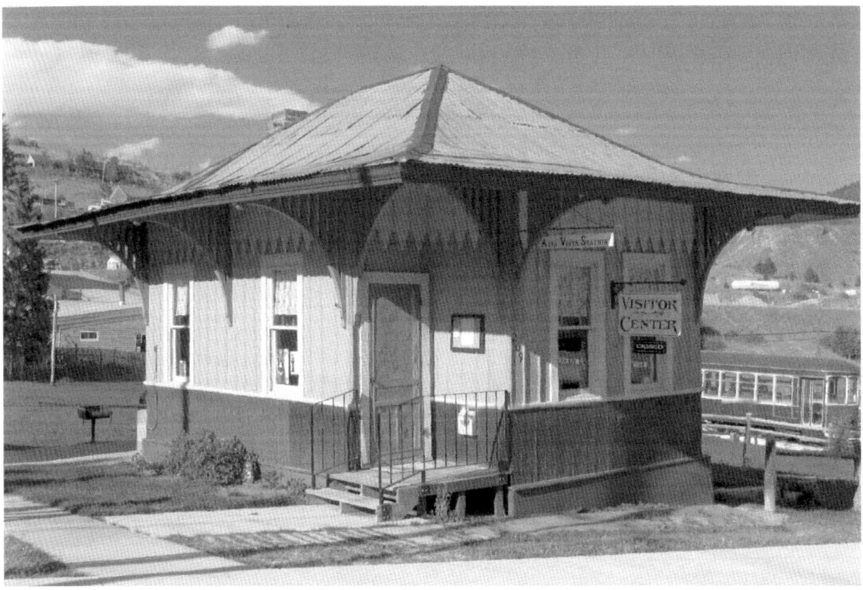

Today, the Alta Vista depot is in Victor, where it serves as a visitor center. *Jan MacKell Collins.*

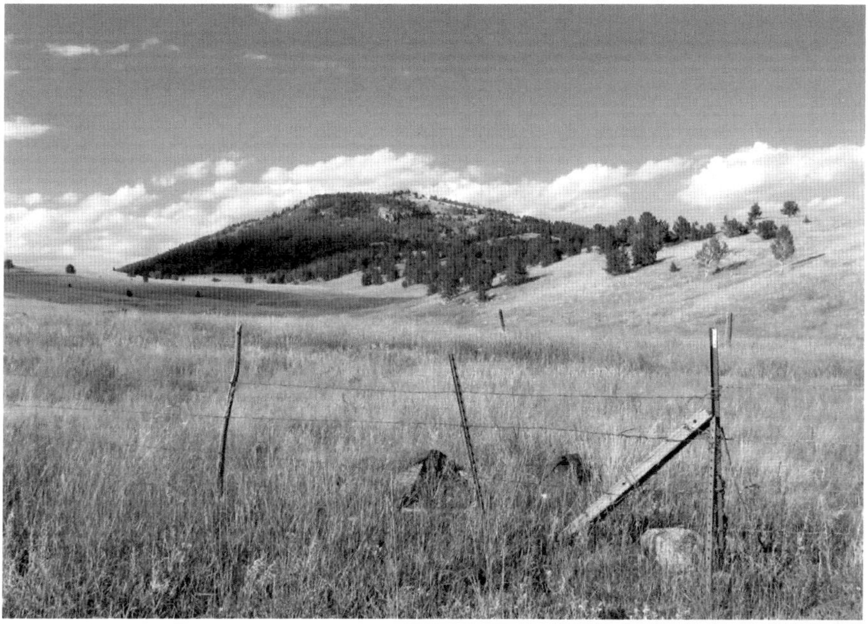

The empty site of Alta Vista along Phantom Canyon Road is now part of a private hunting ranch. *Jan MacKell Collins.*

It cost a bit to rebuild the tracks, but the F&CC was up and running again by November. Four trains passed through Alta Vista daily. By 1899, picnics in Alta Vista's sunny meadows were a favorite daytime destination among locals. Passengers boarded the F&CC at Cripple Creek at 9:00 a.m. and headed toward Alta Vista. At 3:30 p.m., after a day of picking wildflowers and eating picnic lunches, all boarded the train back to Cripple Creek. A round-trip ticket cost twenty-five cents.[266]

Only a few residents were living in Alta Vista in 1900. They were operator S. Aller, F&CC employees Jim Doyle and George Metzger, miner E.H. Niles and Harvey Taylor, who ran a brickyard. Taylor employed Louis Scott as a brick maker. The F&CC tracks washed out a second time in 1912, and the railroad closed. In 1913, the Alta Vista Mining Company announced plans to build a new mill at Alta Vista, but this apparently never happened. In time, only the depot remained, standing in a field along what is now the dirt road of Phantom Canyon.[267] The depot has since been moved to Victor, where it serves today as a visitors' center.

27

DYER

NAMED FOR A BRITISH COLONEL

In April 1897, a group of entrepreneurs banded together to form the Cripple Creek District Railway, an electric trolley line between Cripple Creek and Victor. The line began operations in November 1897, although in its formative years the company went through a number of principal officers who could not seem to agree with one another. When board member John Bolles resigned in late 1897, he was replaced by Colonel Henry Clement Swinnerton Dyer, a British military officer who also was a well-known civil engineer. Newly elected president of the board Irving Howbert was likely hoping Dyer could contribute needed cash to the enterprise. Howbert wanted to pull out anyway, which he did almost as soon as the new line began running. Dyer took his place. In his honor, the small station of Dyer was established between the whistle-stop of Midway and Victor.[268]

In reporting on the progress of the newly named Cripple Creek District Electric Railroad in early 1898, the *Cripple Creek Morning Times* noted that the "switches at Midway, Dyer and Anchoria have been completed and the extra car service will be put on in a few days." By February, Dyer was served by the line several times a day. Colonel Dyer's presidency was short-lived; in March, locals received the news that he had died in London. The *Cripple Creek Morning Times* assured everyone that the "officials of the new electric line state that his death will have no effect whatever on the projected line from [Colorado Springs] to Cripple Creek, but that cars will be running between the two cities by November 1."[269]

As late as 1900, the *Cripple Creek District Directory* recorded several miners at Dyer, as well as engineer Jack Bruce. H.H. Cooper was a leaser. William C. Corson, storekeeper for the Colorado Electric Power Company at the Los Angeles Mine, also lived there. Most of the miners lived at the Modoc Boardinghouse, run by Mrs. M.J. Boyd. Nothing else of note happened at Dyer, and after the electric line ceased operations in 1920, the stop faded into obscurity.[270]

28

EDLOWE

Achieving What Summit Park Could Not

Four years after the demise of Summit Park between today's Woodland Park and Divide in 1892, a new town took its place. The post office, established on June 19, 1896, was called Edlowe after Edgar D. Lowe. In September, the widow of longtime pioneer Wesley Wheeler, Hattie Wheeler, had the old site of Summit Park resurveyed. New names were assigned to the streets and the old name of Summit Park was officially changed to that of the new town.

For the next several years, Edlowe functioned as a literal whistle-stop along the Colorado Midland Railroad. Trains only stopped upon request, but special "Wildflower Excursions" often came there to enjoy the flowers and picnic in area meadows. These special trains were highly popular, running from Colorado Springs all the way to 11-Mile Canyon some forty miles west. In addition, Edlowe sported a school, a church and a ten-room hotel operated by the Hickox family.[271]

By the late 1890s, farming had become quite lucrative at Edlowe. The rich soil was conducive to growing lettuce and potatoes, as well as raising cattle. From all appearances, the community was quiet and peaceful, save for a night in December 1898 when William Ransdell was returning to his home in Edlowe from Cripple Creek. A "tramp" approached the wagon, and Ransdell gave him a ride. All was well until the tramp suddenly "knocked Ransdell off the wagon, picked his pockets, securing about $2, and left him lying by the roadside unconscious." It was such a cold night that by the time Ransdell recovered, his feet had frozen, leading to fears they might have to be amputated.[272]

As Woodland Park and Divide on either side of Edlowe developed, postal authorities saw no need for the post office, which closed on June 16, 1899. By the 1910 census, there were just a few residents left, mostly ranchers but also Dennis Sweeny, who worked for the Colorado Midland Railroad. Ten years later, the census counted Edlowe residents as part of Divide, although the school district now fell under that of Woodland Park. Then in 1928, Colorado businessmen Clarence Coil, Doug Shafer and John Fowler opened the Silver Spruce Ski Club on a hill behind Edlowe. The men spent the summer of 1929 clearing trees for a ski run. A second run was built in 1930, using heavy equipment courtesy of Spencer Penrose of Colorado Springs's Broadmoor Hotel. Penrose also assisted when a blizzard threatened plans for a competition during the winter of 1931–32. That time, Penrose chartered a special engine of the Colorado Midland to ensure the skiers could get up Ute Pass.[273]

The skiing craze at Edlowe peaked in January 1934, when the club sponsored the official First Tournament of the U.S. Western Ski Association there. Two years later, the ski club moved its operations to the slopes on Pikes Peak. The abandoned lodge and club buildings later burned. Next, in 1937, Lee Hermann established the Quarter Circle H Ranch as a dude ranch near Edlowe for young people. "With a guest ranch of their own, without regimentation," Hermann explained, "where the kids would be on their

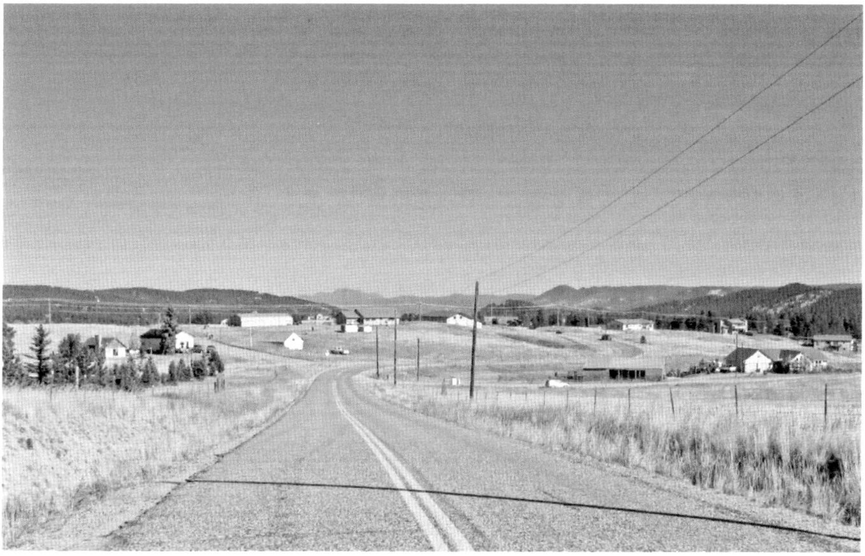

Edlowe as it appears today. Near the few historic buildings, the grade of the Colorado Midland Railroad can still be seen. *Jan MacKell Collins.*

own, run the show, map out their own play and chores—that would have special appeal." Hermann was right; the ranch attracted young campers from wealthy families throughout the United States.[274]

Although the Quarter Circle H Ranch did well, Edlowe ceased growing. The Colorado Midland stopped running in 1949, and during the 1950s, a gas station and café that had opened in an old bunkhouse at Edlowe burned. In 1958, Teller County commissioners ordered the town site to be vacated. The schoolhouse was eventually moved to Woodland Park, and functioned as a church before being converted to the Woodland Park Library in 1967. The building was later torn down.[275] Today only a few homes remain along Edlowe Road.

29

MARIGOLD

Home of the Carlton Tunnel

Although Marigold was never serviced by trains, it did function as a well-used stage stop for travelers going to and from the Cripple Creek District. The place likely came about shortly after the Shelf Road Corporation was formed on November 25, 1891, by William B. "Cap" White and several other men. Together, the group managed to gather $6,000 to improve what was then a precariously high and curvy wagon road leading into the district. Shelf Road's name was no exaggeration; even today, sharp curves and sheer cliff drops landmark the scenic drive. The road was completed by 1892. Toll gates were installed at the upper entrance to the road and at the lower section near Garden Park in Fremont County.[276]

Two main stage stops were along the route, which left Cañon City and spanned roughly ten miles before beginning the tedious climb to the district. Secondary to Marigold was Eldred, where a couple of small one-room log cabins promised hot meals and cool drinks to travelers. Marigold was much more impressive, offering both meals and lodging. The two-story lodging house was constructed of square logs with double-paned glass windows. Stages, pulled by four horses, traveled through four times daily. Stables at Marigold, Eldred, Cripple Creek and Cañon City each kept nine horses, so the coaches always had fresh steeds available. The trip up to Cripple Creek was particularly trying and took two hours longer to make than the trip down to Cañon City.[277]

On October 31, 1895, a post office opened at Marigold. The community was located in Fremont County back then, but when Teller County was

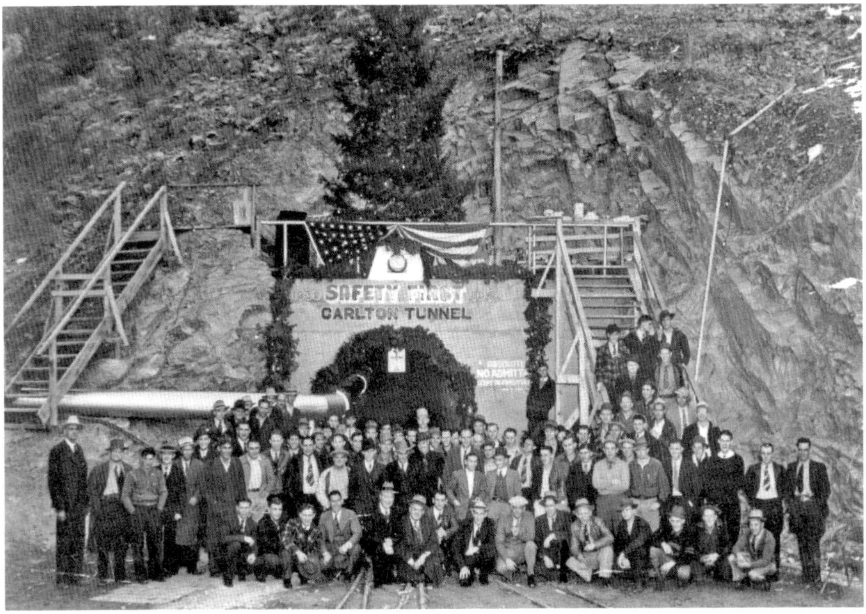

It took nine years to build the Carlton Tunnel near the town of Marigold. This is the dedication of the tunnel in 1941. *Cripple Creek District Museum.*

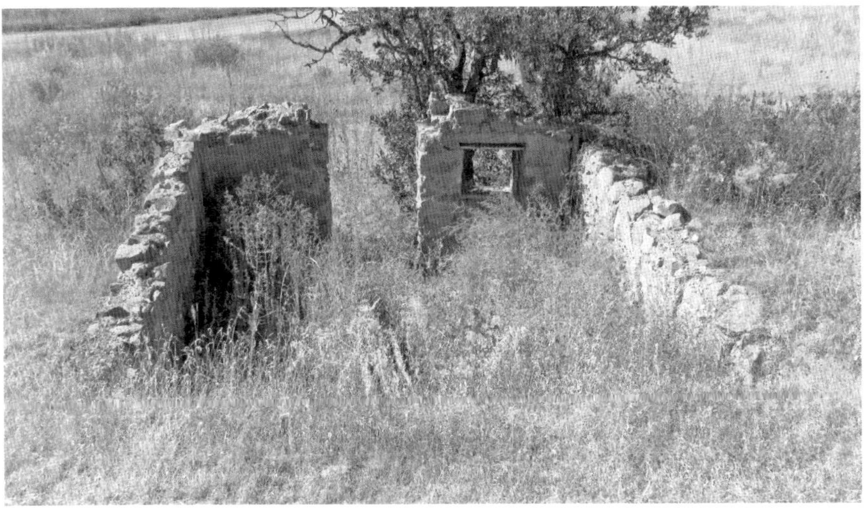

Today, only ruins along Shelf Road between the Cripple Creek District and Cañon City remain to mark the site of Marigold. *Jan MacKell Collins.*

formed in March 1899, Marigold fell within its boundary lines. Eldred remained on the other side of the county line in Fremont County. Enough people lived at Marigold in 1900 to bear mention in the *Cripple Creek District Directory*. With the exception of postmaster Walker Enoch and gardener Frank Allen, the other residents were all miners. Notably, the directory listed some of them as living in Marigold and others as living in West Marigold, although the two neighborhoods were likely right next to each other.[278]

The miners at Marigold soon found that the area had nothing to offer in the way of gold deposits and moved on. Railroads running to the Cripple Creek District diminished the need for stage service, and Marigold's post office closed in June 1902. The community might have been forgotten but for the opening of the Carlton Tunnel in 1939. The tunnel was the dream of railroad and freighting tycoon Albert E. Carlton, who also owned several mines. One of them, the Vindicator, had been plagued by flooding for years.

Carlton died in 1931 before realizing his hope to drain the water via a tunnel. In his place, Carlton's wife, Ethel, along with his brother, Leslie, did it instead. Marigold was chosen as the location of the end of the tunnel. Construction workers probably stayed in some of the old buildings at Marigold, rather than commuting back and forth. The Carlton Tunnel was completed in 1941, with several prominent people attending the dedication. The tunnel proved quite successful and is still in use today.[279] As for Marigold, only a few ruins remain to mark the town.

30

MIDLAND

The Midland Terminal Railroad's First Whistle-stop

Midland was built solely for the benefit of the Midland Terminal Railroad as it built toward the Cripple Creek District. Until 1894, passengers on the Colorado Midland Railroad along Ute Pass had to disembark at Divide, taking the Hundley Stage Line for the remaining eighteen miles to the district. By 1892, it was clear that a train was needed for hauling freight, passengers and precious gold ore. Construction at Midland, a few miles from Divide, began in June 1892, just two months after the town was platted. Midland was intended for housing railroad workers as they built tracks through the area, but grand plans were also made for a fancy hotel and depot. The post office opened on June 27. Those traveling by wagon or horseback could use the Four Mile Toll Road, which cut to the southeast near town and led to Cripple Creek.[280]

Life at early Midland could be harsh. Between 1892 and 1895, seven people were buried there, including an unidentified lumberman and several children. Nearby, Horse Thief Park was so-named for rustlers who hid stolen horses there. According to one source, a gambler visited the Cook & Lannon Sawmill at Midland in 1893 and was subsequently killed during a poker game. He was buried in a huge pile of sawdust, with no one the wiser about his murder until 1933.

Other skirmishes included a night when the bartender of the Midland Saloon was thrown through a window of the tavern by Bill Worley. The assault was justified, as Worley objected to the bartender hitting Gus Green (aka Gus Stoperson) on the head with a whiskey bottle. Another night, a tough calling himself the "Terror of Midland" got in a fight over a girl during a dance. The "Terror" was beaten unconscious. The next day, he discovered his adversary had been national heavyweight boxing champion Bob Fitzsimmons.[281]

Growth at Midland hit a stumbling block when the Midland Terminal Railroad—which had "promised" to reach Midland no later than December 1893—suddenly halted construction so the company could reorganize. Railroad entrepreneurs Henry Collbran, Irving Howbert, Harlan Lillibridge and W.K. Gillett suddenly decided to change the tracks from narrow gauge to the far more sensible standard gauge, which could handle bigger cars. Hence, construction came to a standstill while the group argued with its investors.

Construction resumed in January 1894, and the train reached Midland a few months later. Hundley's stage established a new stop at the town, and other travelers could still obtain horses to take the Four Mile Toll Road. John Riddiough's Glen Road House was located near the "Old Toll Gate" along the road and offered the finest in liquor and cigars, as well as fishing and hunting in season. During the 1893–94 labor war, El Paso County commissioner Winfield Scott Boynton made camp at Midland with upward of one thousand deputies before moving on to Beaver Park.[282]

The initial train fare from Divide to Midland was $1.25 to travel just six miles. One source claims there were many hotels, the largest one being run by Divide pioneer James Loshbaugh. The hotel included a saloon, dining room, store, the post office and, on the second floor, sixteen rooms. Loshbaugh wasn't the best of housekeepers; in time, the hotel became known for its bedbugs, earning Midland the name "Cooty-ville." Later, there were other saloons. One of them was run by a woman from Canterbury, England. The woman painted "Canterbury Falls" on some nearby rocks, and for a time, Midland was sometimes referred to as Canterbury. At its height, Midland had seven saloons.[283]

Once the railroad had been built past the town, there was less need for Midland. Throughout the 1890s, the Midland Terminal did host wildflower excursions to town, but as time went on, fewer people stopped or stayed overnight. The post office closed on January 4, 1895. Locals rallied to reopen it in February, but by 1899, there weren't enough residents to merit postal service. The post office closed again, for good. Finally, only a few people were left at Midland, with poorer folks living in abandoned railroad cars beside the tracks.[284]

But there was yet another industry to be discovered—that of guest ranches and skiing. In 1924, according to resident Don Lawrie, the Fig Leaf Ranch

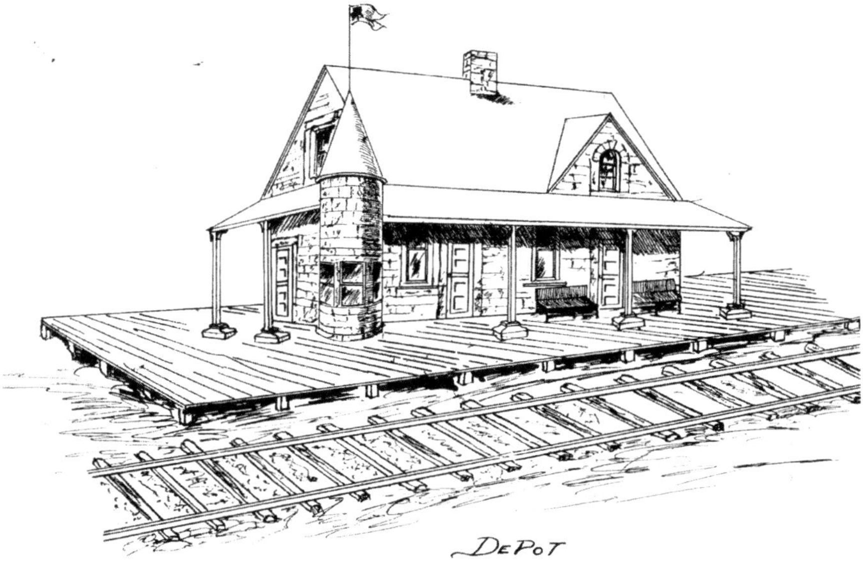

Midland's plat map illustrated what the prestigious Midland Hotel would look like, but the building was never that grand. *El Paso County Clerk and Recorder.*

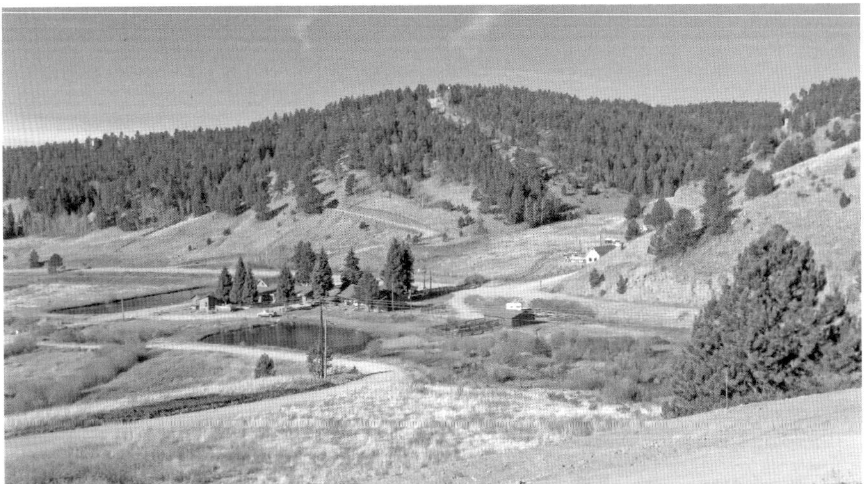

Today, the area around Midland is composed mostly of small ranches, a few homes and Rainbow Valley Guest Ranch. *Jan MacKell Collins.*

was established by his folks at Midland. Lawrie's parents, "Sunny Jim" and "Lady (Jessie) Lawrie," offered log cabins, meals, horses and stocked fish ponds. The price was fifty cents for a bed or meal. Eventually, however, even the Lawries moved on. The last mention of Midland came in 1929, when James Loshbaugh's wife, Margaret, passed away after living at Midland for thirty-five years. Today, the Four Mile Toll Road still exists as another of Teller County's intriguing dirt roads, and a few historic homes remain at the intersection. Nearby is the Rainbow Valley Historical Guest Ranch, whose rustic lodge and cabins were constructed during the 1930s.[285] By accident or design, nearby Canterbury Road leads into a gated residential community.

31

MIDWAY

A Halfway Point in the Cripple Creek District

Midway was so-named because it was conveniently located about halfway between Victor and Cripple Creek. The town likely came about shortly after the Cripple Creek District Interurban Line, aka the High Line, was established. The line ran hourly between 5:00 a.m. and 2:00 a.m. daily. Midway's elevation measured 10,487 feet, making the High Line the highest interurban railroad in North America. From Midway, one could see majestic views of the Cripple Creek District, as well as the Sangre de Cristo Mountains some distance away.

Although Midway was never intended to be more than a stop for miners commuting between their homes and area mines, railcars that were meant to hold no more than forty passengers often carried upward of one hundred men. By about 1896, Archie McKillip and Ed Doyle had built the Grand View Saloon at Midway, providing a place for miners to stay warm and have a drink before catching a ride.[286]

Eventually, a handful of cabins surrounded the Grand View Saloon. About fifty people lived there. One of them was Bathless Bill, a "mucker, skinner, and dance hall sinner" who was particularly known for his odor. Rufus Porter's delightful poem about Bill recounts that his claim paid off, and on a night while buying rounds of drinks, Bill's friends challenged him to take a bath. Bill met the challenge, filling his tub with bottles of expensive champagne at a cost of $1,400. Bill's soaking turned the champagne black, but the story goes:

He dipped a handful up,
And damn his hide, his grin was wide
As he slurped sup after sup
At last all clean like a dance hall queen
Old Bill stepped out to rub—
He'd tasted the wine and said it was fine
And they all made a dive for the tub.
Bill stood there bright, his skin as white
As lilies in the rain—
Admirin' his wealth, they drank to his health
In that filthy black champagne.[287]

In 1900, residents of Midway were getting their mail at Altman. The whistle-stop did feature its own eatery, appropriately named the Midway Restaurant. Things were relatively quiet at Midway for a number of years. A grocery and blacksmith were present by 1912, running through at least 1916. There was also "French Blanche" LaCroix, whose home was located across from the Grand View Saloon. A French immigrant and prostitute by trade, Blanche had once worked for Cripple Creek saloon owner Morris Durant. When Durant's wife found out the two were having an affair, she threw acid in Blanche's face, scarring her badly. Blanche moved to Midway, where she initially served miners before retiring and becoming somewhat of a recluse. Locals remembered seeing her from a distance, sitting in the afternoon sun so wrinkles would eventually mask her scars. They also noted that she wore a brown veil when out in public.[288]

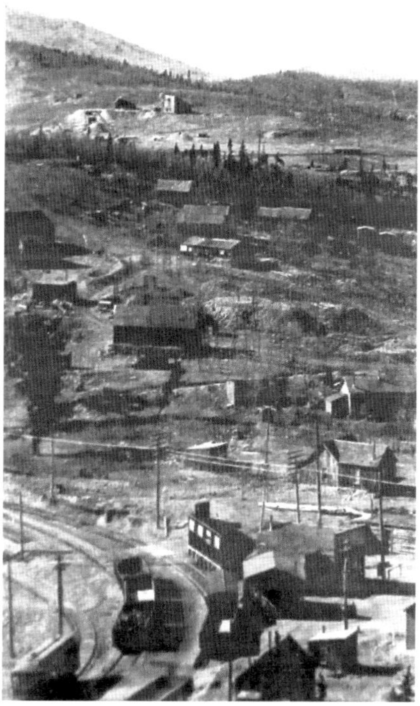

A bird's-eye view of Midway, near Vista Grande. *Library of Congress.*

Although Blanche's face frightened certain children of the Cripple Creek District, others recalled visiting her

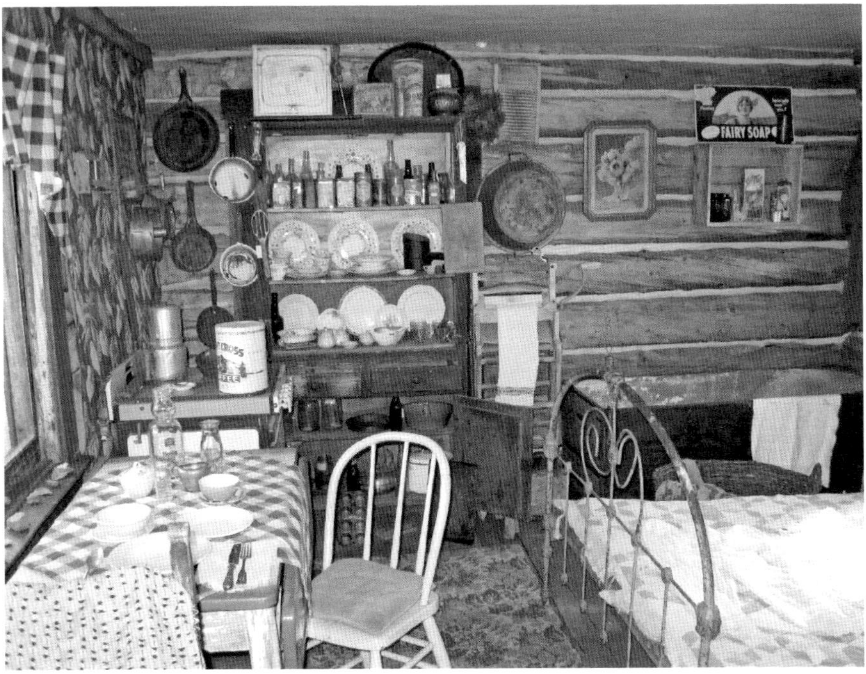

In 2010, French Blanche's cabin was moved to the Cripple Creek District Museum and furnished per descriptions by those who knew her. *Jan MacKell Collins.*

and eating her delicious cookies. In time, Blanche's only other neighbor was Robert T. "Monty" Montgomery, a miner who lived in a tiny cabin across from the Grand View Saloon. The two dated for a time, until Blanche caught Monty seeing another former working girl named Annie Bowers from Independence. Blanche and Annie stayed friends, but Blanche never spoke to Monty again.[289]

Blanche eventually moved to Victor. By the time she died in 1959, Midway was long abandoned. As late as 1994, much of the Grand View Saloon remained intact, but the building and the rest of Midway were bulldozed in 2001 by modern mining operations. The exception was French Blanche's cabin, which the City of Cripple Creek was able to save and move to town. In 2010, the cabin was given to the Cripple Creek District Museum, where today it is furnished to illustrate the way Blanche kept it when she lived there.[290]

32

VISTA GRANDE

TRULY A GRAND VIEW

At 10,486 feet in elevation, Vista Grande's name was no mistake. From the little commuter stop in the Cripple Creek District, one could see views all around the Pikes Peak District, including the majestic Sangre de Cristo mountain range. Vista Grande never had a post office, newspaper, school, church or even a business district in the proper sense. What Vista Grande did have was the High Line, as well as numerous mines and mills all along the surrounding hills.

So what was the purpose of this tiny village? In a nutshell, Vista Grande was a convenient stopover for miners along the High Line beginning in about 1899. In time, there was even a small itinerant population. Vista Grande appears only once in local directories, in 1900. Its locale was west of Midway, and its residents were considered part of that town. Both places utilized Altman's post office. At one time, Midway functioned as the electric station for Vista Grande.[291] In time, however, the whistle-stop simply faded away as quickly as it appeared.

33

WINDY POINT

A Stop Along the High Line

Windy Point first made an appearance in Cripple Creek District newspapers in 1898, when it was noted as one of the stops along the High Line. The tiny whistle-stop might have been of more importance if a proposed new track from Colorado Springs had gone through in September of that year. "The plan now is to start from some point in Colorado Springs and run out to Manitou, where connection will be made with the cog road and its track used to Windy Point," explained the *Cripple Creek Morning Times*. The new railway never materialized, and the *Cripple Creek District Directory* shows Windy Point only in the 1900 edition. The directory noted that due to the number of surrounding mines, "a great many miners have elected to make it their homes." Indeed, nearly every male at Windy Point

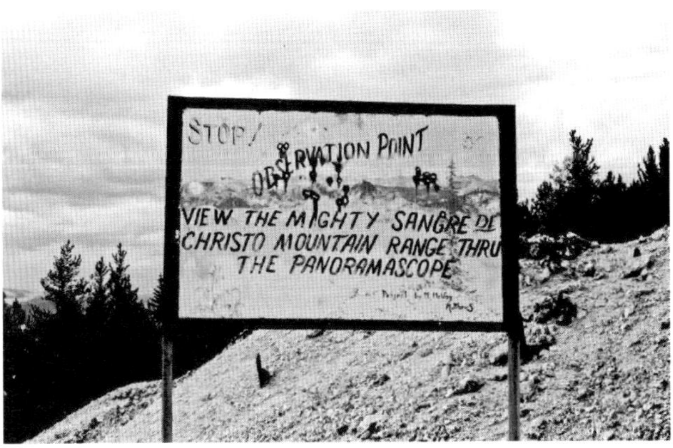

This sign at the American Eagles Mine was originally located at Windy Point, where visitors could view several mountain ranges. *Jan MacKell Collins.*

was employed as a miner. The only business of note was the Windy Point Boardinghouse, which, of course, catered exclusively to miners. But there was also a Miss Brown, who hosted the CCC Club at her "pleasant home" in January.[292]

Long after the gold boom in the Cripple Creek District faded, Windy Point remained a popular stop for tourists wishing to enjoy the scenic views. For many years, a sign pointed out a hand-stamped metal disk whose arrows showed various mountain ranges and landmarks. Both the sign and the disk were moved to the American Eagles Mine site above Goldfield some years ago. As for Windy Point, the place has long been part of the mining operations that obliterated its existence.

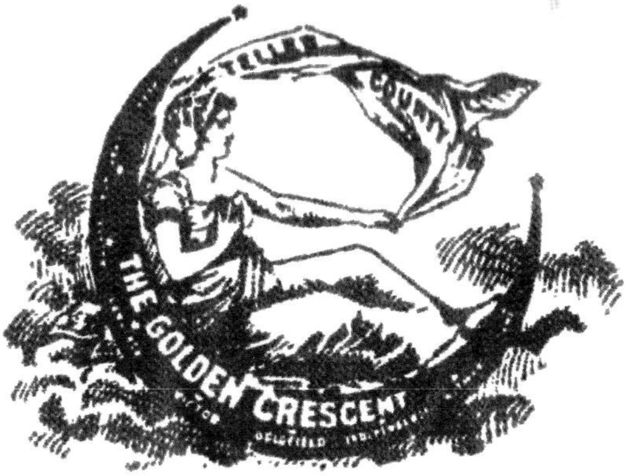
COUNTY
THE GOLDEN CRESCENT

PART IV

HERE ONE DAY, GONE THE NEXT

34

ALNWICK

AN EARLY SUPPLY TOWN

It can only be surmised that the village of Alnwick, located at the confluence of Four Mile Creek and West Four Mile Creek between Cripple Creek and Cañon City, was named for the historic castle of the same name in England. A post office opened there on August 11, 1887, in what was then El Paso County.

Alnwick was one of the earliest places for ranchers and farmers accessing Cañon City from today's Teller County. The hamlet was nestled along a high bank above what was then known as Oil Creek, well out of flash flood danger. Subsequent to the new gold boom in the Cripple Creek District, Alnwick was platted on March 23, 1892. Some of the streets were given the names of Collbran, Hagerman and Howbert, likely in hopes that railroad moguls Henry Collbran, J.J. Hagerman and Irving Howbert might build a railroad through there someday.[293] In November, the U.S. Geological Survey party visited Alnwick. The *Aspen Daily Chronicle* provided details:

> *Mssrs. W.S. Post, W.L. Wilson, and T.M. Bannon, of the United States Geological Survey, have been at Cripple Creek this week. They compose the surveying party which for the last two months has been engaged in surveying this district for the purpose of making an official topographical map. The survey extends from Pikes Peak on the northeast to Florissant and Lake George on the Northwest, and almost to Cañon City on the south. It will be a valuable and thoroughly reliable map and will comprise nearly 30 miles square, with Cripple Creek in the center. The survey is now almost completed, the last camp of the party now being located at Alnwick.*[294]

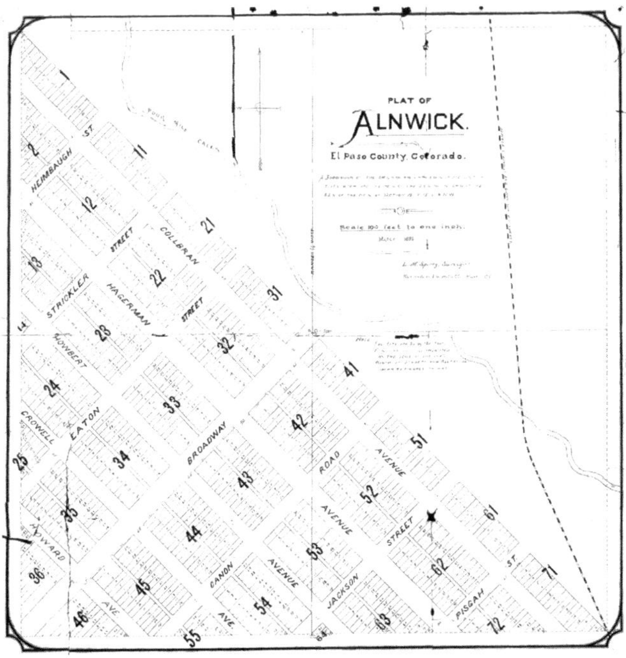

Alnwick served travelers on the High Park Road until the gold boom in the Cripple Creek District began. *El Paso County Clerk and Recorder.*

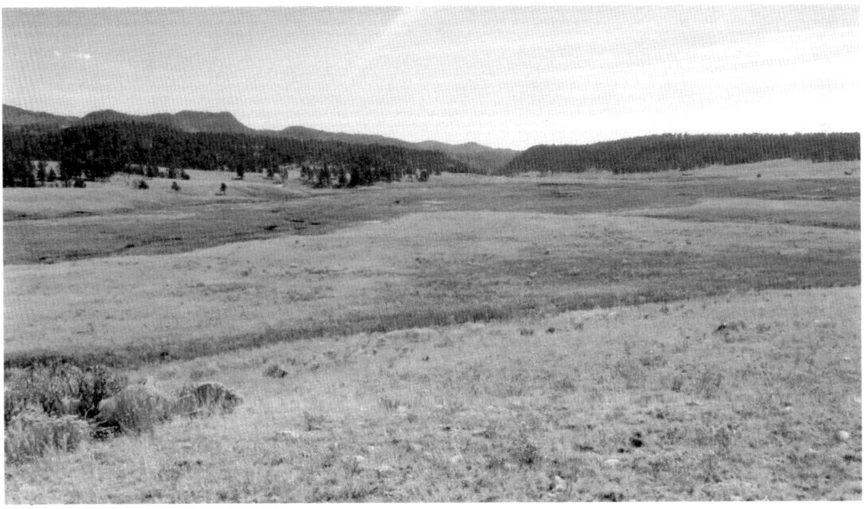

The high creek banks where Alnwick was can still be seen here. The area is now grazing land for a private ranch. *Jan MacKell Collins.*

Plans to make Alnwick the central hub between Cripple Creek and Cañon City quickly dissipated. The post office closed on October 26, 1893. In March 1894, the town was vacated. A short time later, geologist Charles Whitman Cross mentioned the "Alnwick lake beds" in his own geological survey, but nothing was noted about the community. Alnwick Lake was mentioned in passing again in 1906. That same year, Henry Gannett, in his *Gazetteer of Colorado*, called Alnwick "a village." Nothing more was mentioned about Alnwick until 1974, when another report stated the area was "abandoned."[295] Today, Alnwick is composed of nothing more than the meadow of a historic ranch. The road leading to it is privately owned by a local outfitter.

35

HAVERLY

Taken for a Fool

For Jack Haverly, life truly was an up-and-down affair. The man who gained fame and fortune on the theater circuit during the mid-1800s was well known throughout America over his long career. But he also filed bankruptcy so many times that newspapers lost count of just how often he found himself broke. It could be said that in his day, Haverly was a force to be reckoned with, an idea man who tried everything once and twice if he liked it. He was also said to be quite lucky, for as much as he was down, Haverly always bounced back up. His many friends never hesitated to loan him money when he needed it, knowing he would pay it back the next time fortune smiled upon him. "Jack Haverly was a fine man and a lovable character," wrote Edward Le Roy Rice in 1911. "None did more for minstrelsy than he, and some of the greatest names in theatricals were once associated with him.[296]

John H. "Jack" Haverly was named Christopher Heverly when he was born in Pennsylvania in 1837. As a young man he worked as a "train boy" selling peanuts and candy on passenger trains. He also worked as a "baggage smasher" for the railroads and did a brief stint as a tailor's apprentice. He opened his first variety theater in Toledo, Ohio, in 1864. A misspelling on a poster changed his name from Heverly to Haverly, and the new moniker stuck. Over time, Haverly bought and sold numerous theaters, and also headed up a number of performing troupes. He was also remembered by some as "a compulsive gambler and speculator" who sometimes threw his money away as quickly as he made it. Somehow, however, he always made things work out. At the height of his career, Haverly owned six theaters and an amazing thirteen performing road companies.[297]

Haverly's "United Mastadon Minstrels" performed seventeen shows in London in 1880, but Haverly himself was in Colorado. Folks around Gunnison County remembered him as a "colorful and key figure in the development of early Gunnison." Indeed, Haverly "bought up a fine ranch land just east of Gunnison, had a town named for him, invested heavily in mines around the towns of Gothic and Irwin and purchased several ranches and a sawmill along Ohio Creek." The town of Haverly proper consisted of a group of claims, which the entrepreneur advertised "extravagantly."[298]

Not everyone welcomed Haverly in Gunnison County. The town of Irwin's newspaper, the *Elk Mountain Pilot*, had nothing good to say about his investments. "Take a man from his line of business and place him in a business entirely foreign to his own," sniped the paper, "and he will surely make a wreck of it." True to the newspaper's prediction, Haverly's first town ended up being "essentially a promotional scheme." Newcomers almost immediately started squabbling over who owned what claim. Eventually, the forty or so miners at the camp "'jumped' the town and left Mr. Haverly 'out in the cold.'" The town survived only a few years, taking on different names and residents until fading away altogether.[299]

Haverly continued in both showbiz and mining, even as his finances continued their up-and-down collision course. He was still dabbling in theater and doing quite a good job of it when he visited the Cripple Creek District in January 1896. But according to the *Cripple Creek Morning Times*, the minstrel man had "bade farewell to minstrelry several years ago, and when his face becomes sooty now it is from a miner's lamp instead of a makeup box." Haverly told the paper that he planned to be in the area for a couple weeks. "I came here to see if I couldn't get hold of some property in this district," he said. His plan was fortified with some extra cash he had lying around from his mining investments in Clear Creek County.[300]

Within a short time, Haverly had purchased a piece of land near today's Evergreen Station. Due to his poor financial reputation, however, few investors showed much interest in partnering with him. After some fast talking, Haverly was finally able to get some prospects to have a look at his mines. The properties did look mighty promising, enabling Haverly to acquire partners and file a plat for the new town of Haverly. As reports circulated about the findings on Bull Hill, one hundred miners and several saloon keepers converged on the new town within just four days. "Jack Haverly is rich again," announced the *Hoosier State Chronicles* newspaper

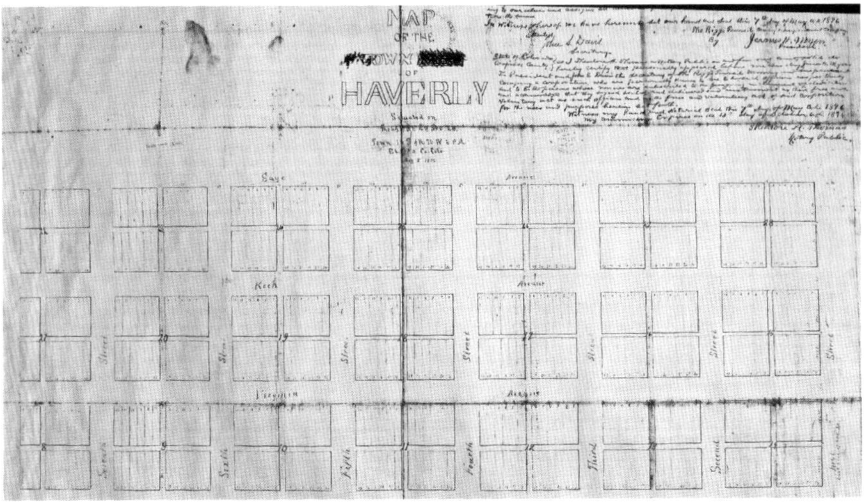

Haverly was the second town that minstrel performer and theater owner Jack Haverly established in Colorado. *Teller County Assessor.*

of Indiana in their July 15, 1896 issue. The paper went on to illuminate Haverly's checkered financial career, but ended by announcing that Lady Luck had smiled upon him once again. This time, he was said to have made upward of $200,000 by investing in mines around the Cripple Creek District. Also, "the story has been further told in Chicago that Jack would soon be a millionaire."[301]

Haverly was back on top. "Colonel Jack Haverly and associates have a shaft down 20 feet on a well-developed vein in Camp Haverly," announced the *Mining Industry & Review* magazine on July 18, 1896. "A new steam hoist has lately been put in operation and ore is being saved for a shipment, which will be made sometime next week. A double shift of men will be put to work on Monday." One source says that Haverly platted his town, sold lots at high prices and skipped with the money, but this might be confused with Haverly's town in Gunnison County. Evidence of this evil deed does not appear in local papers, although neither does news of the new town.

In fact, Jack Haverly's name is curiously absent from Colorado newspapers until June 1897, when it was simply noted that he was staying at the Sheridan Hotel in Telluride. The next mention of him came in September, when it was reported he was on his way back to New York via Kansas with a plan to get back in showbiz. Haverly later declared that he had lost $250,000 in Colorado mines. He died in 1901 and was buried in Pennsylvania.[302]

36

LANTER CITY

A Budding Boomtown

Lanter City—alternately known as Lanter, Lantern, Lander's, Landres and Landen—hoped to become the next thriving metropolis in Teller County. The fleeting town is thought to have been founded in about 1896. BLM land records and Lanter City's plat map locate it in the vicinity of Crystal Creek and North and South Catamount Reservoirs, near the North Star Gold Mine. Roads from Lanter City probably led not just to Ute Pass, but also to the Pikes Peak Toll Road and perhaps even Edlowe between Woodland Park and Divide.[303]

The Fountain Creek Mining District was likely formed at the same time as Lanter City, since the town fell within its boundaries. Though only four miles square, the district was home to thirty-eight claims. The property was owned by one Henry Law, who hired surveyor L.J. Carrington to survey and plat Lanter City. Carrington spent three days on the project in November 1900. At the same time, advertisements were being placed in the *Colorado Springs Gazette*. "Wanted," the ad read, "Men and women to engage in all kinds of business at Lanter City in the Fountain mining district five miles north of Pikes Peak. One shipper and lots of good prospects. Take stage at Woodland Park. For information address Tyler and McDowell, Woodland Park, Colo." The ad was presumably taken out by Robert Lanter, who appeared in various news articles about the budding boomtown.[304]

Promoters of Lanter City were certainly hopeful. On November 30, Robert Beers, who already owned some nearby land, platted his own Robert Beers Addition to Lanter City. Next, the December 3 edition of the *Colorado*

Springs Gazette wondered if Lanter City was not destined to be the next Cripple Creek: "Local mining men have been rather indifferent until very lately but it certainly must be admitted now that the camp…at least calls for respectful attention." Of particular interest, according to the article, was that gold was being found in the area. The news was enough to entice a group from Victor in the Cripple Creek District to hire one of their "experts" to come have a look. The man found several claims and figured that ore in the area was worth between twenty and eighty dollars per ton.[305]

In spite of Lanter City's aspirations, Law was able to sell only eight of the lots at Lanter City, to four different buyers. During the town's heyday, there were twenty homes, a livery stable and a blacksmith shop. News of the town continued drifting into newspapers. "Ed Weston of Lanter City was in [Colorado Springs] Sunday," read an article in January 1901. "Mr. Weston, with Messrs. McDowell, Foster and Wheat, have leased the Rico lode and will proceed at once to find what is in it." On February 27, another article hinted a post office was soon to be established, but that never happened. Other news articles told of "Uncle Billy" Parshall, who staked the Louise claim in April, and progress on the McCleary brothers' mine in May. Also in May, fourteen more lots were sold at Lanter City. By October, plans were underway to build a steam plant on Lord and Dean's claim just southwest of town.[306]

Unfortunately, the gold mines around Lanter City simply didn't pan out. Lanter City's other main industry was intended to be logging, but the Pike National Forest was established in 1907 and the homesteaders at Lanter City were suddenly considered trespassers. The news was no doubt disappointing, but in 1908, Henry Law was able to buy back all of the lots at Lanter City and sell the whole town to the Empire Water and Power Company for just $3,000. The company planned to build four reservoirs. But the project never transpired, and Empire sold the property to the City of Colorado Springs in 1930. Colorado Springs picked up where Empire left off, vacating Lanter City and building two large reservoirs. By 1935, South Catamount Reservoir covered about half the old town site. Five or so ruins and a large "glory hole" survived as late as 2000, and the remaining mines were sealed by the Colorado Division of Reclamation and Mining Safety in 2008. Today, there is nothing left of the town.[307]

37

LEWIN

Pick a Town, Any Town

Lewin, located near Manitou Park in the northern section of Teller County, is a classic case of a town that never was. First mention of the principal players in Lewin's short-lived history appeared in February 1896, when business partners Charles M. Graff, Albert Lewin and George A. Smith filed incorporation papers in El Paso County for the Monument and West Creek Toll Road Company. The proposed road would run north from Woodland Park, through the new town of West Creek in what was then El Paso County and on to Monument. The latter town was also in El Paso County, situated along the Denver & Rio Grande Railroad tracks. The following March, Graff, along with G.W. Thornberg and Edward Lewin, platted West Creek on the El Paso County border with Douglas County.[308] No matter there was already a West Creek in Douglas County; the partners seemed to be scrambling to plat as many towns as they could.

Who were these enterprising men? Thornberg's origins remain a mystery, as he is absent from census records for Colorado. In the 1900 census, however, the other partners were all living in Denver. Graff ran a rooming house. George Smith was a day laborer. Edward and Albert Lewin each ran their own wholesale liquor companies. The latter two must have been related; both were born in Germany and immigrated to America in 1880. They were also both involved with the new toll road and, later, the town of Lewin.

When the West Creek of Douglas County won the battle for its name, the partners apparently decided to begin fresh with a new town. Johns Gulch

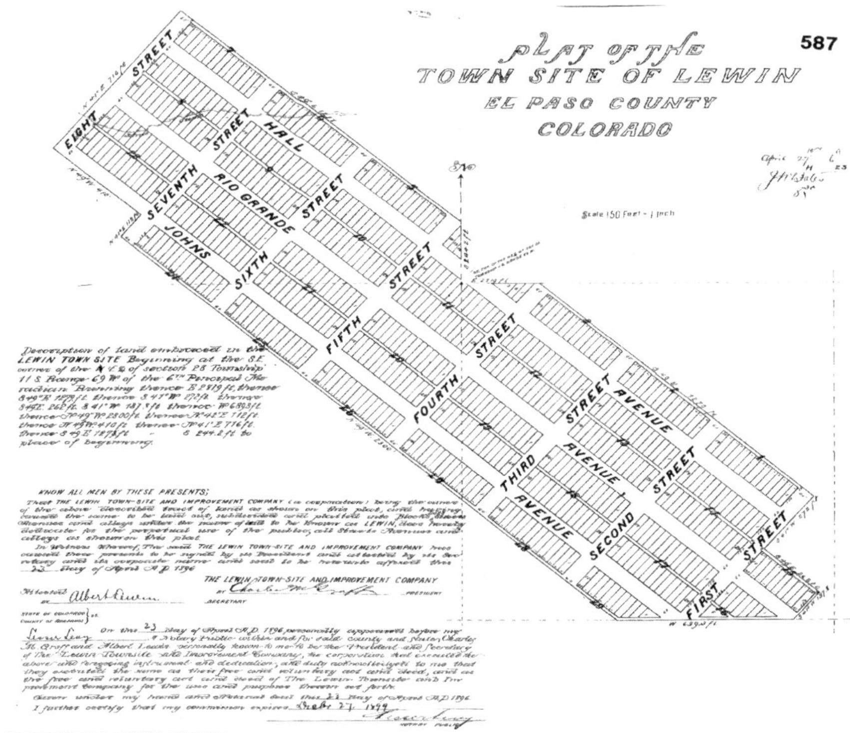

Albert Lewin and his partners hoped their town would be a mining metropolis of the West Creek Mining District. *El Paso County Clerk and Recorder.*

near Manitou Park, named for rancher Henry Thomas Johns, was chosen for the new location. The Lewin Town Site and Improvement Company was formed in April 1900, with Graff as president. Albert Lewin signed the plat map, which was filed on April 23. It appears, however, that Graff, Lewin and company were so busy sinking their time and money into other endeavors that they never had time for their new town of Lewin. The town never developed, and on April 30, 1898, Johns filed a vacation plat for Lewin. There is no evidence to suggest Lewin ever had so much as a building to mark its spot.[309]

38

MANCHESTER

A Gold Mining Bust

The founding of Manchester came about solely due to the gold boom in the Cripple Creek District. While it was likened to other booming towns around Cripple Creek, Manchester actually fell within the boundary lines of the West Creek Mining District in the northern section of today's Teller County. The town site was located six and a half miles from Divide and almost twenty miles from Cripple Creek, along the east branch of West Creek.

A single hint to the new town first appeared with the sale of William J. Burke's mine to the Manchester Gold Mining Company on December 19, 1895. But the budding boomtown was initially known as both North Cripple Creek and Cripple Creek North, probably in hopes that the name would entice more miners to come to the West Creek Mining District. Beginning in January 1896, promoters were advertising lots at North Cripple Creek and promising wealth and prosperity to buyers. "Get in on the ground floor and buy a few lots in North Cripple Creek before the spring boom sets in," advised one ad. "They will make you rich." North Cripple Creek's founding fathers were absolutely certain that gold could be found all through the West Creek Mining District, boasting of "a mineral district which we honestly believe will distance Cripple Creek in two years." Those in Denver who desired a closer look were advised to buy a ticket on the Denver, South Park and Pacific Railroad, get off at the "South Plane" station and take Gabriel's Stage Line to the new town.[310]

Although the town would continue to be known as North Cripple Creek for many years, the name Manchester was applied when the town was officially incorporated on January 30, 1896. Directors of the town company were W.P. and W.A. Gardner, F.A. Yount, Stephen Welch, L.A. Sautter, Lafayette Hiner and F.M. Welch. W.C. Keeline was appointed president. Five hundred lots were laid out along the creek, and the name of the east branch of West Creek was changed to Manchester Creek. Two days later, the *Aspen Daily Times* ran a full report on the new North Cripple Creek Gold Mining and Milling Company. "The company has title to six full claims, all adjoining and comprising sixty acres, thus obliterating all possibility of future litigation from outsiders," said the paper, noting that assays were being valued between $4.80 and $16.00 per ton.

The article also listed as stockholders such important men of the day as H.C. Copeland and Thomas Beck of Aspen, Colorado Midland Railroad agent E.J. Edwards and conductor W.H. Tuttle and J.H. Cragg, formerly an assistant to silver millionaire Horace Tabor. Tuttle was in fact president of the mining company. The men were named, explained the newspaper, because "none would allow his name to be connected with a fake or a fraud." With their reputations intact, promoters of North Cripple Creek/ Manchester began building. By February there was a new hotel, "and the town is assuming an important air. Town lot speculators can now enjoy all the comforts of a first class hotel which is an unusual thing in a young camp." Indeed, the town's buildings were said to be some of the best in the West Creek district, which "indicated rich mining deposits surrounding North Cripple."[311]

A bright future was promised to all who invested in property at Manchester. "To all strangers there is ever a cordial greeting," read a promotional write up on the town, "and the hospitality of their homes is as warm and unselfish as the perpetual sunshine of Colorado." And there was more: the creek promised ample mountain trout, and water rights had been secured. Mail was already running from Divide and served upward of two hundred people, and the application for an official post office had been turned in to the postmaster general. By April, several "first class" buildings stood at Manchester, including "hotels, restaurants, and general supply stores," one of which was run by a Mr. Benton. "That Manchester will soon be the center of a great mining district there is no room left for doubt," the write up promised. The claim was backed up by the presence of several mines in the area, including the Accident and the Lily Lode, owned by Hiner; the Gardner's Tender Foot; and Welch's Badger Boy and "famous" Golden Lode.

Throughout 1896, advertisements and promotions in newspapers across the state kept Manchester in the limelight. The efforts were paying off

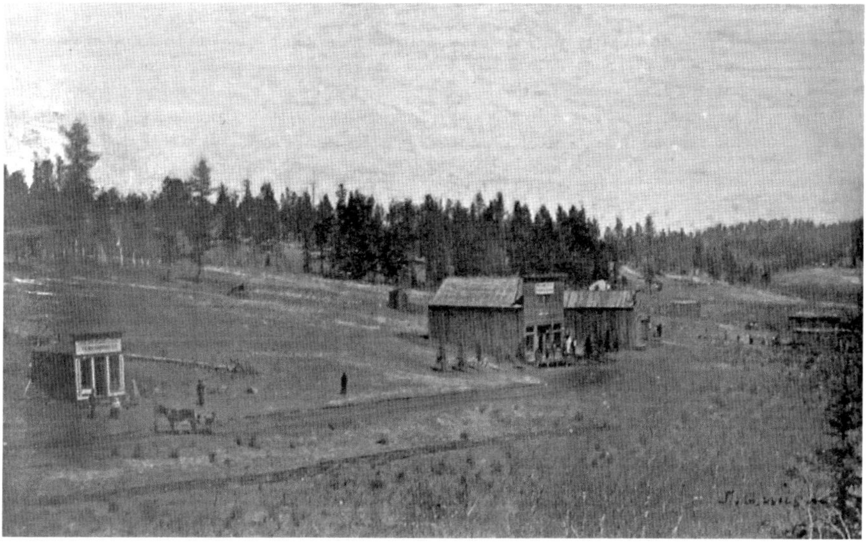

Great plans were made for Manchester, seen here in 1896. *From Hall,* Cripple Creek Up to Date.

somewhat, as evidenced by other mines, such as the Blue Bird, the Blue Eyed Girl, the Lucky Boy and the Red Bird. Out-of-town investors included a group from Nebraska that owned the Omaha Mine, and capitalists from Chicago were due to appear on the scene. "Inexhaustible quantities [of gold] can be mined at small cost, and arrangements are being made to put up a mill for reducing low grade ore."[312] Or, so the founding fathers said.

In the end, the trouble with Manchester was that not enough gold materialized to make everybody's dreams come true. The post office was never approved, and only two news items of note bore mention in newspapers after 1896. One was the mysterious disappearance of Henry Storms at Manchester. In July 1899, Storms's wife reported that two strange men had appeared at the house one morning and offered to buy a team of horses. When Storms declined the offer, the men hired him to take them fishing for a day instead. Neither Storms nor the men ever returned. The other incident took place many years later in 1911, when William Orwig's home burned. The loss of the structure was estimated at $1,000.[313] There was no more news on Manchester after that. The remaining buildings at Manchester disappeared, leaving only a few imprints in the ground where they once stood.

39

PISGAH PARK

A Suburb of Cripple Creek

Mount Pisgah is among the most prominent geographic landmarks in the Cripple Creek District. The tiny extinct volcano's name is a biblical reference to the mountain from which Moses first saw the Promised Land. Because Mount Pisgah was so well known during the district's gold boom of the 1890s, the name was also assigned to other places. They included Pisgah, a small stop on the Colorado Midland Railroad four miles east of Florissant, and Pisgah Junction, the name of the railroad wye just past the Midland Terminal Railroad depot in Cripple Creek.[314]

By 1871, the wide-open meadow at the western base of Mount Pisgah was known as Pisgah Park. Here, rancher Levi Welty and his three sons discovered the meadow with a stream winding through it and decided to settle. The family built a cabin in the area. Following a series of accidents, Levi Welty was said to have exclaimed, "Well boys, this is sure some cripple creek!"[315] Thus, the name Cripple Creek was applied to the stream, as well as the gold mining district that was eventually formed during the early 1890s.

Mining explorations took place around Mount Pisgah for many years. First mention comes in the December 15, 1895 edition of the *Cripple Creek Morning Times*, which reported, "State appraiser W.E. Fine arrived in the city yesterday with a force of men, and soon were on their way to the Mount Pisgah School Section, where they will camp until the work of laying out the ten acre lode claims is completed." Within a year, investors N.B. Wallace, J.F. Murphy and John Lusso platted a town, Pisgah Park, on August 6, 1896. Mining claims with such interesting names as the Grand Humbug, the

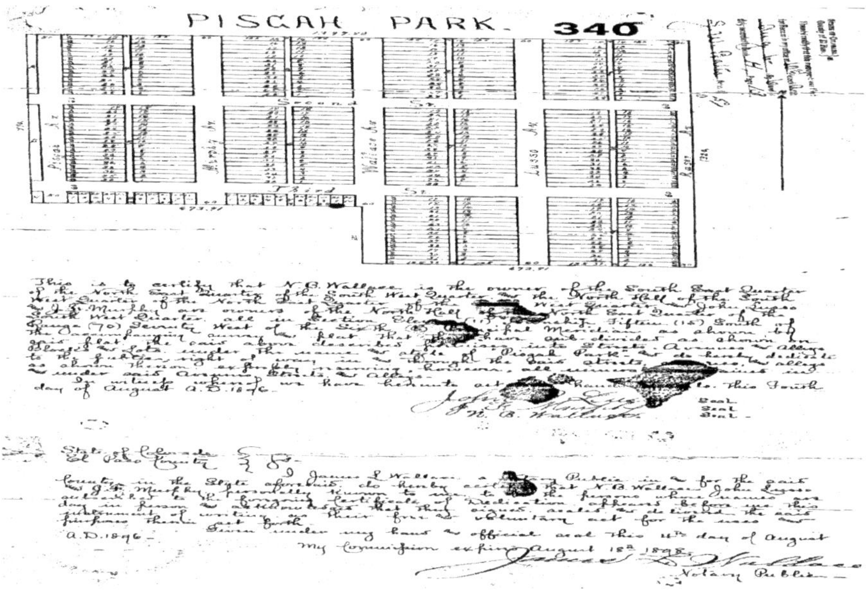

Pisgah Park was intended to be a neighbor to Cripple Creek. The town site is now within Cripple Creek's city limits. *Jan MacKell Collins.*

Belcher, the Thanksgiving and the Happy New Year continued to be staked around the town.[316]

Not much of note happened at Pisgah Park. The new settlement was never even mentioned in newspapers. One source does state that a small pet cemetery was established on the outskirts of town, and there was a park called Pisgah Gardens. Horse races and baseball games were first announced for Pisgah Gardens beginning in 1897. "A big purse will be up for winners of the game between Altman and Anaconda Baseball Clubs," read one advertisement. "The best horses in the District will, on the new racetrack, compete for purses in quarter and half mile dashes. Refreshments, short orders and meals at all hours at Mt. Pisgah Road House." Pisgah Gardens seems to have lasted about a year, for advertisements for the park do not appear after 1897.[317]

The reason Pisgah Park did not survive as a community might be relatively simple. Then, as now, winds blew often enough to make the area uncomfortable, especially in winter. Although a few people built homes during the 1920s and beyond, Teller County now owns most of the old town, and only a few modern houses dot the landscape today.[318]

40

A FLEETING GLIMPSE

GONE WITHOUT A TRACE

Especially during the gold boom years of the 1890s, settlement in Teller County was like a bargain-basement sale. Prospectors by the thousands scrambled from camp to camp and town to town, hoping to cash in on rich minerals and make lots of money. When a mining claim didn't pan out the miners moved on, abandoning each place for the next one. Thus, certain of Teller County's settlements—such as the villages of Arena, Aysee, Critchell and Sampler—came and went so quickly that nobody even knows where they were. Of the settlement of Stamp Mill, only a post office circa 1895 documents its existence.

Other places leave scant clues to their whereabouts. The settlement of Black Forest was near today's Mueller State Park. The camp of January was established in 1894 three miles north of Victor and had a post office until 1911. In 1906, the mining camp of McKinney was located near Victor.[319] The following list of other places in Teller County were prominent long enough to at least merit mention in newspapers and other sources.

BOAZ

There is a biblical reference to Boaz, a wealthy land owner in Bethlehem, whose name might have served this short-lived village near the south fork of Wilson Creek in the vicinity of Teller County Road 861. All that is known for sure is that the town, originally located in Fremont County, was

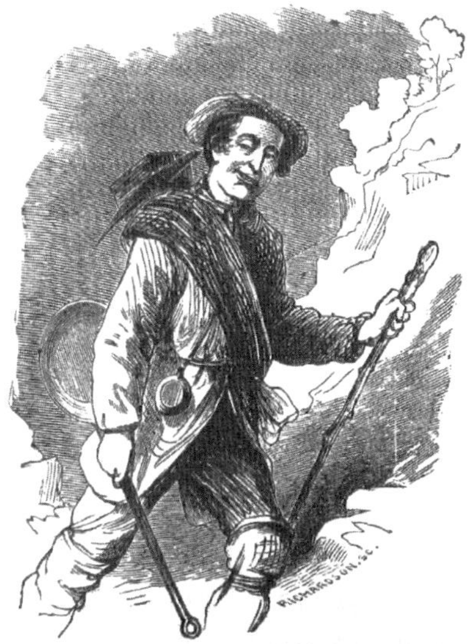

GOING TO THE MINES

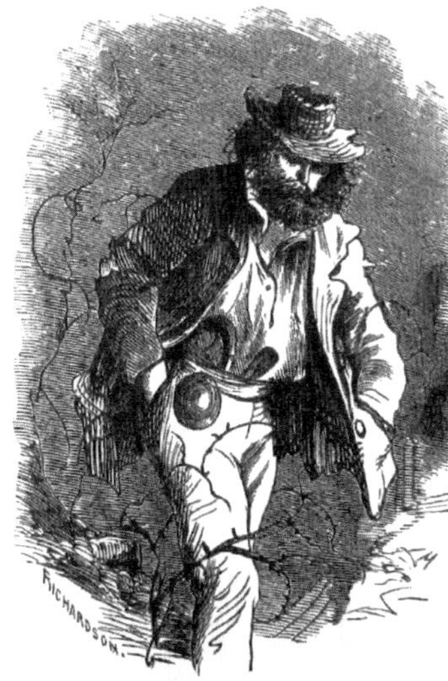

COMING OUT

An early engraving accurately depicts the typical miner at the beginning—and end—of his career. *Jan MacKell Collins.*

granted a post office on March 7, 1895. In 1896, the *Chaffee County Republican* newspaper of March 11 offered a little more insight to Boaz, stating that "the Cripple Creek district is being extended into Fremont County, some 400 claims having been located near Boaz, which lies almost directly west of Victor, some six miles inside the Fremont County line."

By 1897, Boaz was considered part of El Paso County when Fugate's Store was identified as the polling place during the "Silver Republican" primaries. Nothing else of note happened at Boaz, which was too far away from the Cripple Creek District to be of much service to area residents. The post office quietly closed on October 31, 1898.[320] When Teller County was formed in March 1899, Boaz was within the county boundary. By then, however, the community was a thing of the past.

GOLD SPRINGS

Gold Springs is known only by a recorded addition to the budding town that was filed in El Paso County on July 10, 1896. The addition consisted solely of the Rose Thomas and Badger Lode mining claims, which contained only eight blocks between the two of them. Only four of the blocks were useable, the other four being too small to fit into the grid. Airheart, Park and Streit Avenues were intersected by First, Second and Third Streets. The map was signed by Theodore P. Airheart, a noted real estate dealer who resided in Cripple Creek. Advertisements during 1899 identify his office at the Airheart Block in the 200 block of Myers Avenue.[321] Prior to 1899, when Teller County was formed, Gold Springs was probably located in Fremont County. As boundaries for the new county were established, Gold Springs fell just inside the Teller County line.

Airheart surely had some sort of plan for Gold Springs, but unfortunately met with an untimely death. In 1904, Airheart was in a passenger car of the Colorado Springs & Cripple Creek District railway at the Cripple Creek District town of Cameron. As the cars were being switched, the passenger car began rolling and gaining speed as about fifty people jumped to safety. Airheart, J. Kearns and Fred Miller, however, "made an heroic attempt to save their fellow passengers" by trying to work the brake. Before they could stop the car, it jumped the tracks and rolled, killing Airheart and Kearns instantly. Development of Gold Springs was never carried any further. The *Eagle County Times* at Redcliff remembered Airheart as "a man of money" who "stood high in Masonic circles."[322]

SILVER SPRINGS

From all appearances, Silver Springs was the whimsical idea of a woman with an equally whimsical name: Permelia Q. Saunders. Born in Kentucky in 1837, Parmelia married George Saunders in 1852. By 1882, the couple had relocated to Colorado, where George filed for a patent on 120 acres just south of today's Woodland Park. In September 1890, Parmelia hired one Sylvester Johnson to draw up a plat map of Silver Springs. The town was small, bordered by West Avenue, a county road that was probably today's Highway 24, South Avenue and Jackson Avenue. Lots were measured out at 50 by 150 feet. The plat map was not filed until December 22, but Teller County records note that the town was later vacated. Nobody appears to have ever purchased property there.[323]

The Saunderses continued living in the area. In the 1900 census, daughter Alice had joined the elderly couple. George's occupation is listed as a landlord, and he was likely leasing land to neighboring farmers. Ten

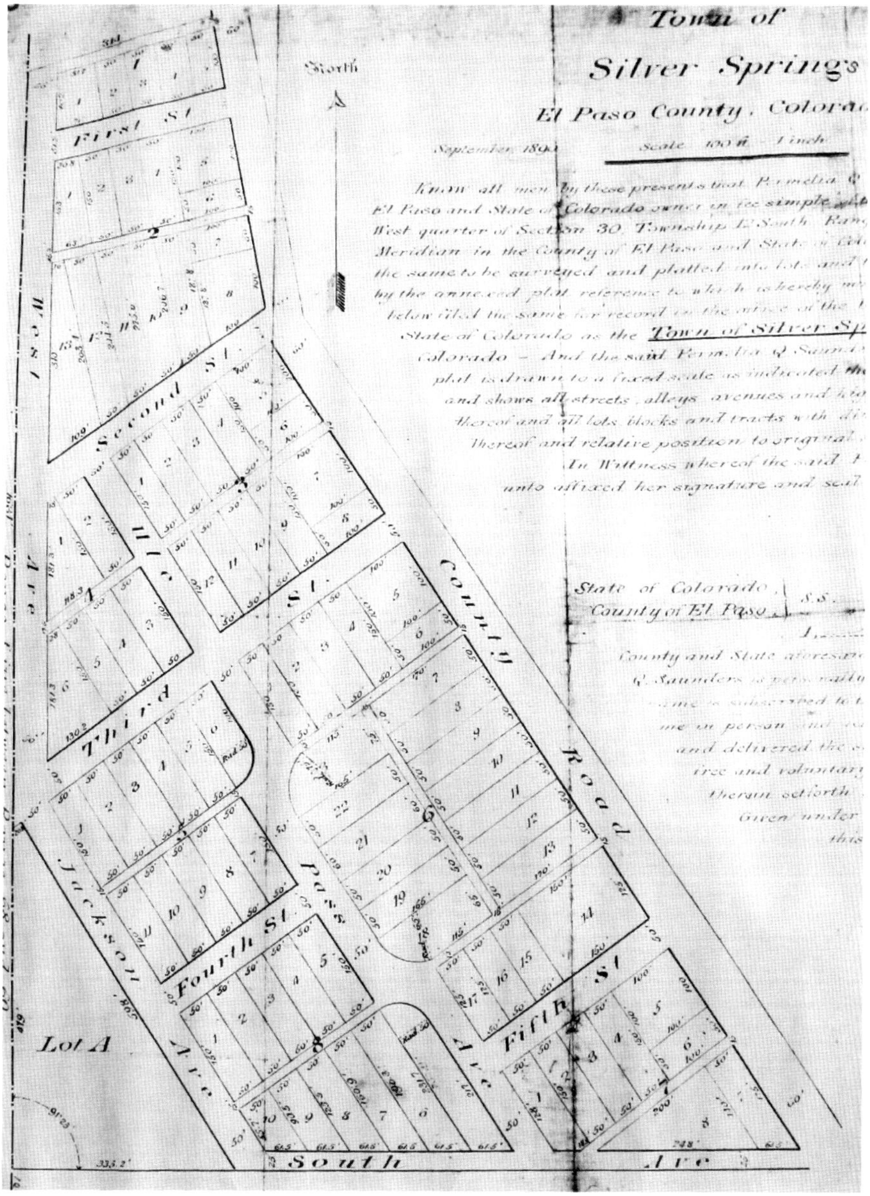

Silver Springs was the whimsical notion of Parmelia Q. Saunders but is now part of Woodland Park. *Teller County Assessor.*

years later, George had died, and most of Permelia's children had joined her at Woodland Park, where her son, George, ran a general merchandise store. Permelia died in February, 1911. She was buried in Woodland Park, her idea for Silver Springs forgotten.[324] Today, Woodland Park's Safeway store is the closest landmark to the site.

STANLEY CITY

First mention of Stanley City comes in the *Castle Rock Journal* of January 24, 1894. An article on the front page proclaimed, "It looks as though Stanley City, the new gold camp near Monument, is going to be a genuine city in the near future." Prospectors at the spot were reporting "plenty of paying ore in sight." The town of Monument was about the nearest landmark to Stanley City, but the budding camp was actually located in Phantom Gulch roughly six miles south of West Creek in today's Teller County. A report in March 1896 claimed the tiny place was "in the midst of what is conceded to be a rich mineral region" and was "being built up as fast as lumber can be hauled upon the ground." Stanley was named for the Honorable M.L. Stanley of Oklahoma, who was employed as manager of the new town's only mine.[325]

Two months later, another news item commented on the "free gold" (gold that required minimal mining techniques) that was being found in the Stanley City vicinity "in considerable quantities." The community headquarters was "literally filled with specimens of ore from the different prospectors in the surrounding country that rank in appearance with those of any camp in the state."[326] In the end, however, Stanley City's free gold was picked clean, and the camp faded as quickly as it began.

SUNOL

Sunol was located in Fremont County when its post office first opened on September 8, 1892. The post office was short-lived, closing on October 18, 1894. Very little is known about the town, and it is only a guess that Sunol was named after a popular racehorse during the 1890s. The town is only mentioned a few times in newspapers. In 1896, a Dr. Emma Hellwig of Chicago purchased a group of mines known as the Parassus Group. Mines owned by the company included the Sunol, but the mine's location is not given. Dr. Hellwig might just be the most interesting character associated with Sunol. Previous to purchasing the Parassus Group, Hellwig was accused of smuggling false teeth into the United States. "Over 5,000 of the contraband molars were found in her apartments," revealed the *Weekly Medical Review* of January–June 1892. "The accused is a widow of middle age, who has a shingle out as a physician."[327]

The other known story of Sunol is nearly as intriguing as Emma Hellwig. In 1897, it was announced that a twenty-mile-long tunnel was being dug from Colorado Springs, under Pikes Peak and its neighboring mountains, to a place "at Four Mile Creek, six miles south of Cripple Creek and near the little town of Sunol." As far as anyone knows, the tunnel never came to fruition. Nothing more of Sunol is mentioned in local papers. As for Dr. Hellwig, she overcame her shame of smuggling teeth. By 1899, she advertised herself as a "graduate physician" of Berlin and Paris and had a stately office in Chicago.[328] When Teller County was formed that same year, Sunol fell within its boundaries but was long gone by then.

WEAVERVILLE

The only clue that really exists about Weaverville is the road by that name, accessible off State Highway 24 just outside Divide. Only four historic buildings are located on Weaverville Road: a home built in 1886; the 1887 Midland Terminal Depot; Divide's Community Center, built in 1900; and another structure built in 1925. The rest of the area and its landscape have been altered drastically in the wake of more modern buildings, including the Teller County Jail.[329] On May 5, 1877, the *Colorado Springs Gazette* reported that a trapper "who made his hunting grounds near Weaverville, Colorado" had taken a number of fox pelts to Chicago, amassing a tidy sum.

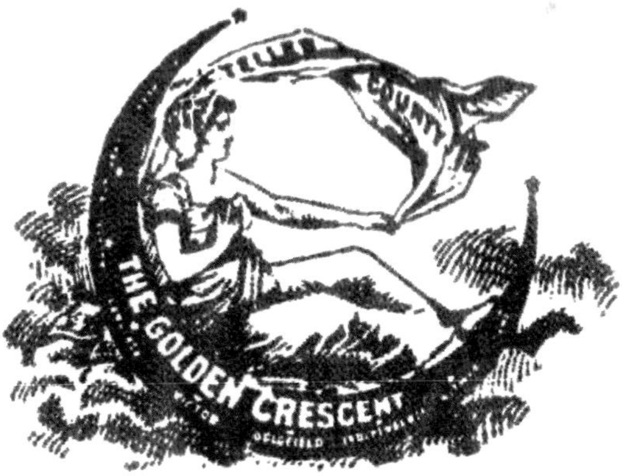
TELLER COUNTY
THE GOLDEN CRESCENT

NOTES

Introduction

1. *History and Description of the Cripple Creek Mining District, Mining and Business Directory City of Cripple Creek and Adjacent Towns* (Cripple Creek, CO: Hazeltine & Co., 1894).
2. *Cripple Creek Complete Directory* (Colorado Springs, CO: Johnson Bros. 1893), 10.

Part I

3. Jan MacKell, *Cripple Creek District: Last of Colorado's Gold Booms* (Charleston, SC: Arcadia Publishing, 2003), 22; Ivan W. Brunk, *Shattered Dreams on Pikes Peak* (Colorado Springs, CO: Pulpit Rock Press, 1989), 39.
4. *Colorado Transcript*, July 31, 1901, 2.
5. "Map and Statement Relative to the Storage and Appropriation of Water by the City of Victor," Teller County Assessor, Cripple Creek, Colorado.
6. Jan MacKell, "Ancient Trails: Gold Camp Road and Ute Pass," *Ute Pass Vacation Guide* (Cascade, CO: Diamond Desktop, 2003), 1.
7. Celeste Black, *Clyde: A Colorado Mountain Town in the Shadow of Pikes Peak* (Cripple Creek, CO: BlackBear, 2005), 15–17, 38.
8. William R. Conte, *The Old Cripple Creek Stage Road* (Colorado Springs, CO: Little London Press, 1984), 5; Brunk, *Shattered Dreams on Pikes Peak*, 44; MacKell, "Ancient Trails"; Black, *Clyde*, 17–18.

9. William Bauer, James L. Ozment and John H. Willard, *Colorado Post Offices 1859 to 1989* (Golden, CO: Colorado Railroad Museum, 1990), 131; Black, *Clyde*, 40.
10. *Tombstone Inscriptions of El Paso and Teller Counties, Colorado*, Version 2.0, CD-ROM (Colorado Springs, CO: Pikes Peak Genealogical Society, 2007).
11. Black, *Clyde*, 19, 29, 33.
12. *Cripple Creek Morning Times*, January 19, 1901, 1. Gerber beat a hasty retreat to Nebraska but was arrested for the crime upon his return in January 1901.
13. Bauer, Ozment and Willard, *Colorado Post Offices*, 131.
14. Tivis E. Wilkins, *Short Line to Cripple Creek*, Colorado Rail Annual, no. 16 (Golden, CO: Colorado Railroad Museum, 1983), 55.
15. Leland Feitz, *Cripple Creek Railroads* (Colorado Springs, CO: Little London Press, 1968), 15; Black, *Clyde*, 40; Bauer, Ozment and Willard, *Colorado Post Offices*, 35.
16. *Colorado, Its Hotels and Resorts* (Denver, CO: Colorado Promotion and Publicity Committee, 1904), 23; Black, *Clyde*, 20–23, 59.
17. Marshall Sprague, *Money Mountain: The Story of Cripple Creek Gold* (Lincoln: University of Nebraska Press, 1979), 254–55.
18. Conte, *Old Cripple Creek Stage Road*, 30; Black, *Clyde*, 41–42.
19. *Colorado State Business Directory, 1908* (Denver, CO: Gazetteer Publishing Co., 1908), 251; Bauer, Ozment and Willard, *Colorado Post Offices*, 35.
20. Bauer, Ozment and Willard, *Colorado Post Offices*, 35; "History of Jones Park and the Colorful Characters that Pioneered the Cheyenne Canyon," http://actionmatrixcom/History/html/JonesPark.htm; "Frosty Park Cache," Geocaching website, http://www.geocaching.com; "History of Jones Park and the Colorful Characters that Pioneered the Cheyenne Canyon."
21. Black, *Clyde*, 22, 54, 72.
22. Ibid., 50–52, 60–61; U.S. census 1920 and 1940; Eveland family tree, ancestry.com; "Isadore Meyers," Findagrave.com.
23. Black, *Clyde*, 29, 33–35, 42, 72; Feitz, *Cripple Creek Railroads*, 15; U.S. census 1920.
24. Black, *Clyde*, 37, 40, 45, 55.
25. Ibid., 45–46, 63–64.
26. Interview with Marlan Bradley, Clyde, Colorado, 2010; Black, *Clyde*, 14, 47.
27. "High Park Road," Gold Belt Byway website, www.goldbeltbyway.com/high-park-road; *Engineering News and American Railway Journal* 35, no. 19 (January–June 1896): 149; *Cripple Creek Morning Times*, August 27, 1897, 1.

28. *Cripple Creek Morning Times*, January 25, 1896, 1.
29. *Colorado Transcript*, February 26, 1896, 7; *Cripple Creek Morning Times*, February 29, 1896, 2; *Leadville Herald Democrat*, March 26, 1896, 4.
30. *Colorado Transcript*, February 26, 1896, 7; *Cripple Creek Morning Times*, February 29, 1896, 2; *Leadville Herald Democrat*, March 26, 1896, 4.
31. Bauer, Ozment and Willard, *Colorado Post Offices*, 73.
32. Allan C. Lewis, *Florence & Cripple Creek Railroad: Forty Miles to Fortune* (Denver, CO: Sundance Publications, 2002), 78; Conte, *Old Cripple Creek Stage Road*, 5; *Journal of the Executive Proclamation of the Senate of the United States of America from December 5, 1887, to March 3, 1889* (Washington, D.C.: Government Printing Office, 1901), 67.
33. Sprague, *Money Mountain*, 69; Conte, *Old Cripple Creek Stage Road*, 6.
34. Kay R. Merrill, ed., *Colorado Cemetery Directory* (Denver: Colorado Council of Genealogy Societies, 1985), 547; *Tombstone Inscriptions of El Paso and Teller Counties, Colorado*, Version 2.0; Jan MacKell. "Looking for Love in All the Wrong Places," *Colorado Gambler* magazine, 2011; interview with Thelma Rathke, Cañon City, CO, 2005.
35. Bauer, Ozment, and Willard, *Colorado Post Offices*, 92; Lewis, *Florence & Cripple Creek Railroad*, 77.
36. Joel F. Love family tree, ancestry.com.
37. *Cripple Creek Morning Times*, June 28, 1899, 1.
38. Ibid., June 29, 1899, 1.
39. Black, *Clyde*, 26.
40. Bauer, Ozment and Willard, *Colorado Post Offices*, 92; *Cripple Creek District Directory 1902–3* (Denver, CO: Gazetteer Publishing Co., 1902); Feitz, *Cripple Creek Railroads*, 15.
41. Kimberly M. Carsell and Kimberle C. Long, "History and Mysteries of Catamount Open Space," prepared for Kevin P. Tanski, parks coordinator, Teller County Division of Parks, September 2000, 4–5.
42. Will Stapp, "Bell, William Abraham (1841–1921)," *Encyclopedia of Nineteenth Century Photography*, vol. 1 (New York: Routledge, 2007), 143–45; Marshall Sprague, *Newport in the Rockies* (Chicago: Swallow Press, 1971), 18–23; "Manitou Experimental Forest," USDA Forest Service website, http://www.fs.usda.gov/detail/manitou/about/?cid=STELPRDB5151964.
43. Carsell and Long, "History and Mysteries," 5, 87; "Manitou Experimental Forest."
44. Carsell and Long, "History and Mysteries," 6.
45. Ibid., 5; Edward M. McFarland, *Midland Route: A Colorado Midland Guide and Data Book* (Boulder, CO: Pruett Publishing Company, 1990), 16.

46. "Colorado's First Resort and Trout Hatchery," Woodland Park Public Library, Woodland Park, Colorado, 4; "Manitou Experimental Forest"; Jan MacKell, "Queen Palmer's Trip Up Ute Pass," *Colorado Gambler*, 2001.
47. Bauer, Ozment and Willard, *Colorado Post Offices*, 95; "Colorado's First Resort and Trout Hatchery," 5; Garden of Eden and Pine Grove plat maps, El Paso County Clerk and Recorder, Colorado Springs, Colorado.
48. Bauer, Ozment and Willard, *Colorado Post Offices*, 95, 142; Torrington plat map, El Paso County Clerk and Recorder, Colorado Springs, Colorado; "Manitou Experimental Forest"; U.S. census 1900.
49. Plat map vacations for Torrington, 1903 and 1909, Teller County Assessor, Cripple Creek Colorado; "Manitou Experimental Forest."
50. Conte, *Old Cripple Creek Stage Road*, 5; Leanne C. Boyd and Glenn H. Carson, *Atlas of Colorado Ghost Towns*, vol. 2 (Deming, NM: Cache Press, a division of Carson Enterprises, 1985), 127.
51. Black, *Clyde*, 8; Brunk, *Shattered Dreams on Pikes Peak*, 44; Henry C. Rathke land patent, GLO/BLM Records website, http://www.glorecords.blm.gov.
52. Carsell and Long, "History and Mysteries," 7; Wilkins, *Short Line to Cripple Creek*, 55; Conte, *Old Cripple Creek Stage Road*, 27.
53. *Aspen Democrat*, September 23, 1901, 3, and September 25, 1901, 4; *Colorado Transcript*, October 2, 1901, 3.
54. Bauer, Ozment and Willard, *Colorado Post Offices*, 124; *Aspen Daily Times*, June 24, 1904, 2; *Colorado Transcript*, August 31, 1905.
55. *Colorado State Business Directory, 1908*, 1, 106.
56. Sprague, *Newport of the Rockies*, 263; "History: Colorado Springs' Water Collection System," https://www.csu.org/CSUDocuments/watertour.pdf; *Colorado State Business Directory, 1919* (Denver, CO: Gazetteer Publishing & Printing Co., 1919), 821.
57. Bauer, Ozment and Willard, *Colorado Post Offices*, 124; Conte, *Old Cripple Creek Stage Road*, 27; "History: Colorado Springs' Water Collection System."
58. King is identified as a carpenter in the 1880 U.S. census; Black, *Clyde*, 11.
59. Brunk, *Shattered Dreams on Pikes Peak*, 39; Black, *Clyde*, 11; Conte, *Old Cripple Creek Stage Road*, 5.
60. Brunk, *Shattered Dreams on Pikes Peak*, 39.
61. Ibid., 42; *Colorado Springs Gazette*, August 31, 1878, 7.
62. Brunk, *Shattered Dreams on Pikes Peak*, 42.
63. Ibid., 39. Jackson's account appeared in the March 1882 issue of *Atlantic* magazine.

64. Black, *Clyde*, 8.
65. Brunk, *Shattered Dreams on Pikes Peak*, 45–46.
66. Ibid.
67. *Fairplay Flume*, September 6, 1883, 4; Brunk, *Shattered Dreams on Pikes Peak*, 47.
68. Black, *Clyde*, 12; Brunk, *Shattered Dreams on Pikes Peak*, 47.
69. Brunk, *Shattered Dreams on Pikes Peak*, 48–50; Mayo G. Smith land patent, GLO/BLM Records website, http://www.glorecords.blm.gov.
70. Brunk, *Shattered Dreams on Pikes Peak*, 50.
71. Ibid.; Black, *Clyde*, 13; *Aspen Evening Chronicle*, July 28, 1892, 3.
72. *Akron Weekly Pioneer Press*, November 15, 1895, 1; Brunk, *Shattered Dreams on Pikes Peak*, 51.
73. *Silver Cliff Rustler*, April 2, 1902, 3, and April 16, 1902, 2; *Fairplay Flume*, May 2, 1902, 1; Black, *Clyde*, 13, 19–20; City of Colorado Springs website, https://parks.coloradosprings.gov/explore-play/explore/open-spaces/south-slope-recreation-area.
74. Merrill, *Colorado Cemetery Directory*, 549; *Tombstone Inscriptions of El Paso and Teller Counties, Colorado*, Version 2.0; Jan MacKell, "Spring Creek: A Forgotten Suburb of Cripple Creek," *Dark Horse Press*, 1997.
75. Spring Creek file, Cripple Creek District Museum, Cripple Creek, Colorado.
76. *Cripple Creek Morning Times*, January 15, 1896, 1.
77. Jacob Abby, findagrave.com; MacKell, "Spring Creek."
78. *Cripple Creek Morning Times*, January 1, 1898, 1, and June 25, 1898, 4.
79. Ibid., August 20, 1898, 1, and August 23, 1898.
80. Hunter family tree, ancestry.com; "Jacob Abby," findagrave.com.
81. MacKell, "Spring Creek."
82. Bauer, Ozment and Willard, *Colorado Post Offices*, 137; *Colorado Springs Gazette*, August 29, 1874, 1.
83. *Colorado Springs Gazette*, June 19, 1875, 1; *Pueblo Chieftain*, August 31, 1876, 2; *Pueblo Weekly Chieftain*, August 24, 1876, 3.
84. Carsell and Long, "History and Mysteries," 10–13; "History of the Cliff House at Pikes Peak," Cliff House website, http://www.thecliffhouse.com/cliff-house-history; Rowenna Blum and Pikes Peak Genealogical Society, "HISTORY: Names and Places Associated with Woodland Park, Teller County, Colorado," December 1988. USGW Archives, http://files.usgwarchives.net.
85. *Denver Daily Times*, September 18, 1877, 1; *Pueblo Weekly Chieftain*, November 1, 1877, 3.
86. *Colorado Springs Gazette*, February 23, 1878.

87. Benjamin Logan and Wesley Wheeler, BLM/GLO records website, http://www.glorecords.blm.gov.
88. George Croffutt, *Crofutt's Grip-Sack Guide of Colorado*, vol. 2 (Omaha, NE: Overland Publishing Co., 1885), 92, 161.
89. Robert L. Brown, *Colorado Ghost Towns Past Present* (Caldwell, ID: Caxton Printers, Ltd. 1981), 305; *Leadville Daily/Evening Chronicle*, June 29, 1886, 4, and December 12, 1886, 1, 5.
90. Summit Park plat map, El Paso County Clerk and Recorder, Colorado Springs, Colorado; Bauer, Ozment and Willard, *Colorado Post Offices*, 137; Carsell and Long, "History and Mysteries," 11.
91. *Leadville Herald Democrat*, October 19, 1889, 4; Carsell and Long, "History and Mysteries," 13.
92. "Henry Truman Williams," Research Association website, http://www.emery.research.pasttracker.com/john-anthony009.EMERY9A2.htm; "Williamite Followers Held Strict but Unorthodox Religious Beliefs," *Old Colorado City Historical Society Newsletter*, no. 1 (March 1991).
93. "Henry Truman Williams," Research Association website; *Aspen Daily Chronicle*, December 10, 1889, 1.
94. "Henry Truman Williams," Research Association website; "Williamite Followers Held Strict but Unorthodox Religious Beliefs."
95. *Aspen Daily Chronicle*, December 10, 1889, 1.
96. Carsell and Long, "History and Mysteries," 14–15; Richard Rhinehart, "Historic Williams Canyon Plaque Stolen"; Colorado Caves website, http://www.coloradocaves.org/?p=455.
97. Bauer, Ozment and Willard, *Colorado Post Offices*, 137; *Aspen Daily Times*, August 22, 1891, 4; *Leadville Daily/Evening Chronicle*, April 13, 1896, 4.

Part II

98. *Directory of the Cripple Creek Mining District for 1900* (Cripple Creek, CO: Cripple Creek District Directory Co., 1900), 511, 514.
99. U.S. census 1880.
100. *Directory of the Cripple Creek Mining District for 1900*, 518–19; U.S. census 1900 and 1910; "William Maxim Hover," findagrave.com.
101. MacKell, *Cripple Creek District*, 90.
102. Interview with David "Bean" McCormick, Victor, Colorado, 2003.
103. *Cripple Creek Morning Times*, August 16, 1898, 1; "Harry Aspey," findagrave.com.

104. Boyd and Carson, *Atlas of Colorado Ghost Towns*, 2:127; Wilkins, *Short Line to Cripple Creek*, 37.
105. Donald R. Elliott, "Place Names of Colorado," edited by Doris L. Elliott, manuscript for the Colorado Council of Genealogical Societies, Inc., Denver Public Library, Denver, Colorado, 1999, 195.
106. Colorado Department of State, *Biennial Report of the Secretary of State of Colorado* (Denver, CO: Smith-Brooks Printing Company, 1896), 144.
107. Bauer, Ozment and Willard, *Colorado Post Offices*, 73; Fred Hills, *The Official Manual of the Cripple Creek District, Colorado, U.S.A.* (Colorado Springs, CO: Fred Hills, 1900), 245.
108. Elliott, "Place Names of Colorado," 291.
109. Bauer, Ozment and Willard, *Colorado Post Offices*, 74; Glenn R. Scott, "USGS Historic Trail Map of the Denver, 1° x 2° Quadrangle, Central Colorado" (Reston, VA: U.S. Department of the Interior, U.S. Geological Survey, 1999); Elliott, "Place Names in Colorado," 292.
110. Lewis, *Florence & Cripple Creek Railroad*, 81–82.
111. Independence plat map, Teller County Assessor, Cripple Creek, Colorado; Rufus L. Porter, *Gold Fever* (Victor, CO: Hard Rock Poet, 1954).
112. *Portrait and Biographical Record of the State of Colorado* (Chicago: Chapman Publishing Company, 1899, 673); *A Complete City Directory of Cripple Creek, Victor and the Towns of the Cripple Creek Mining District* (Denver, CO: Gazetteer Publishing Co., 1896); *Cripple Creek District Directory 1902–3*, 396.
113. Boyd and Carson, *Atlas of Colorado Ghost Towns*, 2:128; Wilkins, *Short Line to Cripple Creek*, 37.
114. MacKell, *Cripple Creek District*, 61.
115. Elliott, "Place Names of Colorado," 436.
116. Ibid., 469; Ken Lorenz, *From the Yellow Gold of Victor to the Black Gold of Prudhoe Bay* (Colorado Springs, CO: Century One Press, 1983), 20.
117. *Cripple Creek Complete Directory* (1893); *Cripple Creek District Directory 1902–3*, 416.
118. U.S. census 1880 and 1900; Antone Reiger land patent, GLO/BLM Records website, http://www.glorecords.blm.gov.
119. Interview with Reed Grainger and Guy Vinyard, Victor, Colorado, October 22, 2015.
120. *Tombstone Inscriptions of El Paso and Teller Counties, Colorado*, Version 2.0.
121. U.S. census 1900; Edward Pell, U.S. World War I Draft Registration Cards, 1917–18 and Pell family tree, ancestry.com.
122. Interview with Reed Grainger and Guy Vinyard; Pell, World U.S. World War I Draft Registration Cards, 1917–18.

123. *Tombstone Inscriptions of El Paso and Teller Counties, Colorado*, Version 2.0; interview with Reed Grainger and Guy Vinyard; Klausmeier family tree and Pell family tree, ancestry.com.
124. *Aspen Evening Chronicle*, November 19, 1892, 2.
125. *Buena Vista Herald*, January 27, 1894, 2.
126. *New Castle News*, July 31, 1896, 2.
127. *Aspen Tribune*, October 6, 1900, 4.
128. *Directory of the Cripple Creek Mining District for 1900.*
129. Sprague, *Money Mountain*, 70, 79, 116; *Cripple Creek Complete Directory* (1893); *Directory of the Cripple Creek Mining District for 1900*, 413.
130. Sprague, *Money Mountain*, 223–24; *Aspen Daily Times*, February 20, 1900, 3.
131. Sprague, *Money Mountain*, 225; *Cripple Creek District Directory 1902–3*, 416.
132. Robert Brown, *Jeep Trails to Colorado Ghost Towns* (Caldwell, ID: Caxton Printers, 1963), 36; *Cripple Creek Morning Times*, January 1, 1898, 18; Robert B. Murray and Russell D. Lee, eds., *Colorado Ghost Town Guide* (Basalt: Colorado Recreation Guides, third printing, 1982), 112.
133. *Aspen Daily Chronicle*, October 11, 1893, 1; *Leadville Democrat*, November 17, 1893, 1.
134. *History and Description of the Cripple Creek Mining District* (1894), 41, 88; Bauer, Ozment and Willard, *Colorado Post Offices*, 11.
135. Lewis, *Florence & Cripple Creek Railroad*, 221; MacKell, *Cripple Creek District*, 40.
136. MacKell, *Cripple Creek District*, 41; George G. Suggs Jr., *Colorado's War on Militant Unionism: James H. Peabody and the Western Federation of Miners*, 2nd ed. (Norman: University of Oklahoma Press, 1991), 19.
137. *History and Description of the Cripple Creek Mining District* (1894), 148–49.
138. *Castle Rock Journal*, January 9, 1895, 2; Bauer, Ozment and Willard, *Colorado Post Offices*, 11.
139. *Aspen Daily Times*, March 13, 1895, 1.
140. *Colorado Springs Gazette-Telegraph*, February 15, 1975, 10.
141. *Boulder Daily Camera*, May 14, 1895, 2; *Colorado Transcript*, May 22, 1895, 7.
142. *Leadville Daily Press*, September 7, 1895, 4.
143. *Boulder Daily Camera*, September 23, 1895, 2; *Cripple Creek Morning Times*, December 13, 1895, 4; *Aspen Tribune*, January 30, 1896, 1.
144. *Complete City Directory of Cripple Creek, Victor and the Towns of the Cripple Creek Mining District* (1896); Lewis, *Florence & Cripple Creek Railroad*, 319.
145. *Silver Cliff Rustler*, October 7, 1896, 1.
146. *Leadville Herald Democrat*, April 12, 1897, 4; *Fairplay Flume*, April 15, 1897, 1; *Telluride Daily Journal*, June 16, 1897, 1.

147. *Cripple Creek Morning Times*, September 9, 1897, 1.
148. Ibid., January 1, 1898, 18.
149. Ibid., January 20, 1898, 4, February 11, 1898, 4; March 10, 1898, 1.
150. Ibid., October 16, 1898, 1.
151. Brown, *Jeep Trails to Colorado Ghost Towns*, 36.
152. *Directory of the Cripple Creek Mining District for 1900*; *Cripple Creek District Directory 1902–3*.
153. *Telluride Daily Journal*, May 23, 1903, 1; *Aspen Daily Times*, May 24, 1903, 1.
154. Jan MacKell, "Altman, The Highest City in the United States," *Colorado Gambler*, 2006.
155. Bauer, Ozment and Willard, *Colorado Post Offices*, 11.
156. *Cripple Creek District Directory 1915–16* (Denver, CO: Gazetteer Publishing Co., 1915); Brown, *Jeep Trails to Colorado Ghost Towns*, 37.
157. Hills, *Official Manual of the Cripple Creek District*, 55; *Aspen Daily Leader*, April 25, 1892, 4.
158. *Aspen Daily Times*, July 11, 1893, 2.
159. *Cripple Creek Complete Directory* (1893); Bauer, Ozment and Willard, *Colorado Post Offices*, 12.
160. Leslie Doyle Spell and Hazel M. Spell, *Forgotten Men of Cripple Creek* (Denver, CO: Big Mountain Press, 1959), 59–60.
161. *Leadville Herald Democrat*, March 15, 1894, 1; Anaconda plat map, El Paso County Clerk and Recorder, Colorado Springs, Colorado; *History and Description of the Cripple Creek Mining District* (1894), 41, 149–50.
162. Lewis, *Florence & Cripple Creek Railroad*, 236; *Leadville Herald Democrat*, July 3, 1894, 1; Boyd and Carson, *Atlas of Colorado Ghost Towns*, 2:127.
163. *Aspen Daily Times*, September 29, 1895, 8; *Aspen Tribune*, November 26, 1895, 1.
164. *Leadville Herald Democrat*, May 17, 1896, 6.
165. *Directory of the Cripple Creek Mining District for 1900*.
166. Josiah Roberts, U.S. World War I Draft Registration Cards, 1917–18, Ancestry.com; "Josiah Roberts," Internet Movie Database, imdb.com. Some websites claim Roberts was born in Anaconda in 1890, but the town did not yet exist. Roberts's World War I draft registration verifies he was actually born in Rockvale, Colorado.
167. Spell and Spell, *Forgotten Men of Cripple Creek*, 125–26.
168. "Texas Guinan," Internet Movie Database, imdb.com.
169. Jan MacKell, "From Squaw Gulch to Big Snake: A History of Anaconda," *Colorado Gambler*, 2006; *Los Angeles Herald*, November 12, 1904; *Aspen Daily Times*, November 13, 1904, 1.

170. *Cripple Creek District Directory, 1905* (Denver, CO: Gazetteer Publishing Co., 1905), 94; Cripple Creek and Victor Narrow Gauge Railroad website, http://cripplecreekrailroad.com/history; *Cripple Creek District Directory, 1907* (Denver, CO: Gazetteer Publishing Co., 1907), 95; *Colorado State Business Directory, 1908*, 131.
171. Bauer, Ozment and Willard, *Colorado Post Offices*, 12; *Cripple Creek District Directory, 1912–13* (Denver, CO: Gazetteer Publishing Co., 1912), 105.
172. MacKell, "History of Anaconda."
173. *Denver Post*, July 8, 2000; *Colorado Springs Gazette*, "Family Hopes Mine Expansion Won't Disturb Son's Memorial," July 29, 2011.
174. Jan MacKell, "Arequa Gulch and That Mysterious 'A,'" *Colorado Gambler*, 2006.
175. "Fountain's Oldest Structure?" Historic Fountain Colorado website, http://fountaincolorado.blogspot.com/2011/03/requa-and-croft.html; Sprague, *Money Mountain*, 3, 7, 13.
176. Sprague, *Money Mountain*, 13–15; *Colorado Springs Gazette*, September 26, 1874, 2; MacKell, "Arequa Gulch and That Mysterious 'A.'"
177. Robert Brown, *Ghost Towns of the Colorado Rockies* (Caldwell, ID: Caxton Printers, Ltd., 1977), 147; Arequa plat map, El Paso County Clerk & Recorder, Colorado Springs, Colorado.
178. MacKell, *Cripple Creek District*, 16.
179. *Tombstone Inscriptions of El Paso and Teller Counties, Colorado*, Version 2.0; Merrill, *Colorado Cemetery Directory*, 547; *Cripple Creek Complete Directory* (1893).
180. Bauer, Ozment and Willard, *Colorado Post Offices*, 3–4, 13; Arequa vacation map, El Paso County Clerk & Recorder, Colorado Springs, Colorado.
181. Hills, *Official Manual of the Cripple Creek District*, 63, 98, 128, 297; MacKell, "Arequa Gulch and That Mysterious 'A.'"
182. *Directory of the Cripple Creek Mining District for 1900*, 129–32.
183. Arequa vacation map; MacKell, "Arequa Gulch and That Mysterious 'A'"; *Cripple Creek District Directory, 1915–16.*
184. MacKell, "Arequa Gulch and That Mysterious 'A.'"
185. Brown, *Jeep Trails to Colorado Ghost Towns*, 43.
186. Spell and Spell, *Forgotten Men of Cripple Creek*, 46, 49–51.
187. *Colorado Springs Daily Gazette*, January 16, 1892; Spell and Spell, *Forgotten Men of Cripple Creek*, 51, 55, 59.
188. Spell and Spell, *Forgotten Men of Cripple Creek*, 47, 113; MacKell, *Cripple Creek District*, 31.
189. Bauer, Ozment and Willard, *Colorado Post Offices*, 12; MacKell, *Cripple Creek District*, 32, 95.

190. Susan Anderson family tree, ancestry.com; Virginia Cornell, *Doc Susie: The True Story of a Country Physician in the Colorado Rockies* (New York: Ivy Books, Published by Ballantine Books, a division of Random House Inc.), 30; MacKell, *Cripple Creek District*, 96.
191. Sprague, *Money Mountain*, 102; Spell and Spell, *Forgotten Men of Cripple Creek*, 119–20.
192. Jan MacKell, "Read All About It: The Newspapers of Teller County," *Colorado Gambler*, 2000; Free Coinage Gold Mining Company stock certificate No. 167, 1893, Cripple Creek District Museum, Cripple Creek, Colorado; Bauer, Ozment and Willard, *Colorado Post Offices*, 12.
193. *Denver City Directory, 1899* (Denver, CO: Ballard & Richards, 1899), 152; Casady Black Shuemaker York Fortune Bradbury family tree, ancestry.com.
194. Black, *Clyde*, 8; Beaver Park plat map, Teller County Assessor, Cripple Creek, Colorado.
195. *Aspen Evening Chronicle*, November 19, 1892, 2; Beaver Park plat map; *History and Description of the Cripple Creek Mining District* (1894), 26–27.
196. Lewis, *Florence & Cripple Creek Railroad*, 229; Sprague, *Money Mountain*, 150–53; "Boynton Family," Carr Manor website, carrmanor.com.
197. "Boynton Family," Carr Manor website.
198. *History and Description of the Cripple Creek Mining District* (1894); Teller County Block Books 1895–97, Teller County Assessor, Cripple Creek, Colorado; *Directory of the Cripple Creek Mining District for 1900*; Beaver Park vacation map and East Cripple Creek plat maps, Teller County Assessor, Cripple Creek, Colorado.
199. Jan MacKell, "Cameron and Pinnacle Park: Ghosts of a Playground Past," *Colorado Gambler*, 2000.
200. Grassy plat map, Teller County Assessor, Cripple Creek, Colorado.
201. Grassy partial vacation map, El Paso County Clerk and Recorder, Colorado Springs, Colorado; S.E. Poet, "The Story of Cameron, Colorado," *Colorado Magazine*, September 1932, 195; Cripple Creek *Morning Times*, August 4, 1899, 2; MacKell, "Read All About It."
202. Poet, "Story of Cameron, Colorado"; Charles O. Brantigan, "Matthew John McBird (And His Children)," manuscript, 2008, published online, drbrantigan.com/history/mcbrdbio%20080330%20public.pdf.
203. Poet, "Story of Cameron, Colorado"; Cameron plat map, Teller County Assessor, Cripple Creek, Colorado.
204. *Cripple Creek Morning Times*, September 30, 1899, 1; October 12, 1899, 5; December 8, 1899, 1; Bauer, Ozment and Willard, *Colorado Post Offices*, 142; *Cripple Creek Morning Times*, December 31, 1899, 5. In the book

Colorado Post Offices 1859 to 1989, the authors report that Touraine's post office opened in 1889 and was moved to Cameron in 1891.

205. *Directory of the Cripple Creek Mining District for 1900*, 133; Poet, "Story of Cameron, Colorado"; Cameron plat map.

206. MacKell, "Cameron and Pinnacle Park"; Dave Southworth, *Colorado Mining Camps* (Round Rock, TX: Wild Horse Publishing, 1997), 118; *Castle Rock Journal*, March 8, 1901, 1; Bauer, Ozment and Willard, *Colorado Post Offices*, 27; *Yuma (Colorado) Pioneer*, September 6, 1901, 4.

207. MacKell, "Cameron and Pinnacle Park"; J. Anthony Lukes, *Big Trouble: A Murder in a Small Western Town Sets Off a Strugg* (New York: Simon & Schuster, 2012), 233.

208. *Cripple Creek District Directory, 1905*, 101; *Cripple Creek District Directory, 1907*; Bauer, Ozment and Willard, *Colorado Post Offices*, 27; Crying Wind, *I Remember Divide* (n.p.: self-published, July 1977); *Cripple Creek District Directory, 1912–13*, 107; Cameron vacation map, March 29, 1904, Teller County Assessor, Cripple Creek, Colorado.

209. Jan MacKell, "A Forgotten Ghost Town: Eclipse," *Colorado Gambler*, 2008.

210. *Cripple Creek Morning Times*, January 19, 1898, 1; Brown, *Ghost Towns of the Colorado Rockies*, 133.

211. Brown, *Ghost Towns of the Colorado Rockies*, 134; Boyd and Carson, *Atlas of Colorado Ghost Towns*, 2:128.

212. *Cripple Creek District Directory, 1902–3*, 347; Brown, *Ghost Towns of the Colorado Rockies*, 134.

213. Brown, *Ghost Towns of the Colorado Rockies*, 146–47; Boyd and Carson, *Atlas of Colorado Ghost Towns*, 2:127. Another source says the Bernards staked the claim, found the antlers and named Elkton and that Bernard sold half of his claim to a local grocer to settle his bill of $36.50.

214. *History and Description of the Cripple Creek Mining District* (1894), 156; Bauer, Ozment and Willard, *Colorado Post Offices*, 50; Brown, *Ghost Towns of the Colorado Rockies*, 149; Lewis, *Florence & Cripple Creek Railroad*, 328; *Complete City Directory of Cripple Creek, Victor and the Towns of the Cripple Creek Mining District* (1896), 311; *Cripple Creek Morning Times*, October 29, 1897, 1.

215. Lewis, *Florence & Cripple Creek Railroad*, 330; *Cripple Creek Morning Times*, July 1, 1898, 1; November 6, 1898, 2; December 1, 1898, 1.

216. Omer Vincent Foxhoven, *The City of God in the City of Gold* (n.p.: self-published, June 1952); *Cripple Creek District Directory, 1902–3*, 348; *Cripple Creek District Directory, 1905*, 293; *Cripple Creek District Directory, 1912–13*, 224.

217. Brown, *Ghost Towns of the Colorado Rockies*, 147–49; *Colorado State Business Directory, 1919*, 474; *Colorado State Business Directory, 1920* (Denver, CO: Gazetteer Publishing and Printing Co., 1920), 500.
218. Bauer, Ozment and Willard, *Colorado Post Offices*, 50.
219. Brown, *Ghost Towns of the Colorado Rockies*, 173–74; Jan MacKell, "Whatever Happened to Gillett?" *Colorado Gambler*, 2008; McFarland, *Midland Route*, 34.
220. Lewis, *Florence & Cripple Creek Railroad*, 324; MacKell, "Whatever Happened to Gillett?"; Southworth, *Colorado Mining Camps*, 116; Brown, *Ghost Towns of the Colorado Rockies*, 173.
221. Brown, *Ghost Towns of the Colorado Rockies*, 173–74; Bauer, Ozment and Willard, *Colorado Post Offices*, 60; Lewis, *Florence & Cripple Creek Railroad*, 244.
222. Lewis, *Florence & Cripple Creek Railroad*, 321; Southworth, *Colorado Mining Camps*, 116; Teller County Block Books 1895–97; MacKell, *Cripple Creek District*, 52.
223. Brown, *Ghost Towns of the Colorado Rockies*, 175; Jan MacKell Collins, "Arizona Charlie Meadows, Cowboy Extraordinaire," *Frontier Gazette* magazine, Summer 2015; Teller County Block Books 1895–97.
224. Sprague, *Money Mountain*, 179.
225. Ibid., 182; Brown, *Ghost Towns of the Colorado Rockies*, 176; Southworth, *Colorado Mining Camps*, 116.
226. MacKell, "Whatever Happened to Gillett?"; *Complete City Directory of Cripple Creek, Victor and the Towns of the Cripple Creek Mining District* (1896); Brown, *Ghost Towns of the Colorado Rockies*, 133, 174; Foxhoven, *City of God in the City of Gold*.
227. Gillett vacation map, El Paso County Clerk and Recorder, Colorado Springs, Colorado; *Directory of the Cripple Creek Mining District for 1900*; *Cripple Creek District Directory, 1902–3*, 365.
228. MacKell, "Whatever Happened to Gillett?"; *Cripple Creek District Directory, 1905*, 303; Bauer, Ozment and Willard, *Colorado Post Offices*, 60; Porter, *Gold Fever*.
229. Merrill, *Colorado Cemetery Directory*, 548; MacKell, "Whatever Happened to Gillett?"; Winfred Ward Clark, *Skaguay: The Miracle of the Gold Camp Near Cripple Creek & Victor* (Colorado Springs, CO: Century One Press, 1989), 26.
230. Independence plat map, El Paso County Clerk and Recorder, Colorado Springs, Colorado; Robert M. Ormes, *Tracking Ghost Railroads in Colorado* (Colorado Springs, CO: Green Light Graphics, 1980), 93; Jan MacKell,

"Independence: One of the Last Ghost Towns," *Cripple Creek & Victor Eagle*, 1996; Bauer, Ozment and Willard, *Colorado Post Offices*, 92; *Complete City Directory of Cripple Creek, Victor and the Towns of the Cripple Creek Mining District* (1896), 352.

231. Bauer, Ozment and Willard, *Colorado Post Offices*, 92; *Directory of the Cripple Creek Mining District for 1900*; MacKell, "Independence."

232. Porter, *Gold Fever*; MacKell, "Independence"; *Cripple Creek District Directory, 1902–3*, 403.

233. Sprague, *Money Mountain*, 253–54.

234. *Cripple Creek District Directory, 1905*, 323; Foxhoven, *City of God in the City of Gold*.

235. *Colorado State Business Directory, 1919*, 611.

236. Sprague, *Money Mountain*, 289–91.

237. MacKell, "Independence"; interview with Kathy Justice, Victor, Colorado, 2003; Bauer, Ozment and Willard, *Colorado Post Offices*, 92; interview with Jane Mannon, Cripple Creek/Victor Gold Mining Company, 2004.

238. U.S. census, 1880; Jan MacKell, "Lawrence, the Earliest Town in the Cripple Creek District," *Colorado Gambler*, 2006; R. Laurie Simmons and Thomas Simmons, "Historic Buildings Survey of Downtown Cañon City, Colorado," manuscript for Front Range Association Inc., Denver, Colorado, 2004–5, 28.

239. MacKell, "Lawrence"; Lewis, *Florence & Cripple Creek Railroad*, 251; Lawrence plat map, El Paso County Clerk and Recorder, Colorado Springs, Colorado.

240. Raynolds Cattle Company stock certificate, http://www.worthpoint.com/worthopedia/1887-stock-raynolds-cattle-company-51555870; "Magdalene Raynolds," findagrave.com; "Decree of the District Court of Fremont County, Colorado, In the Matter of the Priorities of Water Rights in Water District No. 2, approved February 3, 1894," Fremont County Courthouse, Cañon City, Colorado.

241. MacKell, "Lawrence"; Lewis, *Florence & Cripple Creek Railroad*, 251; Bauer, Ozment and Willard, *Colorado Post Offices*, 88; MacKell "Read All About It."

242. Lewis, *Florence & Cripple Creek Railroad*, 251; MacKell, "Lawrence."

243. *History and Description of the Cripple Creek Mining District* (1894), 44; MacKell, "Lawrence"; Lewis, *Florence & Cripple Creek Railroad*, 255; *Complete City Directory of Cripple Creek, Victor and the Towns of the Cripple Creek Mining District* (1896).

244. Lewis, *Florence & Cripple Creek Railroad*, 265; Bauer, Ozment and Willard, *Colorado Post Offices*, 88; MacKell, "Lawrence"; Amended and Additional Plat of the Town of Lawrence, Teller County Assessor, Teller County Courthouse, Cripple Creek, Colorado; *Directory of the Cripple Creek Mining District for 1900*.

245. MacKell, "Lawrence"; *Cripple Creek District Directory, 1902–3*, 415.

246. Brown, *Ghost Towns of the Colorado Rockies*, 230; "Alfred 'Alferd' Packer, The Cannibal of Lake City, Colorado," Sangres.com, http://www.sangres.com/history/alferdpacker.htm#.Vdet3PlViko; Brown, *Jeep Trails to Colorado Ghost Towns*, 43.

247. Bauer, Ozment and Willard, *Colorado Post Offices*, 101; *Cripple Creek Complete Directory*, 1893; Lewis, *Florence & Cripple Creek Railroad*, 73; Brown, *Ghost Towns of the Colorado Rockies*, 231–32.

248. *History and Description of the Cripple Creek Mining District* (1894), 42, 150.

249. Interpretive sign, Mound City site; Bauer, Ozment and Willard, *Colorado Post Offices*, 101; *Complete City Directory of Cripple Creek, Victor and the Towns of the Cripple Creek Mining District* (1896); Lewis, *Florence & Cripple Creek Railroad*, 74; *Directory of the Cripple Creek Mining District for 1900*, 407; Brown, *Ghost Towns of the Colorado Rockies*, 231.

250. *Chaffee County Republican*, February 19, 1896, 4.

251. Signal Butte plat map, El Paso County Clerk and Recorder, Colorado Springs, Colorado; *(Denver, CO) Rocky Mountain Sun*, February 29, 1896, 2.

252. *Castle Rock Journal*, March 11, 1896, 1; Bauer, Ozment and Willard, *Colorado Post Offices*, 132; *Mountain Echo*, May 14, 1898, 1; Signal Butte plat map, Teller County Assessor, Cripple Creek, Colorado.

253. Bauer, Ozment and Willard, *Colorado Post Offices*, 132; *Colorado Republican*, May 24, 1906, 3.

254. MacKell, *Cripple Creek District*, 42.

255. *Cripple Creek Morning Times*, October 31, 1899, 1; *Directory of the Cripple Creek Mining District for 1900*, 4; U.S. census, 1900.

256. *Cripple Creek Morning Times*, February 28, 1899, 3; December 28, 1895, 1; December 29 1895, 1; October 26, 1897, 3.

257. Ibid., April 30, 1899, 1; Kitty Looper, *Road to Gold* (Colorado Springs, CO: Little London Press, 1976), 10; *Directory of the Cripple Creek Mining District for 1900*; Brown, *Colorado Ghost Towns Past Present*, 306; MacKell, *Cripple Creek District*, 84.

258. Brown, *Colorado Ghost Towns Past Present*, 306, 310; MacKell, *Cripple Creek District*, 84; *Aspen Daily Times*, November 28, 1900, 4; interview with Jeff Trenary, Cripple Creek, Colorado, 2002.

259. E-mail correspondence with Shaun Boyd, Douglas County History Research Center, Castle Rock, Colorado, October 2015; West Creek plat map, El Paso County Clerk & Recorder, Colorado Springs, Colorado; Lincoln H. Hall, *Official Cripple Creek Manual Up to Date* (Cripple Creek, CO: Consolidated Publishing Company, 1896).
260. *Castle Rock Journal*, March 11, 1896, 4.
261. *Mountain Echo*, March 5, 1898, 1; *West Creek Mining News*, May 20, 1899; Bauer, Ozment and Willard, *Colorado Post Offices*, 150; West Creek vacation map, 1997, El Paso County Clerk and Recorder, Colorado Springs, Colorado.

Part III

262. Jan MacKell, "Alta Vista: An Important Whistle-Stop in Railroad History," *Colorado Gambler*, 2006. Eight Mile Canyon is now called Phantom Canyon.
263. Lewis, *Florence & Cripple Creek Railroad*, 21, 300–3; MacKell, "Alta Vista."
264. *Aspen Daily Times*, May 29, 1894, 1; MacKell, "Alta Vista."
265. MacKell, "Alta Vista."
266. *Aspen Tribune*, November 8, 1895, 3; *Cripple Creek Morning Times*, August 11, 1899, 2.
267. *Directory of the Cripple Creek Mining District for 1900*, 510; Feitz, *Cripple Creek Railroads*, 5; *Fairplay Flume*, May 9, 1913, 2; interview with Erik Swanson, Cripple Creek, Colorado, 1998.
268. Lewis, *Florence & Cripple Creek Railroad*, 396–97, 402–3; J.H. Tudsberry, ed., *Minutes of Proceedings of the Institution of Civil Engineers*, vol. 133 (London: Great George Street, 1898), 394. Author Allan C. Lewis wrote that Dyer's second middle name was Swerington.
269. *Directory of the Cripple Creek Mining District for 1900*, 525; Wilkins, *Short Line to Cripple Creek*, 37; *Cripple Creek Morning Times*, January 16, 1898, 1; February 8, 1898, 4; March 24, 1898, 1.
270. *Directory of the Cripple Creek Mining District for 1900*, 512–15, 523; Feitz, Cripple Creek Railroads, 21.
271. Bauer, Ozment and Willard, *Colorado Post Offices*, 49; Carsell and Long, "History and Mysteries," 11–13; McFarland, *Midland Route*, 155.
272. Carsell and Long, "History and Mysteries," 13–15; *Wray, Colorado Rattler*, December 11, 1898, 2.

273. Bauer, Ozment and Willard, *Colorado Post Offices*, 49; Carsell and Long, "History and Mysteries," 11; Jean Taylor and Ann Cott, *A Century in the Shadow of Pikes Peak: Don Lawrie, His Mountain, His Life* (Pueblo, CO: Paperwork Inc., 1999), 28.
274. *Steamboat Pilot*, January 5, 1934, 4; Taylor and Cott, *Century in the Shadow of Pikes Peak*, 28; Carsell and Long, "History and Mysteries," 15–18.
275. McFarland, *Midland Route*, 255; Carsell and Long, "History and Mysteries," 11–12.
276. Mabel Hall, *The Story of Phantom Canyon* (n.p.: self-published, third printing, June 1973), 5.
277. MacKell, *Cripple Creek District*, 47; Lewis, *Florence & Cripple Creek Railroad*, 83–84.
278. Bauer, Ozment and Willard, *Colorado Post Offices*, 95.
279. MacKell, *Cripple Creek District*, 122–23; Bauer, Ozment and Willard, *Colorado Post Offices*, 95; Sprague, *Money Mountain*, 289–91.
280. McFarland, *Midland Route*, 34; MacKell, *Cripple Creek District*, 3; Bauer, Ozment and Willard, *Colorado Post Offices*, 98.
281. Merrill, *Colorado Cemetery Directory*, 548–49; Crying Wind, *I Remember Divide.*
282. Lewis, *Florence & Cripple Creek Railroad*, 225–26; McFarland, *Midland Route*, 34; Linda Irene Tingvik, "Rail Dates," Cripple Creek Railroads website, http://www.cripplecreekrailroads.com/index.shtm; Feitz, *Cripple Creek Railroads*, 3; *History and Description of the Cripple Creek Mining District* (1894), 32.
283. Crying Wind, *I Remember Divide.*
284. McFarland, *Midland Route*, 255; Bauer, Ozment and Willard, *Colorado Post Offices*, 98.
285. Crying Wind, *I Remember Divide*; Taylor and Cott, *Century in the Shadow of Pikes Peak*, 26; *Colorado Springs Gazette Telegraph*, February 16, 1929; Rainbow Valley Historical Guest Ranch, http://www.vacationhomerentals.com/Divide/proID-37103.
286. Lewis, *Florence & Cripple Creek Railroad*, 321; Feitz, *Cripple Creek Railroads*, 21; *Directory of the Cripple Creek Mining District for 1900*, 405.
287. Rufus Porter, "Ballad of Bathless Bill," *Gold Fever.*
288. *Directory of the Cripple Creek Mining District for 1900*, 405; *Cripple Creek District Directory, 1912–13*; *Cripple Creek District Directory, 1915–16*; Jan MacKell, *Brothels, Bordellos & Bad Girls: Prostitution in Colorado 1860–1930* (Albuquerque: University of New Mexico Press, 2003), 257–60.
289. Interview with Steve Mackin, Cripple Creek, Colorado, 2002; Looper, *Road to Gold*, 13–15.

290. Interview with Sally McCready, Cripple Creek, Colorado, 1995.
291. Lewis, *Florence & Cripple Creek Railroad*, 311, 321–23; MacKell, *Cripple Creek District*, 84; *Directory of the Cripple Creek Mining District for 1900*, 405.
292. *Cripple Creek Morning Times*, September 28, 1898, 3; January 14, 1900, 2.

Part IV

293. Bauer, Ozment and Willard, *Colorado Post Offices*, 11; Alnwick plat map, El Paso County Clerk & Recorder, Colorado Springs, Colorado.
294. *Aspen Daily Chronicle*, November 17, 1892, 2.
295. Bauer, Ozment and Willard, *Colorado Post Offices*, 11; Alnwick plat map; Charles Whitman Cross, "Pikes Peak Folio, Colorado," *U.S. Geological Survey Geologic Atlas of the United States Folio*, GF-7, 7, *United States Geological Survey Bulletin*, 1896, 36; Francis Ramaley, ed., *University of Colorado Studies*, vol. 3 (Boulder: University of Colorado, November 1905–August 1906), 151; Henry Gannett, *Gazetteer of Colorado* (Washington, D.C.: Government Printing Office, 1906), 14; R.C. Epis and C.E. Chapin, "Stratigraphic Nomenclature of the Thirty-nine Mile Volcanic Field, Central Colorado," *Contributions to Stratigraphy: U.S. Geological Survey Bulletin, 1395-C* (Denver, CO: GNU Records, USGS DDS-6 GNULEX, 1974), C1–C23.
296. *Hoosier State Chronicles*, July 15, 1896; Edward Le Roy Rice, "Blackface! Famous Blackface Minstrel Performers," excerpts from Monarchs of Minstrelsy, 1911, http://black-face.com/blackface-minstrel-performers.htm.
297. *Hoosier State Chronicles*, July 15, 1896; "Jack Haverly," American National Biography Online, http://oxfordindex.oup.com/view/10.1093/anb/9780198606697.article.1001826; Rice, "Blackface!"; Stephen E. Busch, "Haverly's Comic Opera Companies," http://www.operaoldcolo.info/personages/company6.html. The *Toledo City Directory* for 1864 actually lists Jack Haverly as the owner of a saloon.
298. Rice, "Blackface!"; Busch, "Haverly's Comic Opera Companies"; "Place Names in Colorado (H)," prepared by the Colorado Writer's Program and the State Historical Society's WPA Project, *Colorado Magazine* 18, no. 4 (1941): 146.
299. Busch, "Haverly's Comic Opera Companies."
300. Ibid.; *Cripple Creek Morning Times*, January 26, 1896, 1.
301. Haverly plat map, Teller County Assessor, Cripple Creek, Colorado; Busch, "Haverly's Comic Opera Companies."

302. Boyd and Carson, *Atlas of Colorado Ghost Towns*, 2:28; *Telluride Daily Journal*, June 15, 1897, 4; September 7, 1897, 1; Busch, "Haverly's Comic Opera Companies."

303. Carsell and Long, "History and Mysteries," 28; "Lander's City," Ghost Town file, Penrose Public Library, Colorado Springs, Colorado.

304. Eric Swab, "Lanter City—The Next Cripple Creek?" *Friends of the Peak* newsletter, May 2012, 6; Lanter City plat map, Teller County Assessor, Cripple Creek, Colorado; *Colorado Springs Gazette*, November 19, 1900; April 10, 1901, 8; "Lander's City," Penrose Public Library.

305. Robert Beers addition to Lanter City plat map, Teller County Assessor, Cripple Creek, Colorado; Swab, "Lanter City," 6.

306. Swab, "Lanter City," 6; *Colorado Springs Gazette*, January 30, 1901, 8; February 27, 1901, 8; April 24, 1901, 8; May 4, 1901, 8; October 12, 1901, 12.

307. "Lander's City," Penrose Public Library; "History of the Pike National Forest," USDA website, 44, http://www.fs.usda.gov; Swab, "Lanter City," 6–7; Carsell and Long, "History and Mysteries," 27.

308. Amanda Hardin, "A Pioneer in Colorado-Wyoming," *Colorado Magazine* 35, no. 3 (July 1958): 199; *Mining Industry and Review*, 1896, 491; West Creek plat map, El Paso County Clerk and Recorder, Colorado Springs, Colorado.

309. Henry Thomas Johns Jr. family tree, ancestry.com; Lewin vacation map, El Paso County Clerk and Recorder, Colorado Springs, Colorado.

310. *Cripple Creek Morning Times*, January 3, 1896, 4; *Boulder Daily Camera*, January 9, 1896, 2.

311. Hall, *Official Cripple Creek Up to Date*; *Aspen Daily Times*, February 1, 1896, 1; *Golden Transcript*, February 26, 1896, 5; *Castle Rock Journal*, March 11, 1896, 1.

312. Hall, *Official Cripple Creek Up to Date.*

313. Bauer, Ozment and Willard, *Colorado Post Offices*; *Cripple Creek Morning Times*, August 1, 1899, 1; *Grand Valley News*, February 9, 1911, 4.

314. Boyd and Carson, *Atlas of Colorado Ghost Towns*, 2:129; Dell A. McCoy, "Cripple Creek 1899," Sanborn-based map included in Lewis, *Florence & Cripple Creek Railroad.*

315. Sprague, *Money Mountain*, 11–12, 303.

316. Pisgah Park plat map, El Paso County Clerk and Recorder, Colorado Springs, Colorado; Pisgah Park, Teller County website map, http://cdsd.co.teller.co.us/flexviewers/parcel/index.html?search=R0001953.

317. Interview with Melissa Trenary, Cripple Creek, Colorado, 2015; *Cripple Creek Morning Times*, August 14, 1897, 4.

318. Pisgah Park, Teller County Assessor website, http://www.co.teller.co.us/Data/sa.tc?R0001953.

319. Elliott, "Place Names of Colorado," 19, 28, 147, 537, 586, 56, 314, 391.

320. Ibid., 62; Bauer, Ozment and Willard, *Colorado Post Offices*, 21; *Cripple Creek Morning Times*, September 14, 1897, 4.

321. "First Addition to the Town of Gold Springs," Teller County Assessor, Teller County Courthouse, Cripple Creek, Colorado.

322. *Eagle County Times*, July 9, 1904, 2.

323. "Parmelia Saunders," Allen family tree, ancestry.com; George Saunders land patent, GLO/BLM Records website, http://www.glorecords.blm.gov; Silver Springs plat map, Teller County Assessor, Cripple Creek, Colorado.

324. U.S. census, 1910; *Tombstone Inscriptions of El Paso and Teller Counties, Colorado*, Version 2.0.

325. *Castle Rock Journal*, March 11, 1896, 1.

326. *Silverton Standard*, May 2, 1896, 5.

327. Bauer, Ozment and Willard, *Colorado Post Offices*, 137; *Cripple Creek Morning Times*, January 15, 1896, 1; A.H. Ohmann-Dumesnil, HM, MD, ed., *Weekly Medical Review* 25 (January–June, 1892): 279.

328. *Littleton, Colorado Independent*, April 30 1897, 4; Frank Kraft, MD, ed., *American Homeopathist* 25 (1899): 274.

329. Teller County Assessor, Cripple Creek, Colorado.

ABOUT THE AUTHOR

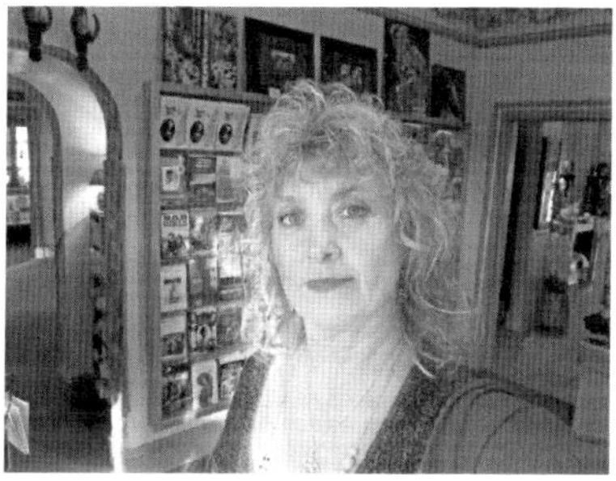

Jan MacKell Collins writes about ghost towns and other interesting aspects of the West. She is formerly the director of the Cripple Creek District Museum and the Old Homestead Museum in Cripple Creek, Colorado. She also had the pleasure of working for Sharlot Hall Museum in Prescott, Arizona. In addition, Ms. Collins has written over two thousand western history articles for magazines in Colorado, Montana and Arizona, including for *True West* magazine. In 2010, she was nominated for Women Writing the West's WILLA award for her 2009 book, *Red Light Women of the Rocky Mountains*; also, she was a co-nominee in 2011 for the 2010 anthology *Extraordinary Women of the Rocky Mountain West.* In addition to her writing, Collins has given over forty programs on the subject of prostitution and western history and has been featured on Rocky Mountain PBS.